S0-ARX-861

FLORIDA STATE
UNIVERSITY LIBRARIES

JUL 14 1995

TALLAHASSEE, FLORIDA

National Interest
and Foreign Aid

National Interest and Foreign Aid

Steven W. Hook

LYNNE
RIENNER
PUBLISHERS

BOULDER
LONDON

HC
60
H6668
1995

Published in the United States of America in 1995 by
Lynne Rienner Publishers, Inc.
1800 30th Street, Boulder, Colorado 80301

and in the United Kingdom by
Lynne Rienner Publishers, Inc.
3 Henrietta Street, Covent Garden, London WC2E 8LU

© 1995 by Lynne Rienner Publishers, Inc. All rights reserved

Library of Congress Cataloging-in-Publication Data
Hook, Steven W., 1959–
    National interest and foreign aid / Steven W. Hook.
    Includes bibliographical references and index.
    ISBN 1-55587-502-5 (alk. paper)
    1. Economic assistance—Case studies. 2. Technical assistance—
Case studies. I. Title.
HC60.H6668 1995
338.9'1—dc20   94-31379
                                                                      CIP

British Cataloguing in Publication Data
A Cataloguing in Publication record for this book
is available from the British Library.

Printed and bound in the United States of America

The paper used in this publication meets the requirements
of the American National Standard for Permanence of
Paper for Printed Library Materials Z39.48-1984.

5 4 3 2 1

To my mother and father

Contents

Tables and Figures

Tables

Figures

Preface

Foreign assistance has emerged as a central component of international relations since World War II. Virtually every nation-state is currently engaged on a regular basis as either a donor or recipient of foreign aid. Concessional aid flows have proven to be malleable instruments of foreign policy whose applications equal the number of donors and recipients in the international system.

The following study examines the most common form of foreign aid, Official Development Assistance (ODA), whose ostensible function is the promotion of sustained economic growth among the world's impoverished countries. The number of ODA donors, many of which have only recently "graduated" from the status of aid recipients, has consistently increased throughout the postwar period. The number of recipients, which now includes many Eastern European states and members of the Commonwealth of Independent States, has also steadily increased.

Although the economic, social, and political development of aid recipients has remained the explicit objective of most ODA flows, the tendency of donor states to pursue their own interests through the transfer of ODA is widely assumed. The rhetoric of aid donors may belie their self-interest on many occasions, but among thoughtful observers of foreign aid—and among many of its recipients—the linkage between national interest and foreign aid is virtually axiomatic.

Beyond this statement, however, the substantive relationship is far less clear. A state's national interest varies with its position within the international hierarchy, its physical and human resources, cultural traditions, and ongoing ties to other states. These factors are often obscure, given the discrepancy between the words and deeds of state leaders. One may intuitively suspect that national interests are at play in a given policy area, but what those interests are and how they are manifested in behavior remains ambiguous. Nevertheless, leaders (and their critics) commonly cast foreign policy in the context of national interest, as the recent U.S. intervention in Haiti attests.

More generally, industrialized states' disbursement of development assistance challenges established assumptions about foreign-policy behavior.

As sovereign actors in a structurally anarchic international system, nation-states must often place egoistic interests above altruistic concerns that benefit foreign populations at the cost of the donor states' own citizens. This presumption represents the basis of realism in international-relations theory. It is often argued, conversely, that the activity of wealthy states in dispensing aid to the world's poor reflects cooperative propensities in world politics, which suggests that relations among states may transcend the Hobbesian struggle for power often portrayed by realists. To proponents of idealism, a growing sense of global community has added the concept of *international* interest to modern statecraft.

Four interrelated propositions are considered in the following pages. First, the foreign policies of modern nation-states have historically been informed, and continue to be informed, by widely shared conceptions of national interest. Second, the substantive content of these national interests in contemporary world politics varies widely among states, depending on their internal characteristics, both physical and social, and their role within the international system. Third, the most salient interests of states may be identified through systematic evaluation of their behavior in specific areas of foreign policy. Finally, the observable behavior of industrialized states in the area of development assistance provides such an opportunity to establish the linkage between national interest and foreign policy. In short, the well-documented paths of these financial flows open a window through which we can view the broader objectives of wealthy states, regardless of the declared statements of their political leaders.

This study is designed to provide detailed substantive information to students of foreign aid, foreign policy, comparative politics, and international political economy. The case studies may be considered in isolation for more limited purposes or collectively for broader comparative analysis and theoretical speculation. Extensive citations are provided to facilitate ongoing research in any or all of these areas. By establishing empirical linkages between donor interests and aid flows, I address theoretical issues regarding the behavior of states in contemporary world politics, an era in which the "low politics" of social and economic concerns have achieved a degree of importance comparable to that of the "high politics" of war and peace. Further, the study pursues the meta-analytic function of promoting future research in the comparative study of foreign policy. Progress in this subfield of international relations has been limited by largely methodological obstacles, which this study attempts to surmount.

Though the phenomenon of foreign assistance has received great attention within scholarly and policymaking circles, its role in contemporary world politics has remained elusive. Analysts have only recently undertaken systematic efforts to identify empirical linkages between aid programs and their broader roles in the foreign policies of donor and recipient states. For much of the postwar period, the scholarly literature on foreign aid has been largely polemical, characterized by such titles as *Billions, Blunders, and Baloney* (Castle, 1955), *Aid as Imperialism* (Hayter, 1971), and *Zapping the Third World* (Linear, 1985). Cross-national studies of foreign assistance and research that documents aid patterns over time have been rare. More fundamentally, the lack of attention to foreign assistance as a sui generis tool of contemporary foreign policy has inhibited understanding and theoretical cumulation. The observation of Hans Morgenthau (1963: 70), though made long ago, remains true to this day:

> Of the seeming and real innovations which the modern age has introduced into the practice of foreign policy, none has proved more baffling to both understanding and action than foreign aid. Nothing even approaching a coherent philosophy of foreign aid has been developed.

Given the recent origin of ODA as a component of world politics, its lack of theoretical refinement may be understandable, particularly as compared to more established policy instruments such as alliance ties, military armament, and trade policy. Problems relating to comparative analysis in the area of development assistance are indeed formidable. States observe differing criteria in defining and reporting foreign-assistance transfers; the line between military and economic assistance is rarely definitive; and the burdens of equating currencies and differing terms of bilateral aid programs add to the complexity.

Many of these problems have been resolved by the emergence of a foreign-aid regime that has brought some order to the diffuse network of concessional flows from rich to poor states. The Development Assistance Committee (DAC) of the Organization for Economic Cooperation and Development (OECD) has defined the parameters of ODA, identified qualitative standards of aid transfers, established guidelines for the reporting and monitoring of ODA flows, and compiled these data in annual tables that provide a statistical basis for cross-national comparison. Like other transnational regimes, that involving development assistance responds to collective concerns, many of which are transnational in nature, as well as the perceived and persistent self-interests of its most powerful members.

This book is divided into three parts. In Part 1 I explore the historical and conceptual context of national interest and foreign aid. In Part 2 I detail the experiences of four major donors—France, Japan, Sweden, and the United States—in transferring ODA to less developed countries, with particular emphasis on their behavior during the 1980s. In Part 3 I contrast the four donors' aid patterns, consider their relationships to the foreign-policy objectives of each state from several perspectives, and evaluate the prospects for aid policy of the donor states and the ODA regime in general.

In Chapter 1, the dynamics of the nation-state system are briefly reviewed, with particular attention to the often conflicting relations among states resulting from the self-help nature of the state system. The concept of national interest is then examined, along with its various connotations, which have often reflected prevailing norms of international relations during their evolution. Finally, the phenomenon of foreign assistance is introduced as an element of contemporary international relations and as a challenge to conventional presumptions and expectations of state behavior. Chapter 2 contains a broader review of the global aid regime—its evolution, principal actors, institutional structures, and the varying forms ODA transfers have taken since World War II. Contending normative approaches to understanding development assistance are then examined.

In Chapters 3 through 6, the ODA programs of France, Japan, Sweden, and the United States are considered in detail. Each chapter includes a review of the historical roots of one state's ODA program and its relationship to that donor's broader national interests and foreign-policy behavior. After a substantive discussion of these programs, the empirical record of each donor during the 1980s is given special emphasis. The behavior of these donors is assessed from four vantage points: their aggregate disbursements of ODA, the direction and functional distribution of aid flows, their "quality" as defined by the aid regime, and their statistical relation to the donors' potential foreign-policy interests. Criteria of aid quality include the demonstrable human needs of countries receiving assistance, the proportion of aid given as grants as opposed to loans, and the degree to which aid transfers are tied to goods and services originating within the donor country. Drawing upon a ten-year data set that includes annual aid commitments by each donor and the characteristics of recipient states, I then advance the statistical linkages between aid flows and the donors' broader foreign-policy interests. A foreign-policy model of ODA, developed by R. D. McKinlay and Richard Little (1977, 1978, 1979) in their analyses of aid programs of the 1960s, is applied to each case (see Appendix 1 for a summary of this research strategy).

In Chapter 7, the four case studies are contrasted from a variety of perspectives. The aid patterns are first considered relative to the potential presence of three donor, foreign-policy interests: humanitarian, economic, and security. The findings are considered from the perspective of the donors' broader roles within the international system and in the context of their societal relations and political institutions. The relationship between the quantity and quality of their aid flows, as well as those from other OECD members, is considered along with the relationship between the absolute size of their economies and their observable behavior in providing development aid. Finally, their patterns of behavior are compared to those expected of actors within an international economic regime. In Chapter 8 I explore the theoretical implications of these findings, review the more general patterns of development, and consider ongoing challenges to its norms and principles. I then anticipate future ODA patterns in the four donor states and the future of national interest as an orienting principle in foreign policy.

Attention in this study is limited to the *sources* of bilateral development assistance—the donor countries—and to *development* assistance. Security assistance, particularly prevalent in the aid policies of the United States and the former Soviet Union during the Cold War, generally serves explicit foreign-policy interests and is thus less open to interpretation. In the case of development aid, ambiguities regarding donor motivation are pervasive and inhibit understanding, especially in comparative analysis. For analysts attempting to identify the determinants of ODA policy, however, this murkiness must not preclude systematic study. Given the increasing salience of ODA as a tool of foreign policy, understanding its role becomes all the more critical.

It is a central presumption of this study that a combination of historical review, substantive description, and statistical analysis is essential in enhancing apprehension of comparative foreign-policy behavior. In isolation, none of these approaches adequately brings to light the linkage between national interest and foreign aid. Taken together, they illuminate the relationship. As is the case with other aspects of this book, our statistical presentations are designed to be accessible to a diverse readership, including students and administrators of aid policy in donor and recipient states. As such these techniques are relatively simple, but their findings are nonetheless instructive and their implications compelling.

As the chapters to follow suggest, debates over foreign assistance have largely reflected broader normative disagreements about the appropriate roles and responsibilities of wealthy states in world politics. In the mid-1990s, these normative debates have been tempered by the absence of Cold War tensions and a growing consensus regarding the function of foreign assistance in promoting social, political, and economic development in the Third World. Transnational concerns regarding the effects of economic disparities between North and South have increasingly been accepted by donor states within the ODA regime. However, their ongoing aid programs continue to reflect their individual prerogatives and self-proclaimed national interests. The presence of both considerations throughout the Cold War period and toward the millennium is the primary subject of this book.

—*Steven W. Hook*

Acknowledgments

This book would not have been possible without the assistance, cooperation, and patience of many close friends and colleagues. Among the most instructive was Charles W. Kegley, Jr., whose work on comparative foreign policy energized the field and who supported this project from the beginning. Harvey Starr also brought his methodological expertise to bear on this project, as did Neil Richardson, a pioneer in the study of foreign economic policy, and James Kuhlman, a skillful political economist and valued colleague. David Cingranelli, Maurice East, C. Roe Goddard, Michael Link, Donald Puchala, and Jerel Rosati, who have commented on early sections of this book, also deserve my long-lasting gratitude.

At the University of Florida, I was provided with generous research support by Ken Wald, chairman of the Department of Political Science, and Pat Sivinski, director of the Faculty Support Center. Martin Ingram, Martina Jones, Richard Nolan, Steven Snook, and others contributed greatly to this effort. I was strongly encouraged by John Spanier, who showed interest in my work along the way and invited me to join him in his ongoing examination of U.S. foreign policy. In the final stages, Peter J. Schraeder provided thoughtful and invaluable guidance. All of these individuals perused parts of this manuscript and provided insightful critiques; none, however, should be held responsible for its deficiencies.

I would also like to thank Fred Hindley, a mentor of long standing, for his enduring support. Most important, my wife, Debra-Lynn B. Hook, a gifted journalist who has wisely preserved her writing skills in the Fourth Estate, has patiently tolerated my frequent absences, physical and otherwise. My son Christopher and daughter Emily also deserve all the love and attention they have coming to them.

—*S. W. H.*

PART 1

The Context of National Interest and Foreign Aid

1

Introduction

The accepted standard of international morality in regard to the altruistic
virtues appears to be that a state should indulge in them in so far as this
is not seriously incompatible with its more important interests.
                                                              —*E. H. Carr*

The privation and suffering of much of the world's population has presented its affluent minority with a humanitarian challenge to which the traditional imperatives of national interest seemingly do not apply. More than
80 percent of the world's population lived in low- or middle-income countries in 1990 and produced less than 15 percent of global wealth (World
Bank, 1992). Of the world's 5.3 billion inhabitants, more than 1 billion
lived in "absolute poverty," and another 1 billion survived on a subsistence
basis. Though many parts of the world experienced unprecedented prosperity during the 1980s, the gap between the world's richest and poorest
peoples widened considerably during this period, the "lost decade" of
Third World development.[1]

Leaders of industrialized states responded by sharing their wealth with
impoverished peoples in the form of foreign assistance. In so doing, they
ostensibly were motivated by the need to ease malnutrition, prevent the
spread of disease, limit the suffering that results from natural disasters,
construct stable and representative political systems, curb population
growth, and promote long-term economic expansion in less developed
countries (LDCs). Throughout the post–World War II period, foreign assistance took on an air of moral obligation among affluent states, which responded by committing more than $500 billion to LDCs (OECD, 1994a).

Contrary to widespread expectations that foreign aid flows would
weaken or disappear with the demise of the Cold War, which provided its
own strong impetus for North-South "cooperation," the scope and complexity of aid relations has only increased in the 1990s. The developmental needs of transformed states in Eastern Europe and the former Soviet
Union have been added to those of existing recipients in Africa, Latin
America, and southern Asia, which have been receiving annual infusions
of aid for decades and are in the midst of structural-adjustment programs

3

to manage growing debt obligations and qualify for continued assistance.[2] At the same time, a growing number of industrialized states, many of them former aid recipients, have become active as donors. Though established aid programs have been reduced or eliminated in the 1990s because of domestic constraints within donor countries, new programs have been widely adopted based upon standards of "sustainable" economic development and other priorities defined by major donors and international organizations.

At one level, this increasingly common aspect of contemporary world politics represents an apparent exception to the prevailing rules of statecraft, in which state actions are justified on the basis of (frequently "vital") national interests. These self-interested concerns inform the decisions of political leaders in many areas of domestic governance but more often influence foreign policy, a distinctive realm in which nation-states frequently compete for power, prosperity, and prestige in a contentious international system. From antiquity to the present age, the ends of national interest have commonly been used to justify any means necessary to achieve them.

Yet even as foreign aid seemingly departed from the prevailing egoism of international relations, it became evident that aid programs were often motivated as much by the self-interests of donors as by the human needs of recipients. The failure of bilateral and multilateral aid programs to achieve their stated objectives, as reflected in the growing gap between rich and poor during the 1980s, only deepened public and scholarly skepticism about the practice. "When other benefits to the donor are taken into account, the imagery of gift-giving embedded in most discussions of aid becomes questionable" (Wood, 1986: 14).

In this study, the tension between national interest and foreign aid is considered as it pertains to four major donors—France, Japan, Sweden, and the United States. Of particular concern is their use of Official Development Assistance (ODA), the primary form of such transfers in the post–World War II period, which has become "a highly significant and long-lasting part of the financial relations" between rich and poor (Lumsdaine, 1993: 34). In the 1990s nearly every nation-state is participating in a global ODA regime either as a donor or recipient of concessional resources. Although united by their use of this form of foreign assistance, nation-states' application of ODA varies widely in practice, reflecting the independent prerogatives of each. Their contrasting but highly visible behavior in dispensing ODA reveals much about national interest and its role in guiding foreign-policy behavior during the postwar period.

As with any other aspect of foreign policy, an examination of national interest and foreign aid must first be placed within the broader context of international relations. This study thus begins by considering the concept of national interest, its varied connotations and applications throughout history, and its role in contemporary world politics. The uneasy marriage between national interest and foreign aid is then explored before I turn, in subsequent chapters, to a more concrete examination of the aid regime and the involvement of the four donor countries in sharing their wealth with developing countries.

The Evolution of National Interest

Although the concept of national interest is a relative newcomer to statecraft, it has become "an inescapable rule for the nation—a rule written in the nature of things" (Beard, 1934). Either explicitly or implicitly, leaders rely upon this concept to rationalize their actions both at home and abroad. National interest must consequently be reckoned with as states continue to play a decisive role in contemporary world politics. As Crabb (1986: 213) observed,

> The concept of national interest has established itself as part of the lexicon of diplomacy and it continues to be used widely by the officials of the United States and other governments as a term that collectively describes the nation's highest-ranking diplomatic goals, especially as these relate to the protection of national security.[3]

As the following brief historical review illustrates, national interest has proven to be a very elastic concept with multiple meanings across time and space. State leaders have invoked national interest in pursuit of widely varying strategies of foreign policy, including isolationism, neutralism, regional or global hegemony, collective security, and transnational cooperation. The shifting relationships between church and state, between state and society, between political and economic forces, and between states and international organizations all have influenced interpretations and applications of national interest.

Though their applications of national interest have varied, the behavior of leaders has reflected the prevailing tenor of world politics of each historical period. Specifically, widespread conceptions of national interest have alternated cyclically between provincial, conflictive, or egoistic strains (which inform the evolving realist paradigm in international-relations theory), on one hand, and cosmopolitan, cooperative, or altruistic strains (which collectively influence the alternative theory of idealism), on the other. As will be demonstrated in subsequent chapters, both views have found expression in the utilization of foreign assistance.

Thucydides (1951 [ca. 402 B.C.]) was among the first to observe that the overriding interest of political leaders in self-protection often dictated their actions in both domestic and foreign affairs. Further, in a world of multiple centers of power in which each possessed differing levels of economic and military resources, the primacy of self-interest would frequently lead to conflict. These elementary though profound insights were given expression by Thucydides in his history of the Peloponnesian War. Leaders of both Sparta and Athens were forced to consider their incompatible claims as a basis for action. Citizens of other city-states, often caught between these two regional powers, found their options limited and largely defined by their dominant neighbors. As the Athenians bluntly informed the inhabitants of the island of Melos, who sought to remain neutral and isolated from the regional conflict: "You know as well as we do that right, as the world goes, is only a question between equals in power, while the strong do what they can and the weak suffer what they must" (Thucydides, 1951: 331).

This early conception, a forebearer of contemporary realist theories and definitions of national interest, was often eclipsed during the Middle Ages by theological doctrines emphasizing transcendent interests of mankind in adherence to universal laws and moral codes of behavior. The Catholic Church and the Holy Roman Empire promoted these values in Europe; the doctrine of "just war" provided an ethical justification for the extension of Christian theology by violent means (Johnson, 1987). Relying on the alliance of church and state, monarchs defended their divine right to impose their will on their subjects at home and their adversaries abroad. National interests were equated with universal norms during this period, a practice that, paradoxically, would be repeated by idealists of the twentieth century.[4]

Beginning in the fifteenth century, the secular foundations of national interest were established as world politics entered its modern phase. The emerging basis of foreign policy, often articulated in the context of *raison d'état* (reason of state), guided the domestic and foreign policies of a relatively small number of elites, who acted without the knowledge, assent, or involvement of their citizens. The notion that states maintained interests distinct from religious institutions, or indeed from universal norms, represented a fundamental departure in thinking about national interest. These conceptions of the early Renaissance, articulated by Niccolo Machiavelli (1985 [1532]) and other pioneers of realpolitik, were popularly associated with the amoral pursuit of state power and survival as ends in themselves. Intended to guide the Florentine city-state through the rivalries that plagued Renaissance Italy, "Machiavelli's political writings are mantels on how to thrive in a completely chaotic and immoral world" (Forde, 1992: 64).

These lessons extended beyond the Italian peninsula, touching on all sovereign territories faced with internal unrest or external encroachments. At a time when feudal structures were under assault both internally and externally and commercial ties were expanding across borders at an accelerating rate, the responsibilities of the state grew steadily. Its activities "included the establishment of a diplomatic system, a network of permanent embassies with accredited diplomats, foreign-policy analysts and advisors in addition to an elaborate structure for the rapid transport and the safe storage of diplomatic dispatches" (Knutsen, 1992: 27). All of these developments reinforced the state's power, facilitated economic activity, and brought some degree of order, if not peace, to international relations.

Among his other concerns, Machiavelli attempted to reconcile the dissonant coexistence of good and evil in both human nature and societal relations. In his view, the state served a vital mediating function, enforcing laws to moderate the egoistic consequences of its citizens' selfish passions and to prevent internal conflicts from undermining the state's authority. Differing standards of individual ethics, which had previously been beyond compromise or resolution, were to be brought under the direction of state authorities: "Moral goodness and justice were produced and could be produced only by the constraining power of the state" (Meinecke, 1957: 33).

Of course, for the state to serve this mediating role, it would have to ensure its own self-preservation. Herein lay the functional basis of *raison d'état*, articulated most concretely by Cardinal de Richelieu in the early seventeenth century as he devised French strategy in the Thirty Years' War. Despite his adherence to Catholic theology, Richelieu rejected the notion that French policy must be driven by universal moral laws. "Man is immortal, his salvation is hereafter," Richelieu argued. "The state has no immortality, its salvation is now or never." He concluded that France's survival would best be protected if it allied with Protestant forces in northern Europe, a view that gave pragmatic diplomacy priority over theological maxims. By the end of the war, France's strategy had proved successful, and it later served as a model for subsequent leaders. Richelieu's formulation of *raison d'état* underscored the moral paradox of state power earlier identified by Machiavelli: The state facilitates domestic order and moral behavior only through the tacitly amoral means of foreign policy. In this view, "The state is entirely independent but at the same time completely isolated. . . . The political world has lost all its connection not only with religion or metaphysics but also with all other forms of man's ethical and cultural life. It stands alone—in an empty space" (Cassirer, 1946: 140).[5]

The current legal status of nation-states, vested with internal sovereignty and, in principle, protection from external threats, was most directly enunciated in the 1648 Treaty of Westphalia, which ended the Thirty Years' War in Central Europe. The emergence of the modern state, "a self-originating, self-empowered unit operating exclusively in pursuit of its own interests" (Poggi, 1978: 88), was accompanied by the gradual demise of feudalism in the West as a basis for societal organization. Expanding commercial exchanges necessitated administrative reform at the domestic level as well as steps toward the regulation of trade and colonial settlement through international law and treaties. Yet in affirming the legal rights and roles of states, Westphalia merely reinforced and formalized the anarchic nature of interstate relations. The emerging state system was likened to a "pre-political" domain in which egoistic actors were required to subordinate collective needs to the defense and promotion of their own. The continuing absence of centralized authority at the systemic level produced the same consequences that Thomas Hobbes identified at the societal level: State actors, like individuals in the ideal-typical "state of nature," were prone to pursue self-interests at the expense of collective welfare (see Watkins, 1934).

Under the nascent state system, the dictates of national interest would be determined by each sovereign, whose formulations would be based, presumably, on a rational calculation of its available resources and alternatives. Rationality, the product of modern education and the liberation of modern leaders from religious dogma, was expected to fill the "empty space" of the secular era in world politics. Whereas political philosophers such as Jean Bodin and Giovanni Botero attempted to reconcile national interest with broader normative principles, most leaders considered their options more narrowly. They favored the prevailing emphasis of the Enlightenment period on rationalism, which had produced theoretical breakthroughs in the fields of physics, astronomy, and biology and which seemingly could be applied to the behavior of states. In the early nineteenth century, leaders of the great powers placed their faith in the coordinated maintenance of a balance of power, or "equilibrium," among nations. As Prince Metternich of Austria (quoted in Guluck, 1967: 32) noted,

> Politics is the science of the vital interests of States in its widest meanings. Since, however, an isolated state no longer exists, and is found only in the annals of the heathen world . . . we must always view the society of states as the essential condition of the modern world. . . . The great axioms of political science proceed from the knowledge of the true political interests of all states; it is upon these general interests that rests the guarantee of their existence.

Metternich and other European leaders thus perceived the state system as an integrated, interdependent whole. The pursuit of national interest was to become an essentially mechanical function, and the ambitions of individual states were to be subordinated to the collective interest of systemic stability.

This experiment in "concert diplomacy" by the major European states, relying as it did upon a fluid and precarious balance of power, could not be sustained indefinitely. It failed in the late nineteenth century with the rise of new powers—namely, the newly unified Germany and the United States—and the concurrent decline of other powers, particularly Great Britain. Upon Germany's defeat of Austria and France and its unification under Otto von Bismarck, the notion of national interest was widely infused with the predatory logic of social Darwinism. National interest was reduced to survival of the fittest among the traditional and emerging great powers of the period. This view was embraced by U.S. President Theodore

Roosevelt, who viewed national survival through military competition as a reflection of martial virtues. The concept of realpolitik returned to the European continent and expanded westward to the Americas and beyond, where the United States carried a "big stick" in Latin America and assumed control of the Philippines and other Pacific nations. All of these changes further undermined the mechanistic basis of great-power stability and paved the way for world war in 1914.

The simultaneous collapse of the Russian, Austro-Hungarian, and Ottoman empires contributed to the rise of nationalism across Eurasia, resulting in the emergence of new nation-states based upon the principle of self-determination. This development after World War I prompted another reformulation of national interest. Woodrow Wilson revived cosmopolitan notions of a world order based upon universal standards of morality, democratic development, and international restraint, the latter of which was to be ensured by the collective-security provisions of the League of Nations. Wilson's prescriptions were rejected by the U.S. Senate, which preserved its constitutional prerogatives in defending its perceived national interests, but were widely adopted by other nation-states. The effectiveness of his program in dampening international conflict was short-lived, however, as lingering animosities from World War I and a prolonged economic depression weakened the sense of shared interests epitomized by the League of Nations. In Germany, Italy, and Japan these deteriorating conditions encouraged fascist movements predicated on the narrowest of conceptions of national interest, contributing to the onset of World War II.

While the West's experiment in collective security cracked under growing strains, the newly formed Soviet Union espoused the tenets of Marxism-Leninism, which viewed conventional definitions of national interest as agents for capitalist control. Soviet leaders promoted universal aspirations of solidarity among propertyless classes within industrialized countries and their overseas colonies. In the absence of worldwide support for these assumptions and their prescriptions, which was viewed as temporary, the Soviet Union segregated itself from the political and economic structures of the West. (Many of these structuralist assumptions gained adherents in the postcolonization period and found expression within the United Nations and other international organizations, a point that will be explored further in the next chapter.)

Both world wars were widely viewed in the 1950s as the result of naive assumptions about universal "power politics" interests and quixotic expectations about the conduct of states. Realism reemerged as the dominant theoretical paradigm of the postwar period, as theorists returned to Machiavellian, Hobbesian, and Bismarckian notions of power politics. Among other scholars who refined a "scientific" theory of international relations, Hans Morgenthau (1951) viewed international relations as rooted in human nature, unchanging over time and inherently conflictive (see also

Aron, 1966, and Waltz, 1964). To these analysts, transnational solutions and moral imperatives were worse than useless in preserving the interwar peace; they effectively *encouraged* World War II by intoxicating responsible leaders, thus giving aggressors a free hand.

Morgenthau was joined in his critique of idealism by other realists who had assumed positions of power within the U.S. government. In basing U.S. foreign policy upon the objective of "containing" communism in the Soviet Union, George Kennan (1951: 95) rejected the presence of "legalistic-moralistic" considerations, which "run like a red skein through our foreign policy of the last fifty years." Kennan suggested that concrete and explicit national interests, rather than normative values, should guide U.S. foreign policy. Other U.S. statesmen, particularly Henry Kissinger during the late 1960s and early 1970s, resigned themselves to continuing differences between the superpowers and a world order based on the bipolar balance of power, regional alliances, nuclear deterrence, and arms control.

Finally, as the Cold War began to thaw in the midst of superpower détente in the 1970s, yet another formulation of national interest was widely adopted, this one recognizing the interdependence not only between East and West but also between North and South. According to the "world-order politics" of the 1960s and 1970s, partly a revival of Kantian and Wilsonian principles, the fates of all countries were inextricably linked. This worldview dictated that the centrality of the Cold War conflict give way to the socioeconomic development of the Third World and that national interests be accommodated to transnational concerns. Most member states of the United Nations advanced this perspective in the late 1970s, including the United States under Jimmy Carter, who departed from the earlier emphasis of U.S. foreign policy. To some observers of the period, the emergence of transnational interdependence suggested that a "modified Westphalia" system had emerged in which "spheres of influence modify the principal of equality; supranational actors modify the principles of no external earthly superior authority; an ever more complex pattern of interconnectedness of decisions, events, and developments modifies the principle of independence" (Ruggie, 1972: 877).

After the revival and subsequent termination of the Cold War in the 1980s and early 1990s, the UN again embraced global priorities and expanded its efforts to promote socioeconomic development in the Third World, pursuing measures to protect the environment, control population growth, and curb the proliferation of weaponry. The UN-sponsored Conference on Environment and Development ("Earth Summit"), which in the summer of 1992 brought together the largest assembly of world leaders in history, reflected an unusual convergence of national interests and established a basis for future collaboration. The UN also expanded its humanitarian-relief and peacekeeping efforts; though it was frustrated in Somalia and Bosnia-Herzegovina, it contributed to the establishment of civil order in El Salvador, Nicaragua, Angola, Cambodia, and parts of the Middle East.

The immediate post–Cold War period, though marked by a resurgence of nationalism and ethnic conflict in many areas, also witnessed the diffusion of democratic principles in a growing number of regions, particularly Latin America, Eastern Europe, the former Soviet Union, and parts of Africa. In this respect, many scholars (e.g., Russett, 1990; Doyle, 1986) advanced empirical evidence to support the eighteenth-century formulations of Immanuel Kant that democratic societies, in which dissent is tolerated and political rights protected, would be largely peaceful in their relations toward each other (if not toward other, nondemocratic societies).

International relations at the end of the twentieth century reflect the presence of both the realist and idealist traditions in world politics and their related applications of national interest. The contemporary system is fraught with great volatility, and "even the slightest fluctuations can seem portentous, with each shift confirming that change is the norm, that patterns are fragile, and that expectations can be frustrated" (Rosenau, 1990: 12). To an unprecedented degree, the perceived national interests of states have become conditioned upon the behavior of other states; consequently, single-state interests have become aligned with transnational concerns, promoting cooperative undertakings. In other areas, the divisions between states and societies have deepened, and appeals to an egoistic orientation have been revived. It is under such circumstances that a greater understanding of national interest and its contemporary manifestations is most crucial.

National Interest: Contemporary Perspectives

The preceding historical review illustrates the multiple dimensions of national interest. More important, it reveals the intimate connection between the theory and practice of international relations as they have developed in tandem for centuries. Prevailing conceptions of national interest reflected ongoing changes in world politics and, in turn, influenced the foreign policies of states in widely varying ways. The concept of national interest thus serves as a valuable heuristic device for foreign-policy analysis. It draws attention to the importance of statehood as a response to disorder at the societal level as well as to its open-ended role in meeting the challenge of systemic anarchy. Attention must be paid to the frequent invocation of national interest by state leaders, even in the absence of an agreed-upon analytic basis of the term. Noted Cerny: "No matter what the disagreements about foreign policy may be, they have in common a quite specific operational framework, which is that of the concept of national interest, whatever the content which is explicitly or implicitly included in various conceptions of that national interest" (1980: 110).

As national interest has become common diplomatic currency, it has drawn criticism for its ambiguities and, in some cases, pernicious prescriptions. To many, the very notion that a nation-state has a discernible national interest is empirically and morally dubious, "oversimplified and wrongheadedly dogmatic" (Hoffmann, 1978: 133). These critics argue that such a notion commits the multiple sins of reifying the inanimate state; of presupposing a consensual set of values and priorities that is untenable in a pluralistic society; and of presuming, accepting, or advocating competitive rather than cooperative foreign policies (see Cook and Moos, 1953). To some, the multiplicity of domestic priorities prevents a coherent definition of national interest.[6] Others contend that the narrow adherence to national interest in the nuclear era threatens international stability. The Cold War rivalry, in this view, provoked the superpowers "to secure resources and power for one national or regional segment of the species while letting other segments of the species suffer or die" (Johansen, 1980: 391; see also Barnet, 1971).

These critiques of national interest illuminate its analytic and occasionally normative limitations. But they fail to negate the continuing reality that, given the utility of the sovereign state as a mechanism for social, political, and economic organization, and given its unique capacity for external protection, its preservation and security remain collective goods for which its leaders are held accountable (Olson, 1971; see also Russett and Sullivan, 1971, and Ruggie, 1972). Acknowledging the presence of collective interests need not entail the reification of the state. To the contrary, given the functional basis of international relations in legally autonomous and competitive states, it is appropriate to conceive of objective criteria for the self-preservation of each actor. "It is by no means the case that national interest has been without value to conscientious policy makers who were determined to set reasonable objectives, to judge carefully what was at stake in particular situations, and to act prudently in any given situation," observed George and Keohane (1980: 218).

This interpretation of national interest rejects the vision of citizens as purely atomistic and of domestic groups as ultimately exclusive. The state may instead be regarded as an autonomous actor whose objectives "cannot be reduced to some summation of private desires" (Krasner, 1978: 5–6). State leaders must balance and reconcile conflicting domestic interests, as envisioned by the dominant liberal paradigm. Those interests are often distorted or overwhelmed by powerful economic actors, a central presumption of Marxism. Beyond these limitations, however, leaders pursue holistic concerns that regulate and, in some cases, moderate subnational interests. The state may more productively be viewed as

> a large group itself, with common standards of political ethics, with ties of mutual respect and appreciation (not only coinciding interests) binding its members together, and with a real common good that in the long run benefits all those within the group, in their role as members of the whole,

if not always in their capacity of members of a subgroup. Individuals in a society join together for purposes broader than convenience and the promotion of their own unshared aims. (Clinton, 1994: 50)

The coherence of these objectives, of course, relies upon the cohesion of the state. In some cases, internal divisions may be so deep that no sense of "common good" develops. The legitimacy of the state and its leaders is then brought into question, the basis of national interest is undermined, and the society often falls into civil war or disintegration. Such was the case in the former Soviet Union and Yugoslavia; it also explains the recent collapse of societal order in Afghanistan, Haiti, and the African countries of Somalia, Liberia, and Rwanda, among others.

In most other cases, however, the record is less cataclysmic. Despite the presence of crosscutting domestic interest groups, cultural and ethnic cleavages, and some degree of societal unrest, most modern states have inculcated a sense of collective identity in their populations and an underlying notion of shared national purpose. Leaders of these states (including the four under review in this study) frequently act upon widely shared perceptions of collective identity and conceptions about the ends and means of their states' involvement in foreign affairs. Their objectives are often distorted by the narrow interests of powerful subnational groups; governments have in countless instances sacrificed lives in ideological crusades lacking broad public support. But "between these extremes exist the vast majority of modern states, which seek to achieve collective objectives of national security; welfare of citizens; access to trade routes, markets, and vital resources; and sometimes the territory of their neighbors" (Holsti, 1988: 122).

All of this presents an analytic challenge to students of foreign policy, who must discern both the transcendent interests and the related policy actions of states inductively by observing their behavior over time and across a wide range of issue areas. In some cases national interest may be limited to the Hobbesian minimum of simple survival in a hostile environment; in other cases it may encompass other values that incorporate issues of transnational welfare. The predisposition of states to seek either egoistic or altruistic objectives is thus highly variable, as is clear from the historical record. As Morgenthau and Thompson (1985: 11) argued:

> The kind of interest determining political action in a particular period of history depends upon the political and cultural context within which foreign policy is formulated. The goals that might be pursued by nations in their foreign policy can run the whole gamut of objectives any nation has ever pursued or might actually pursue.

The number of nation-states has grown rapidly in the post–World War II period, first with the breakup of the European colonial empires in the

1950s and 1960s and then with the disintegration of the Soviet Union in the early 1990s. National interest consequently remains a critical aspect of international life whose application in practice may be discerned, if not reliably from the rhetoric of political leaders, then from systematic observation of state behavior in specific areas of policy. As we will find, the area of foreign assistance provides such an opportunity.

National Interest and Foreign Aid

The half-century of ideological, economic, and geopolitical struggle between the Cold War superpowers profoundly influenced the domestic politics and foreign policies of all nation-states. Though it produced a degree of systemic stability (Gaddis, 1987), the Cold War created and in some cases exacerbated regional conflicts among impoverished and politically fragile countries in the Southern hemisphere, many of which were in the process of extricating themselves from colonial domination. This convergence of superpower rivalry and Third World state building, coming at a time of unprecedented prosperity in the industrialized world, continues to shape relations between North and South well beyond the Cold War.

In this setting, "economic statecraft" (Baldwin, 1985) has become a vital aspect of international relations. Private investment flows and trade across national borders have increased rapidly in the late twentieth century, critically affecting living standards and political relations. As the world economy has become more tightly integrated, the fortunes of many LDCs have increasingly depended upon the willingness of private lenders to make capital available. When private funds have not been forthcoming, LDCs have sought economic support from the governments of industrialized states and international organizations in the form of foreign aid, defined by Mosley (1987: 21) as "money transferred on concessional terms by the governments of rich countries to the governments of poor countries." Foreign assistance programs have been established by virtually every nation-state in pursuit of widely varying short- and long-term objectives. Wealthy states shared their financial resources with allies long before World War II, but "the use of public funds on subsidized terms to assist in the development and growth of sovereign nations has no significant precedent before the Marshall Plan" (Frank and Baird, 1975: 135).

Official Development Assistance, the most common form of economic aid, involves bilateral and multilateral transfers of goods and services for the ostensible purpose of promoting economic development in poor countries. Leaders of industrialized states have generally agreed to uphold certain norms, and their ODA flows have been sufficiently coordinated and routinized so as to constitute a cohesive international regime, an "institutionalized system of cooperation in a given issue-area" (Kegley and

Wittkopf, 1993: 33). To the Organization for Economic Cooperation and Development (OECD), public funds are an essential complement to private capital, which often cannot be profitably invested in LDCs and is thus unable to improve their living standards:

> The basic proposition of international cooperation for development has been that pre-industrial and relatively stagnant economies could be launched on a course of dynamic economic and social transformation, ultimately sustainable without prolonged dependence on concessional aid; further, that this process could be set in motion, broadened, and accelerated by the efficient use of internal and external resources in combinations appropriate to the particular case, in an environment of policies and leadership conducive to sustained development. (OECD, 1985a: 11)

As noted above, development aid appears to be founded on altruistic and humanitarian principles. Upon closer inspection, a variety of donor self-interests appear, along with subnational interests within both donor and recipient states. "Aid has always been seen as a tool of policy and a policy in its own right, an approach which has created ambivalence about what aid is and does," argued Rix (1980: 83). At a time of great import for the emerging foreign-aid program in the United States, Liska (1960: 127) made the case for embedding such assistance in the context of foreign policy: "The sole test of foreign aid is the national interest of the United States. Foreign aid is not something to be done, as a Government enterprise, for its own sake or for the sake of others. The United States Government is not a charitable institution, nor is it an appropriate outlet for the charitable spirit of the American people."

The contemporary aid regime, involving more than $50 billion in concessional transfers transferred annually to more than 100 developing states, has experienced constant change since assuming its current structure in the 1960s. The number of donors and recipients of foreign assistance steadily increased during the aid regime's first three decades, subsuming almost every sovereign state in complex, ongoing aid relationships by the mid-1990s. Concurrently, normative approaches toward aid reflected the geopolitical environment of each period, as well as accumulated lessons from past development efforts. Foreign assistance thus exists as an additional tool of foreign policy, serving as a vehicle for the distinctive domestic, regional, and global interests of all participants. As Baldwin (1966: 3) argued, "[F]oreign aid is first and foremost a technique of statecraft. It is, in other words, a means by which one nation tries to get other nations to act in desired ways. . . . Thus, foreign aid policy is foreign policy, and as such it is a subject of controversy in both the international and the domestic political arenas."

Just as the foundations of national interest vary across cases, the singular instrument of ODA reflects the individual designs of donors as they disburse public funds to distant governments. "A country's programme for development cooperation is inevitably part of its foreign policy," wrote Thord Palmlund (1986: 109), a former Swedish aid official. "Sometimes it gives substance to policy intentions better than words." Foreign aid has served as a microcosm of donor states' foreign policies; for every donor, a different story can be told about the use of aid as an agent of national interest. The same can be said of recipients, who have relied upon annual infusions of ODA and incorporated this source of funding into their long-term fiscal planning and development strategies (see Lele and Nabi, 1991). Recipients recognized the Cold War superpowers' competition for their allegiance during the Cold War and exploited the ensuing "aid rivalry" to their advantage. To receive further assistance, however, leaders in LDCs had to demonstrate its effectiveness and value in promoting their benefactors' stated goals. In the 1990s, poor nations' debts to donor states, international organizations, and private banks—and their requirements for ongoing economic support—bound them closely to their creditors, who in turn had assumed a long-lasting stake in the recipients' economic fortunes. In this way, foreign assistance strengthened the sense of interdependence between North and South, the most significant aspect of contemporary global relations.

The relationship between national interest and foreign aid is complex and often obscure. But it represents a central facet of the contemporary world order, in which the "low politics" of social and economic welfare have become as salient to international relations as the "high politics" of military security (Keohane and Nye, 1989). Understanding this relationship becomes more important as a growing number of states provide or receive foreign assistance and as rich and poor states pursue increasingly common interests alongside their more narrowly defined national interests.

Notes

1. In many LDCs, average life expectancy, per capita food consumption, and other standards of social welfare fell steadily during the decade.

2. Developing countries in Latin American owed nearly $500 billion to public and private creditors in the early 1990s, and states in sub-Saharan Africa owed nearly $200 billion. These African LDCs spent four times more public funds on interest payments than they did for health programs during the period (*The Economist*, 1993: 52).

3. Crabb (1986: 113–116) identified several contributions of the concept of national interest to international relations. Among these, the concept "calls attention to the essentially competitive and sometimes violent nature" of world politics; it makes explicit "vital interests" of states and establishes a "scale of priorities"; it thereby renders foreign policy more consistent over time and more understandable to potential adversaries; and it creates the possibility that common interests among states may be identified.

4. An early articulation of this view can be found in St. Augustine (1954 [425]). See also Vitoria (1934 [1532]) for an application of this view to Spanish colonization in the Western Hemisphere.

5. Kissinger (1994) provides a useful review of the origins of national interest during this period.

6. See Dahl (1971) for a consideration of this view. Also, see Balbus (1978) for an application of Marxist analysis to the concept of public or national interest. Beard (1934) and Osgood (1953) are among the early analysts of U.S. foreign policy to explore the multiplicity of domestic priorities based upon the uneven distribution of wealth in the society.

2

The Setting of
Development Assistance

As Chapter 1 demonstrated, both the concept of national interest and the practice of foreign aid have provoked great controversy among foreign-policy makers and analysts. In this chapter, the structure of Official Development Assistance (ODA) is reviewed in some detail, along with conflicting normative perspectives that have been advanced regarding ODA during the post–World War II period. Familiarity with this debate will be helpful as the French, Japanese, Swedish, and U.S. ODA programs are examined respectively in the following four chapters.

In its short history, ODA has become an important foreign-policy tool of donor and recipient states alike. But what constitutes ODA? How is it substantively different from commercial loans, trade, foreign investment, and other forms of international resource transfers? The answers to these seemingly straightforward questions are elusive given the overlapping objectives underlying all such exchanges and given the fungible nature of foreign aid; as Parkinson remarked, "The whole is a complicated skein of imperfect understanding, differing value judgements and conflicting political aspirations" (1983: 11). Even within the single category of ODA, donor states commit funds in many forms, through many channels, under widely varying terms, and for multiple reasons.

For analytic purposes, boundaries may be constructed to distinguish ODA from other forms of foreign assistance and financial flows. The twenty-one-member Development Assistance Committee (DAC), the coordinating agency of the Organization for Economic Cooperation and Development, defines ODA as

> those flows to developing countries and multilateral institutions provided by official agencies, including state and local governments or by their executive agencies, each transaction of which meets the following tests: a) it is administered with the promotion of the economic development and welfare of developing countries as its main objective, and b) it is concessional in character and contains a grant element of at least 25 per cent. (OECD, 1974: 115)

Stated more succinctly, ODA applies to *public* transfers of *economic* resources on *concessional* terms for *developmental* purposes. Public transfers are those in which the resources travel from the donor government to the recipient government either directly or through transnational organizations. Economic resources are distinct from military resources, which are explicitly designed to pursue the security interests of both donors and recipients. The terms of ODA, or subsequent obligations imposed on recipients, may be minimal in the case of grant aid or more demanding in the case of concessional loans, but in all cases they must be more favorable than the terms recipients would be able to receive on commercial capital markets. Finally, ODA involves the explicit requirement that the funds be used for purposes of economic development, defined by the World Bank (1992: 31) as "a sustainable increase in living standards that encompass material consumption, education, health, and environmental protection."

The patterns of aid flows fluctuated as ODA networks took shape during the 1960s and 1970s in response to shifting domestic conditions within donor states and prevailing trends in world politics. On the whole, the aggregate volume of aid grew steadily throughout the postwar period. The volume of ODA transfers more than doubled between 1970 and 1990 in inflation-adjusted dollars; annual flows of concessional aid reached levels in excess of $50 billion by 1990. Although bilateral flows decreased slightly in the early 1990s, multilateral aid increased to a record $16.8 billion in 1992. More donors entered the aid business during this period through both bilateral and multilateral channels, offering assistance to an expanding set of recipients. When private financial flows, including investments and commercial loans, are added to the picture, total resource flows from North to South amounted to nearly $200 billion in 1992 (OECD, 1994a: 65).[1]

Despite the ongoing pressures of global economic recession, domestic political opposition, the demonstrable shortcomings of past aid programs, and the demise of the Cold War, wealthy states consistently increased their volumes of aid to the Third World. Although some major donors, most notably Saudi Arabia and other members of the Organization of Petroleum Exporting Countries (OPEC), reduced annual transfers in the 1980s, members of the DAC continued to increase assistance into the 1990s. In so doing, they coordinated aid policy to a considerable extent, basing ODA calculations upon widely circulated data regarding the socioeconomic conditions in recipient states, collaboratively reporting aid transfers, and monitoring their implementation. Although these donors steadfastly resisted incursions against their sovereign authority to dispense public funds in the form of ODA, they adopted and generally adhered to "rules of the game" and expected fair play on the part of others. This pattern of behavior affirms the presence of a foreign-aid regime in contemporary world politics, one of a growing number of transnational regimes that has emerged since World War II.[2] In fact, as Wood (1986) demonstrated, a separate and distinctive ODA regime has emerged within the overall aid regime, which involves other concessional flows. Each of the commonly cited regime components—principles, norms, rules, and decisionmaking procedures—is evident in the formulation and execution of ODA.

The fundamental principle of aid giving as "the price of affluence" has been accepted by nearly all industrialized states, which have added the fiscal and institutional components of foreign aid to their diplomatic arsenal. Donors and recipients generally observe a complex set of norms regarding the minimal qualifications for aid, the preferences for market or commercial resources when available, the functions aid is intended to serve, and the anticipation that recipients will uphold standards of "good government," promote environmental conservation and population control, and implement fiscal reforms under the guise of "structural adjustment." Explicit targets have also been adopted involving the proportion of donor GNP devoted to ODA, with 0.7 percent serving as the standard for OECD members. Other norms involve the proportion of "tied" aid to overall assistance and the degree to which aid is extended in the form of grants versus low-interest loans.[3] Numerous and complex rules exist that regulate the process by which ODA transfers are negotiated, documented, implemented, and monitored. And decisionmaking procedures for all of these functions have been codified by the donors and international organizations that dispense assistance. Many additional components of contemporary ODA are suggestive of regime behavior, including an emergent division of labor among donors and multilateral institutions, both in terms of the geographical distribution of ODA and the varying repayment terms imposed upon recipients. Overall, conditions imposed upon recipients in the 1980s and 1990s for managing their social, economic, and political policies reflect a growing consensus within international organizations, private lending institutions, industrialized states, and LDCs.

The coordinated flow of concessional aid emerged in response to widely perceived economic disparities between North and South (and, more recently, between the West and the former Soviet bloc). Evolving conditionalities for aid have reflected a bias against statist macroeconomic policies and in favor of market-driven, export-led growth strategies. Additionally, more recent aid programs have responded to a recognition that "human capital" is as critical to economic development as financial and technological transfers (see Lucas, 1988). Expectations of long-term development that is sensitive to demographic, socioeconomic, and environmental concerns have been emphasized in the 1990s.

The aid regime has not displaced the foreign-policy prerogatives of donor states, who continue to incorporate aid programs into broader economic, political, and security relations with LDCs. In some cases, these interests have been acknowledged and accommodated by the OECD: The spheres of influence of some ODA donors (e.g., Japan in East Asia, France in francophone Africa) have been preserved, while additional geographic concentrations (e.g., Germany in Eastern Europe and Russia) have been outlined in more recent OECD deliberations. In other cases (e.g., the Japanese preference for loans rather than grants), the disparities between OECD norms and donor practices have remained wide.

These tensions between the national interests of donors and the collective standards of the ODA regime, which existed throughout the Cold War and persist in the mid-1990s, remain one of the defining features of international aid. Its manifestation in the observable patterns of aid flows, to be examined in subsequent chapters, is a primary subject of this study.

Evolution of the ODA Regime

Although ODA in its current incarnation did not exist prior to World War II, foreign assistance was not unknown to diplomats of the eighteenth or nineteenth centuries. Developed countries had long supplied allies with military equipment on concessional terms, and states often transferred funds overseas for disaster relief or other purposes. For example, French aid to the United States was critical to U.S. success in the Revolutionary War against Great Britain. Almost two centuries later U.S. military transfers to Great Britain, the Soviet Union, and other allied states tipped the balance of forces against Nazi Germany during World War II. But the elaborate, routinized ODA regime of the late twentieth century is a by-product of World War II and its immediate aftermath. The contemporary ODA regime took shape rapidly during the two decades after World War II (see Table 2.1). Its roots lie in three important and related developments that emerged after the war.

First, development assistance served as a functional extension of the ideological schism between East and West that displaced European rivalries as the centerpiece of world politics after World War II. Both Cold War superpowers transferred massive amounts of economic assistance to selected LDCs, which often received military support in addition. Other donors, including Sweden and France, directed assistance as a means of *preventing* LDCs' subordination to either of the superpowers. Second, and more broadly, the emergence of North-South "cooperation" reflected the growing emphasis on economic growth as a determinant of political stability in developing countries, a perspective that adopted Western liberal assumptions of a "harmony of interests" among market-driven states. In this view, economic growth was a prerequisite for democratic development in the Third World.

Finally, the formation of the ODA regime coincided with the liberation of most European colonies between 1945 and 1965, an additional manifestation of the postwar international system. The dismantling of Europe's colonial empires was a priority of Franklin Roosevelt, who anticipated the support for Third World development as a postwar priority. "I am

Table 2.1   Origins of the ODA Regime, 1944–1965

1944	Bretton Woods conference establishes International Bank for Reconstruction and Development (World Bank) and International Monetary Fund (IMF)
1945	Approval of UN Charter, pledging to "employ international machinery for the promotion of the economic and social advancement of all peoples"
1946	Decolonization process begins with Philippines; India and Pakistan follow in 1947; France establishes FIDES program to support overseas territories
1947	U.S. Marshall Plan directed toward European recovery; Truman Doctrine calls for aid to Greece, Turkey, and other states resisting internal and external subversion
1948	Formation of Organization for European Economic Cooperation (OEEC), precursor to the Organization for Economic Cooperation and Development (OECD)
1950	Colombo Plan establishes a six-year aid program to LDCs in South and Southeast Asia
1952	Mutual Security Program establishes long-term basis for U.S. foreign aid
1954	Sweden appoints special minister for development assistance, beginning large-scale aid program
1957	Treaty of Rome creates European Economic Community and European Development Fund for Overseas Countries and Territories
1960	Peak year of decolonization in Africa; World Bank creates International Development Association (IDA)
1961	UN proclaims "Development Decade"; U.S. president Kennedy announces Alliance for Progress; Japan creates Overseas Economic Cooperation Fund
1963	Formation of OECD's Development Assistance Committee (DAC), designed to coordinate and monitor member ODA programs
1964	First meeting of UN Conference on Trade and Development (UNCTAD); establishment of African Development Bank (ADB); *Jeanneney Report* published in France
1965	UN's "International Cooperation Year"; diversion of U.S. aid funds to Southeast Asia

firmly of the belief that if we are to arrive at a stable peace it must involve the development of backward countries," Roosevelt told Winston Churchill. "I can't believe that we can fight a war against fascist slavery, and at the same time not work to free people all over the world from a backward colonial policy."

Amid the expansion of the ODA regime, qualitative approaches to Third World development and ODA shifted and grew more diverse. The ebbs and flows in ODA reflected changing political, military, and economic alignments among states and a deepening intellectual understanding of national development that came with experience.[4] Donors originally focused on state building as a primary objective of ODA, then shifted to the promotion of "basic human needs" in the 1970s. Many LDCs struggled with growing fiscal crises in the 1980s, so donors linked aid flows to recipients' creation of market-oriented economies and broader forms of structural adjustment. Respect for human rights became an additional condition during this period, and in the 1990s aid programs were designed to promote "sustainable" development that responded to the need for population control and environmental protection.

As the dominant international power at the end of World War II, the United States was central to the origin and development of the contemporary aid regime.[5] Among its other initiatives in creating the postwar political and economic order, the Truman administration identified foreign assistance as a useful means of rebuilding decimated societies and hastening their return to economic vitality. The European Recovery Program (ERP), more widely known as the Marshall Plan, provided for the transfer of $13 billion between 1948 and 1952. Although most of these funds were transferred to Western European states, approximately $3 billion flowed to non-European states (e.g., Korea, the Philippines, Taiwan, and Turkey) for a variety of developmental purposes.[6] The Truman administration's motives underlying the Marshall Plan and the subsequent "Four Points" program were multiple, overlapping, and often ambiguous; hence, they have become the source of extensive post hoc speculation among historians and political scientists. Among its primary objectives, the Truman administration attempted to establish a postwar political and economic order that would encourage (and reward) democratic governments that pursued liberal macroeconomic policies. Secondary objectives included reestablishing markets for exports from the United States and Western Europe, helping domestic manufacturers and farmers dispose of surplus stocks, bolstering allies who had liquidated their overseas investments during the war and faced the impending loss of colonial possessions, and preserving the goodwill of LDCs as sources of raw materials and potential markets needed by the United States and other industrialized states.[7]

This process occurred alongside coordinated efforts by the Western industrialized powers to create a postwar security system. The Brussels Pact of 1948 linked France, Great Britain, and the Benelux countries, and the 1949 North Atlantic Treaty Organization (NATO) brought together the United States, Canada, Iceland, and thirteen Western European states. The Soviet Union and its Eastern European allies subsequently established the Warsaw Pact in 1955, in large part to counter NATO. In response, many LDCs, led by Egypt and India, subsequently formed the nonaligned movement to assert their independence from the superpowers. In this critical sense, the geopolitical maneuvering of the Cold War coincided with the formation of the aid regime; both processes, in fact, may best be viewed as two sides of the same coin.

The economic and Eurocentric character of the early aid regime shifted in the early 1950s as U.S. concerns stemming from the Chinese Revolution and the Korean War influenced development strategies. In the United States, the newly formed Mutual Security Agency (MSA) assumed control of the aid effort, overseeing the Economic Cooperation Administration (ECA), the Technical Cooperation Administration (TCA), and other agencies within the U.S. government. Institutional refinements continued in the mid-1950s, as the Mutual Security Act of 1954 created the International

Cooperation Administration (ICA) to coordinate U.S. aid transfers. Continuing assistance to Western Europe resulted from a trans-Atlantic "dollar gap" that threatened trade relations and heightened concern for the internal political stability of recipient states.

Other industrialized states joined the aid effort in the early 1950s. Under the 1950 Colombo Plan, members of the British Commonwealth, along with the U.S. government, provided economic and technical assistance to newly independent India and other developing countries in southern Asia. Other aid programs were established in the late 1950s by the Council for Mutual Economic Assistance (CMEA), primarily funded by the Soviet Union. Among recipients of CMEA assistance in the mid-1980s, those receiving the largest volumes included Vietnam, Cuba, Mongolia, Afghanistan, Ethiopia, and India (OECD, 1985a: 115). Thus, the seeds of "aid rivalry" were sown, as the Western-led effort to assist the economic recovery of the industrialized world gave way to competition among Cold War blocs.[8]

In the 1960s, amid continuing geopolitical tensions, ODA donors again shifted their focus, this time toward supporting decolonization and state-building efforts throughout the Third World, particularly in Africa. Aggregate aid flows doubled during this period as the institutional basis of the contemporary aid regime was established. The UN General Assembly proclaimed the 1960s the (first) "Development Decade" and established a target of 5 percent annual economic growth for LDCs.[9] To help them reach that target, wealthy states pledged increasing amounts of bilateral and multilateral funds. Leaders of the UN named global economic development as one of their central objectives in supporting the process of decolonization. Through the General Assembly, which included growing numbers of newly independent Third World states, and within its various specialized units, the UN emerged as an important multilateral conduit for economic assistance. Developing states, through the Group of 77 (G-77) and other coalitions, used the UN as a forum to study and articulate their collective needs.

Among its major initiatives, the UN sponsored conferences on world hunger and population growth and declared 1965 the "International Cooperation Year." The first UN Conference on Trade and Development (UNCTAD) was held in Geneva in 1964, during which representatives of 119 countries formulated collaborative efforts to support North-South economic cooperation. The UNCTAD meetings became routinized and "may well have laid the basis for a new constructive relationship between the industrialized countries of the middle latitudes and the developing nations of the tropics" (Black, 1968: 11). At the second UNCTAD meeting in 1968, members adopted the standard that donor states should provide at least 0.7 percent of their gross national products to development assistance by 1980, the first of several such targets for future aid flows. This and other long-term goals were outlined in the 1969 Pearson Report, which reflected the growing consensus among donors about the promising impact of aid on Third World development.

Within industrialized donor states during the 1960s, the Organization for European Economic Cooperation (OEEC) was reorganized as the Organization for Economic Cooperation and Development. The name change reflected the members' shift in emphasis from European postwar reconstruction to Third World development.[10] In 1963, OECD members formed the Development Assistance Committee, the coordinating agency for bilateral and multilateral transfers from member states. Immediately upon its inception, the DAC became "the leading forum of the richer nations for discussing their mutual interests involved in the policies, administration, and effectiveness of aid" (Rubin, 1966: 4).[11]

In the United States, this dynamism within the aid regime was reflected in John F. Kennedy's Alliance for Progress. Congress approved Kennedy's funding requests as well as his program to establish the U.S. Agency for International Development (USAID), the Peace Corps, and other organizations to promote Third World development. Whereas other ODA donors were encouraged to funnel assistance to Asian and African recipients, the United States targeted Latin America as a primary beneficiary of its Alliance for Progress. The U.S. aid effort, however, became entangled in the Vietnam War by decade's end and further complicated by aid rivalry with the Soviet Union and China, but the institutional restructuring overseen by the Kennedy administration remained intact three decades later.

The 1970s witnessed a sevenfold increase in concessional flows and a continuing proliferation of aid sources. Members of OPEC turned to ODA as an outlet for capital surpluses resulting from the price shocks of 1973–1974; by the early 1980s they accounted for more than 20 percent of global ODA flows. Led by Saudi Arabia, Kuwait, and the United Arab Emirates, these oil-producing states supported a relatively small number of developing nations, predominantly Islamic states such as Syria, Jordan, Bahrain, Yemen, and Sudan. Their selection in large measure reflected the contentious political alignments that took shape after the 1973 OPEC oil embargo. OPEC funding reached a peak of about $10 billion annually in the late 1970s, about 20 percent of global aid flows, before falling to less than $3 billion in the early 1990s.

As noted earlier, growing recognition of the shortcomings of past aid programs, particularly the failure of large-scale, capital-intensive projects to stimulate economic growth, resulted in a redirected focus on the basic human needs of Third World populations. In 1974 members of the G-77 proposed a New International Economic Order (NIEO), which called for

a new way of ordering the international economic system so as to bring about, first, improved terms of trade between the present-day center and periphery countries . . . ; secondly, more control by the periphery over the world economic cycles that pass through them . . . ; and, thirdly, increased and improved trade between the periphery countries themselves.[12]

These reforms were passed in December 1974 by the UN General Assembly as the Charter of Economic Rights and Duties of States. Though the stipulations in the charter were advisory in nature, the proposed NIEO identified structural problems in the world economy as the basis of LDC underdevelopment and articulated the preference of LDCs for fundamental changes in North-South relations. The proposals covered a wide range of issue areas, including development assistance. Whereas in the past ODA transfers had been directed toward industrialization and long-term economic development, often involving the construction of large government office buildings, power plants, and hydroelectric dams, new aid programs were directed toward agricultural programs and the day-to-day needs of individuals and small villages.

Private financial flows, in the form of loans rather than direct investment, became more common in the late 1970s and ultimately exceeded the volume of public transfers. This pattern continued in the early 1980s, as "recycled" OPEC revenues were transferred to Third World states that were unwilling or unable to apply for further ODA. These private flows, particularly to Mexico, Brazil, and Argentina, exacerbated the debt crisis of the early 1980s, which in turn prompted another shift in the focus of the ODA regime.

State creditors formed the Paris Club and private creditors the London Club to coordinate their efforts in managing nearly $1 trillion in Third World debt. Through the Baker and Brady plans (named after the U.S. treasury secretaries who promoted them), many of these debts were either rescheduled (i.e., given extended reimbursement periods) or, to a much smaller extent, forgiven outright. In return for these concessions, many Third World states agreed to submit to oversight by the World Bank and International Monetary Fund (IMF) of their fiscal, monetary, and trade policies. Recipients were encouraged to pursue fiscal policies that protected private enterprises from government intervention, preserved open markets and export-led growth, and discouraged inflation and the continued accumulation of transnational debt. These efforts effectively reduced the debt burdens of many LDCs, particularly those in Latin America, where economic growth rates began to accelerate in the early 1990s. Most African LDCs, however, continued to experience stagnant growth and sought further concessions from their public and private creditors.

This brief overview of the evolution of the ODA regime illustrates its intimate connection to other aspects of North-South relations and to the intensifying conflict between East and West. To a large extent, development aid flows have been coordinated with other forms of foreign aid and private capital transfers. The management of the resulting "debt overhang," which includes ODA and other capital flows, has required extensive coordination among states and between private and public sectors. Thus, ODA must not be viewed in isolation; the ODA regime is one among many that have become involved with the management of debt, the promotion of free trade, the coordination of global monetary policies, and the resolution of social and environmental problems that cross political boundaries.

Sources and Recipients of ODA

One of the most significant trends in postwar foreign assistance has been the ongoing proliferation of both donor and recipient states. Whereas immediately after World War II foreign aid was dominated by bilateral assistance from the United States, by the 1990s assistance was widely distributed among bilateral (i.e., national), multilateral, and private sources. And whereas a handful of European states received most foreign assistance in the late 1940s, almost every developing country sought or received ODA by 1990.

Among bilateral donors, the United States was by far the world's primary supplier of military and security assistance during the post–World War II period, transferring almost $400 billion to more than 120 states during the first 45 years after World War II (USAID, 1991: 4). In fiscal year 1991, a time of deepening economic recession, burgeoning trade and budget deficits, and widespread domestic opposition to foreign aid, the United States transferred more than $16 billion in economic assistance. The aid flows produced their own complex web of large and competing bureaucracies in Washington, D.C., and within recipient states, as well as a diffuse spectrum of policy objectives and expectations. The U.S. share of world ODA flows declined steadily (along with its share of global GNP) as other industrialized countries recovered from the devastation of World War II and initiated their own bilateral aid programs. The U.S. share exceeded 90 percent in the immediate postwar period, dipped to about 60 percent in the 1960s, and fell below 20 percent by the 1990s.

A major factor in this trend was the emergence of Japan as a major ODA donor. With memories of Japan's previous status as a recipient of U.S. economic support still in the minds of many government officials, Japan reached ODA parity with the United States in the late 1980s (see Figure 2.1). As it did so, its leaders pledged to broaden the distribution of Japanese development aid beyond the Pacific Rim, to direct increasing amounts through multilateral organizations and regional banks, and generally to increase its adherence to DAC standards of aid "quality." The U.S. government and other OECD members strongly encouraged this expansion of Japanese aid, which, given the externally imposed constraints on its military program, represented an important means by which Japan could become reintegrated within the network of industrialized states.

France attained its current status as the world's third largest donor of ODA by disbursing more than $4 billion in aid annually during the 1980s. Germany ($3.2 billion in 1981), the United Kingdom ($2.2 billion), and other Western European states also managed large-scale bilateral aid programs. As some LDCs, emulating Japan's approach to development, experienced rapid economic growth and thus "graduated" from recipient to donor status, they joined other affluent states in offering ODA packages; South Korea, for example, made such a transition and is scheduled to join the OECD in 1996. Taiwan, Singapore, Malaysia, and Thailand are expected to become aid donors by the end of the century. The World Bank (1993) hailed such cases as "models" of economic growth and published a guidebook for other LDCs entitled *The East Asian Economic Miracle.*

Additionally, multilateral organizations such as the European Community and various components of the United Nations tripled their share of global foreign assistance between 1956 and 1980. The growth in assistance channeled through multilateral agencies paralleled the ODA regime's increased emphasis on "high-quality" aid transfers. International organizations presumably eliminate the coercive strings and expectations that are attached to bilateral assistance and thus can more efficiently respond to the needs of developing states. More so than bilateral aid, foreign assistance from multilateral sources was distributed to least less-developed countries (LLDCs) and carried "softer" terms for reimbursement, often requiring no reciprocal obligations from recipients. Yet despite the growth in multilateral funding, most development assistance continued to be transferred bilaterally from donor to recipient states. Although bilateral transfers were less predominant by the 1980s, they remained the primary mode of ODA transfers. Bilateral assistance from developed countries accounted for 92 percent of aid transfers in 1956, compared to 57 percent in 1980. The proportion of multilateral aid varied dramatically among donors in the late 1980s, ranging from 12 percent in the case of New Zealand to more than 60 percent in the case of Ireland (OECD, 1991a: 178).

Regardless of the relative composition of bilateral and multilateral ODA flows, one must be mindful that both originate in legislative or executive bodies of the donor states and must ultimately be regarded as tools of those countries' foreign policies. And although multilateral aid is widely regarded as less "political," it must not be presumed that donor states provide these funds without regard to their use, efficacy, or domestic benefits. In some cases, multilateral ODA commitments serve the perceived national interests of donors as effectively as bilateral arrangements. Benefits include the enhanced credibility donors achieve by such collaborations. In other cases, particularly those involving environmental policy, multilateral agencies address regional or global problems of consequence to the donor states that cannot be resolved through bilateral channels.

Immediately after World War II, wealthy states organized their efforts within the World Bank, one of the central institutional manifestations of

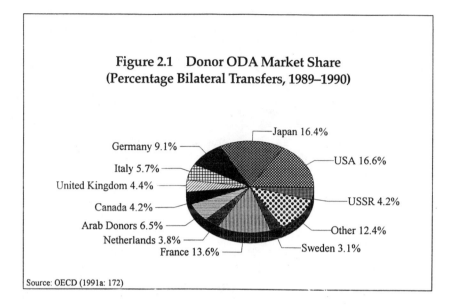

**Figure 2.1   Donor ODA Market Share
(Percentage Bilateral Transfers, 1989–1990)**

Japan 16.4%
Germany 9.1%
Italy 5.7%
United Kingdom 4.4%
Canada 4.2%
Arab Donors 6.5%
Netherlands 3.8%
France 13.6%
USA 16.6%
USSR 4.2%
Other 12.4%
Sweden 3.1%

Source: OECD (1991a: 172)

the Bretton Woods system. The International Bank for Reconstruction and Development (IBRD) was given responsibility for providing development capital to LDCs when private funds were unavailable. The IBRD emerged as the World Bank's "hard" loan window, from which it transferred low-interest loans obtained on international financial markets. Its initial objectives were articulated by Eugene Black, World Bank president from 1949 to 1962: "The function of foreign aid is to promote and marginally supplement the flow of private loan and direct investment capital to the developing countries and to assist these countries in mobilizing their own resources for achieving their developmental goals."[13]

Also during this period, leaders of the World Bank created the International Development Association (IDA) to promote and coordinate the transfer of "soft loans" (with little or no interest) from industrialized countries to LDCs.[14] Through the IDA, the World Bank continued to secure capital for developing countries despite their growing indebtedness and frequent domestic crises. After receiving periodic replenishments from the World Bank's wealthiest members, the IDA provided funds to recipients on more favorable terms than those extended through the IBRD. In addition, IDA funds were limited to the poorest of LDCs; only states with per capita annual incomes of less than $765 were eligible for IDA funds in the mid-1990s. In addition, the World Bank's International Finance Corporation (IFC) channeled aid to private industry within LDCs. This represented one of the most rapidly growing conduits of ODA in the 1980s and 1990s, as donor states promoted private-sector development projects rather than those controlled by recipient governments. Through the IFC, donors committed about $4 billion in 1993, almost six times more than the sum committed in the early 1980s.

Finally, an increasingly important outlet for multilateral financing was the array of regional development banks that emerged in the 1960s in response to appeals by developing states for assistance better suited to their specific needs. These included the Inter-American Development Bank, the African Development Bank, the Asian Development Bank, and the Caribbean Development Bank. In addition, such consortia as the Arab Fund for Economic and Social Development and the Islamic Development Bank made concessional funding available.

As noted previously, the role of private bank lending to developing states expanded widely in the 1970s and early 1980s. Whereas an almost imperceptible share of external financing came in the form of bank lending in the 1950s, by 1980 such transfers accounted for 45 percent of private capital flows, replacing direct investment as the primary source of private funds. For leaders of LDCs, private capital presumably liberated them from the potentially compromising position of accepting concessional funds from other nation-states, funds that were often tied to imports from the donors or to externally managed technical assistance projects. In an effort to avoid being subjected to the leverage of industrialized states, Third World leaders often turned to private sources of capital, which offered funds with fewer strings attached regarding LDCs' internal political structures, economic practices, and diplomatic positions, all of which became increasingly central to the calculations of government leaders in the 1980s and 1990s.

The proliferation of aid sources, as noted previously, has been accompanied by a widening population of actual and potential aid recipients. This group of recipients expanded steadily throughout the postwar period, reflecting the overall proliferation of nation-states in the world system. Many of the new recipients were in sub-Saharan Africa, where political independence did not translate into economic growth. To the contrary, poverty grew worse in many of these LDCs, which in turn provoked greater demands on their governments and undermined their political stability. As they attempted to resolve these internal problems, they increasingly relied upon foreign assistance for short-term relief and long-term economic development.[15]

In the early 1990s, with the demise of the Soviet Union and the independence of its former territories and satellite states, a new set of candidates for economic assistance emerged, including Russia, the Ukraine, the

Baltic states, Poland, Hungary, and other former members of the Warsaw Pact. Their political viability in large part depended upon rapid economic development, which in turn required large volumes of capital from industrialized countries. Some analysts saw these flows as a "grand bargain" by which Western states could ensure long-term stability and create lucrative markets for future commerce. OECD members contributed about $8 billion to these countries in 1991 and 1992, with Germany disbursing about half that total. Among recipients, Poland and Hungary received about 60 percent of OECD funding in 1992, with the remaining aid distributed evenly among Ukraine, Belarus, and former members of the Warsaw Pact (World Bank, 1994: 128–130).[16]

The end of the Cold War did not produce the end of the aid regime, as many had predicted, but it imposed new demands on donors and added a transformed East-West dimension to international development atop its continuing North-South orientation. The ability of developed countries to respond to these new demands was limited both by their own domestic economic problems and by preexisting commitments and long-term aid relationships that wedded donor states to recipients over an extended period of time. Enduring bilateral aid relationships would be threatened by a diversion of limited funds. Thus, despite the emergence of new potential recipients in Eastern Europe, LDCs in sub-Saharan Africa and South Asia still received nearly two-thirds of global ODA transfers in the early 1990s, with the remaining share being largely concentrated among recipients in East Asia and Latin America (see Figure 2.2).

Foreign assistance was a vital source of capital for these recipients, encouraging long-term bilateral ODA relationships and furthering the institutionalization of the aid regime. Foreign assistance accounted for 10 to 20 percent of the gross national products of many aid recipients during this period, and in some cases the level exceeded 50 percent. Both donors and recipients discouraged one-time infusions of aid, or "quick fixes" to resolve momentary needs, instead favoring sustained and predictable development support. Thus, the maintenance of ODA ties became a central area of contact between donors and recipients.

The diversity of bilateral aid programs was reflected in the multiple purposes and terms under which resources were transferred. By far the most common form of ODA in the late 1980s was grant aid, which constituted 70 percent of bilateral ODA in 1989–1990. The rest was transferred in the form of concessional loans, technically considered ODA because of their provisions for submarket interest rates and longer reimbursement periods than those offered by private sources. Among the emergent norms of the contemporary ODA regime, donors were encouraged to minimize the loan component of total ODA transfers and to extend aid on terms that did not require burdensome obligations by recipients. Interest rates for ODA loans varied across countries, with some countries

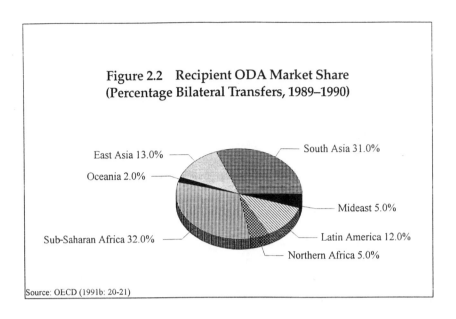

Figure 2.2   Recipient ODA Market Share
(Percentage Bilateral Transfers, 1989–1990)

East Asia 13.0%

Oceania 2.0%

South Asia 31.0%

Mideast 5.0%

Sub-Saharan Africa 32.0%

Latin America 12.0%

Northern Africa 5.0%

Source: OECD (1991b: 20-21)

(e.g., Canada and Denmark) expecting no interest and others (e.g., Austria) seeking interest of approximately 5 percent; average interest rates during the mid-1980s were about 3 percent. Further, donor states allowed varying grace periods before the first reimbursements on ODA loans were expected; the range extended from 5.7 years (West Germany) to 12.8 years (Switzerland), with an average grace period of about 8 years being reported by OECD members during the mid-1980s. Finally, the amount of time recipient states were given to repay these concessional loans ranged in 1984 from 13.9 years in the case of Norway to 50 years in that of Canada (OECD, 1985a: 108).

Donor states have long been able to require that ODA resources be spent on their own goods and services, a practice known as "tying" of foreign aid. In 1989, 63.5 percent of bilateral aid was at least partially tied by members of the DAC, mainly through requirements that donors be allowed to participate in technical cooperation projects funded by their ODA. Of untied aid, approximately half was transferred in the form of cash to recipients, with the remainder designated for open-ended technical cooperation projects and import financing.

Nearly 25 percent of foreign assistance was designated in 1988–1989 for social and political infrastructure. The construction or expansion of schools, hospitals, and government offices were included in this category. About 22 percent was directed toward economic infrastructure, including the construction of utilities, roads, and communication facilities. The remaining bilateral flows were directed toward, in order of magnitude, program assistance, agriculture, industrial production, and food aid (OECD, 1991a: 181). As in many other areas of development aid, the purposes for which concessional flows were extended were largely determined by donor states and thus reflected their overall foreign-policy prerogatives.

Foreign Assistance: Theoretical Perspectives

A central premise of this study is that foreign assistance may productively be viewed as a microcosm of nation-states' broader efforts in foreign affairs. Thus, it should not be surprising that interpretations of foreign aid commonly reflect the paradigmatic orientations of analysts toward political economy and international relations in general. In this section these theoretical perspectives are briefly reviewed, and their applications to foreign assistance are considered. At the risk of oversimplification and of obscuring important divisions within these categories, the common division of realist, idealist, and structuralist paradigms is applied in contrasting these theoretical perceptions of development aid (see Table 2.2).

To those adhering to the realist paradigm, international relations are conducted in a Hobbesian state of nature, a "war of all against all" that remains intractable given the inherent flaws in human nature, deep-seated cultural differences, and the absence of an overarching sovereign in world politics. Interstate relations are seen as generally conflictive in this view, and foreign policies are self-serving by necessity. *Raison d'état* is the operating principle for diplomats, who pursue national self-preservation as their primary, if not exclusive, objective. Given that realists generally define "good in terms of interest rather than morality . . . a realist ethic of the national interest is therefore typically both statist and amoral" (Donnelly, 1992: 91).

From the realist perspective, foreign assistance should primarily, if not exclusively, be designed to facilitate donor interests. Humanitarian objectives are deemphasized; aid is viewed as minimally related to recipient economic development. If an effect is identified, it is significant only to the extent that it increases the donor's political influence, military security, trade programs, and foreign investments. Foreign aid in this view is "inseparable from the problem of power. Politics is the governing factor, not an incidental factor which can be dispensed with" (Liska, 1960: 15). Prescriptions range from the elimination of aid programs that have little bearing on the donor's interests to qualified support for aid based on demonstrable benefits to the donor. To Singer (1972: 319), decisionmakers in

Table 2.2   Contrasting Views of Development Aid: Evaluations and Prescriptions

Normative Perspective	Evaluation of Current ODA	Prescription for Future ODA
Realist	Appropriate only to advance donor interests	Should be minimized; security assistance should take priority; economic funds should be linked to efficiency of LDCs and "return on investment"
Idealist	Potentially beneficial in addressing collective interests of donors and recipients	Should be expanded; "basic needs" and transnational problems should be priorities; donor and recipient states must reform aid bureaucracies
Structuralist	Instrument by which wealthy states exploit LDCs and institutionalize their dependence on the First World	Should be abolished in current form; international organizations should control redistribution of economic resources in pursuit of global economic equality

powerful states "are well aware that, rhetoric to the contrary, every economic or military aid package is tied in political strings." Relating this view to early U.S. aid policy, Brown and Opie (1953: 580) believed "the egalitarian principle has not been in the past and should not be in the future the basis of action in any phase of American foreign assistance. . . . [F]oreign assistance must be rooted in the interest of the United States."

Many realists have questioned the assumed linkages between the transfer of foreign assistance, recipient economic development, and subsequently harmonious relations between donor and recipient. Morgenthau (1963: 79), for example, found these assumptions to be "borne out neither by the experiences we have had nor by general historic experience." In his view, U.S. foreign assistance could better be understood as "bribes" from rich to poor countries. Similarly, Banfield (1963: 26–27) criticized the "fog of moralizing" that often accompanies foreign-aid rhetoric. "The most influential writings about aid doctrine are full of cliches and sweeping statements that turn out on close examination to be meaningless or else entirely unsupported by evidence." Moralistic analysis, he argued, "tells us how we ought to act in a world that is not the one in which we must act." Ten years later, Knorr (1973: 166) dismissed notions of "genuine philanthropy or humanitarianism" and added that "merely a small fraction of foreign economic aid can be safely attributed to a plain sense of human solidarity or to a sincere feeling that the wealthy . . . have the responsibility to share with the destitute two-thirds of mankind." He identified altruistic goals as one factor in aid calculations but considered them subordinate to other motivations, including economic and military needs, postcolonial control, long-term stability, and bureaucratic inertia. More recently, Gilpin (1987: 32) concluded that humanitarian concerns played an important role in foreign assistance allocations, but "the primary motives for official aid by governments have been political, military, and commercial."

Other realists have based their opposition to foreign assistance on the inability of recipient states to utilize the resources effectively. Wolfson (1979), for example, argued that the nondemocratic and crisis-prone political cultures in many LDCs limit their responsiveness to First World economic models and development assistance. This perspective convinced Bauer (1984) and Eberstadt (1988), among others, that aid programs must be more "businesslike" and therefore limited to recipients that could effectively convert the funds into sustained economic development. An assumption underlying this view is that ODA must provide some return on the investment for the donor, including the recipient's long-term presence as a market for exports and, through sustained growth, its diminished need for future concessional financing.

The idealist paradigm challenges realist assumptions and prescriptions in virtually every respect, advancing a vision that is more positive regarding the motivations of individuals and state actors and more optimistic about their potential for cooperative relations. To idealists, a conception of interstate relations based upon relentless competition both ignores the record of cooperation that emerged in the late twentieth century and serves as a self-fulfilling prophecy of future conflict. The debate between realists and idealists, predictably, has found expression in the area of foreign assistance. In the view of most idealists, national interests should be minimized or eliminated from aid calculations, which should instead be guided by transnational humanitarian concerns.

Some idealist assessments (e.g., Lumsdaine, 1993) have challenged the prevalent view that foreign aid has served primarily as a vehicle for the interests of donors and only secondarily addressed the developmental needs of LDC populations. These views emphasize the empirical relationships between many bilateral aid flows and the demonstrable human needs of Third World populations, as well as the proven success of many aid programs in alleviating poverty and suffering within LDCs. The role of the United States has distorted the crossnational record of development assistance from this perspective; when the aid policies of more numerous smaller aid donors are considered, the altruistic dimensions of global foreign aid are revealed.

Idealist critiques of ODA tend to focus more on its execution than its legitimacy, condemning the transfer of aid to repressive elites, large landholders, agribusiness concerns, and recipients that only marginally qualify as needy or less developed. Widely cited examples include U.S. economic aid to Egypt and Israel, the latter of which reported one of the highest living standards in the world during the 1980s. Japanese assistance to middle-income recipients along the Pacific Rim is also seen as violating the proclaimed goal of the aid regime to reduce suffering in LDCs and LLDCs. These critiques often emphasize specific ODA programs that have backfired, bringing more harm than good to recipient populations and producing ill will between donors and recipients. To Seitz (1980), U.S. policies in Iran during the 1970s merely bought resentment among the recipient population. Citing another example, Boyd (1982: 63) concluded that French ODA to its former colonies in Africa exacerbated the economic and political dependence of these LDCs. Similarly, Lappé et al. (1981) contended that many aid relationships merely compound domestic inequalities in Third World states. They stopped short of condemning the practice altogether but argued that "foreign assistance programs will help the poor and hungry abroad only if they attack the root causes of their suffering."

The integration of military and economic assistance is criticized by idealists for a variety of reasons: It promotes the militarization of developing countries, diverts funds otherwise available for development, subsumes LDCs in great-power conflicts, and undermines the developmental basis of foreign aid. Most aid donors have not established programs for military assistance, so such criticism has been most frequently directed toward the United States and the former Soviet Union but in some cases also toward France, Great Britain, and China. Many of the same criticisms were raised, especially during the 1990s, regarding the transfer of military technology, in particular that involving biological, chemical, or nuclear weaponry, to LDCs on commercial terms.

Others within the idealist paradigm emphasize the often inefficient institutional mechanisms by which aid programs are implemented. The decentralized structure for disbursing Japanese aid has often been criticized in this respect, as have the cumbersome bureaucratic processes associated with the U.S. Agency for International Development. Critics point to the tendency of bureaucratic inertia to drive these aid programs and of single development programs to be reproduced within many recipient states. These critics often advocate streamlined aid bureaucracies and aid programs more responsive to the specific needs of each recipient state. As Tendler (1975: 12) observed,

> The rationale behind development assistance . . . causes donor organizations to surround themselves with a protective aura of technical competence—an aura which must be maintained if they are to survive in their institutional world. This makes it difficult to generate the experimental environment necessary for their work. It also tends to result in placing the blame for failure on the wrong thing.[17]

The idealist paradigm is largely reflected in the existing standards of aid quality that continue to be advanced by the OECD and the United Nations: Multilateral aid is preferable to bilateral aid, given its less "political" nature; aid transfers should not be tied to donor goods and services; grants are more appropriate than low-interest loans; and aid should be directed toward recipients with the greatest demonstrable human needs. In the 1990s, standards of "sustainable" development have been added, promoting aid relationships that reward recipients that undertake population-control measures and preserve environmental quality. In addition, expectations of democratic practice within recipient states are most often advanced by idealists.

Structuralist critiques of foreign assistance are often based upon Marxist-Leninist assumptions about the role of economic wealth in enhancing the political power of elites in both industrialized and developing countries, as well as beliefs about the function of foreign aid in preserving or widening economic disparities between wealthy states and LDCs. Among structuralist critiques of ODA, Wood (1986: 5) found that world-systems analysis offers a "useful starting point" in considering aid.[18] Leaders of aid-donating "core" states, through their control of both public and private sources of financing, are able to dictate the development strategies of "peripheral" states in the Third World. Specifically, aid donors impose "outward, export-oriented" approaches to growth, thus depriving LDCs of "real inward-oriented, self-reliant strategies" (Wood, 1986: 314). Donor states and transnational organizations are often seen as engaged in collusive behavior in extending aid, unfairly coordinating resource flows to exploit their individual and collective advantages (Weissman, 1975).

This perspective was broadly shared within the Group of 77, UNCTAD, and other international organizations in the 1970s. Their members argued that a First World division of labor had emerged in the three decades after World War II in which foreign-aid programs were coordinated by donors to perpetuate their structural advantages over poorer states. "In an environment of essentially unmoderated competition, [donor] states employ control and influence strategies in order to protect their interests and thereby preserve their dominance," argued McKinlay (1979: 450). Traditional cultures and political economies were seen as corrupted by ODA relationships; the donor-recipient ties that resulted merely aggravated the preexisting inequalities in the world economy. Within recipient states, aid transfers strengthened the economic and political hegemony of elites, enabling them to impose their self-serving development schemes on the lower classes (see Hayter and Watson, 1985).

The perceived effects of this manipulation of foreign assistance include the increased reliance of LDCs on the monetary policies, consumption patterns, and export policies of core states; restricted political autonomy among leaders in developing states; and the overall subjugation of LDC economies to the Western-led global economy. In short, aid policies further encourage the "dependent development" of peripheral states.[19]

These critics further emphasize that in the case of many aid programs, particularly those of France and Great Britain, aid is primarily directed toward former colonies and effectively serves as a means by which they retain influence over their former colonial holdings: "Those countries which have had to relinquish control over their empires have found in aid the most convenient instrument to prolong and strengthen their influence and power" (Mende, 1973: 71). As Martin observed in relation to French policy toward its former colonies in Africa, "From the very beginning, France's process of decolonization was designed in such a way as to perpetuate dependency links after independence" (1985: 190). Japan's concentration of aid among the former members of its Greater East Asian Co-Prosperity Sphere is cited as another example of neocolonialism, as is the U.S. emphasis on bilateral aid programs to Central American states, many of which concurrently receive large infusions of military assistance (see Brynes, 1966). To Steven (1990: 64), "The movement abroad by Japanese capital is essentially the extension of a social relation, in which the Japanese bourgeoisie forms alliances with foreign ruling classes against both the Japanese and foreign working classes."

Critics from the structuralist perspective are generally pessimistic about the capacity of aid donors to change under the current system of dispensing ODA; their historical domination of the world economy precludes their rehabilitation into beneficent aid donors. For adherents of this view, the inequalities within the existing aid regime demand that it be abolished. Some contend that the practice of distributing foreign aid is fundamentally incompatible with international development; others believe international organizations must assume responsibility for the redistribution of wealth from North to South. Further resources should only be given to countries that demonstrate their willingness to use them in an egalitarian manner. Proponents of this view believe that industrialized states must ultimately commit greatly increased volumes of economic aid as a step toward global economic equality and that these transfers should be effectively disconnected from donors' self-interests.

These competing views were widely debated within the United Nations, the OECD, the World Bank, and other multilateral arenas.[20] The tenor of debate reflected the broader climate of world politics during each period; thus the Cold War infused the debate with ideological polemics. In addition, accumulating experience with development efforts contributed to the aid debate. Both the linear developmental model, predominant in the 1940s and 1950s, and that premised upon the nationalization of industries and import-substitution strategies, popular in the 1960s and 1970s, were weakened by their failed applications, whereas the success of other approaches, particularly the East Asian model of centrally directed, export-led growth, gained adherents. Throughout the post–World War II period, mounting empirical evidence relating to previous efforts was widely circulated and became manifested in ODA reforms and initiatives (see Todaro, 1977).

By the mid-1990s the ODA regime had become so institutionalized that ongoing criticism from the left and the right had limited impact on the scope and direction of aid flows. However contentious the debate, a consensus emerged in favor of the expansion of North-South development cooperation and the maintenance of qualitative standards along the lines favored by many idealists. But the presumptions of realists were also recognized by the aid regime, which acknowledged the intrusion of donor self-interests into aid relationships and the need for aid programs that were incorporated into "businesslike" macroeconomic policies. In general, a pragmatic approach to ODA emerged that recognized the inseparable coexistence of national interests and foreign aid. As Lairson and Skidmore (1993: 249) concluded,

> Given the political stakes associated with aid, the poor's lack of participation in the aid process is hardly accidental. Indeed, were aid to be reformed to focus more directly and effectively on the poor and to provide them with substantial input and control, aid would undoubtedly lose much of the appeal it presently holds for political elites in both donor and recipient nations. Ironically, taking the "politics" out of foreign aid might simply undercut the motivation for governments to go on spending and receiving foreign aid, leading to a massive contraction of such programs.

As the parameters of the aid debate narrowed in the 1980s and 1990s, one central assumption was shared by analysts of all normative persuasions: The relationship between political stability and economic development is truly symbiotic. Governments cannot govern effectively or judiciously in the midst of prolonged economic privation. Conversely, economic growth cannot be sustained in the midst of debilitating political turmoil. Consensus on this issue has resulted in the concurrent direction of ODA toward both goals through the construction of legislatures, magistracies, and town halls on the one hand and the delivery of fertilizer, tractors, and power generators on the other. Donors of ODA select recipients based on the expectation that the resources will contribute to both processes and that their combined effect will result in sustained progress that may lead the recipient toward self-sufficiency and promote greater economic integration between North and South. The interdependence of political and economic development, then, is appreciated by realists, idealists, and structuralists alike, although their ultimate assessments of and prescriptions for ODA continue to vary widely.

Four "Stories" of Development Aid

The next four chapters will consider the behavior of the French, Japanese, Swedish, and U.S. governments during the 1980s in the area of development aid to LDCs and LLDCs. The historical context of their aid policies and the empirical patterns of their aid flows will be reviewed, along with the implications for the linkage between national interest and foreign aid. These donor states were selected on the basis of their divergent but dynamic roles in world politics during the 1980s and their equally distinctive foreign assistance strategies and programs. They represented widely varying levels of economic output and other indicators of economic activity (see Table 2.3); each exhibited strengths and weaknesses in different categories of economic performance. In terms of gross output, for example, the United States was the preponderant economic power, with a GNP nearly double that of Japan and larger than the combined GNP of Japan, France, and Sweden. Japanese GNP growth was greatest among the four in 1990. Sweden reported the slowest pace of economic growth and the greatest relative level of external debt but also the highest per capita GNP and the lowest level of 1990 unemployment. France, despite its large size and active regional and global role, recorded the lowest per capita income and suffered the highest unemployment. In terms of government spending, an important factor in any discussion of foreign-assistance policy, Sweden reported the greatest spending rate, nearly twice that of Japan and the United States.

These differences in the French, Japanese, Swedish, and U.S. economic profiles are indicative of the countries' broader diversity, located as they are on three continents and having distinct languages, cultural traditions, and military and political systems. Yet these four nations also had much in common. They all achieved unprecedented prosperity during the post–World War II period, and all directed part of their wealth toward

Table 2.3　　Economic Profile of ODA Donors

	France	Japan	Sweden	United States
GNP 1989 (in U.S. $ billions)	$958	$2,900	$188	$5,100
Per capita-GNP (1990)	$21,100	$24,000	$26,000	$21,700
% GNP growth (1987–1990)	3.3	5.2	1.8	3.6
% Unemployment (1990)	9.0	2.1	1.5	5.5
Balance of payments (% 1990 GNP)	−0.7	1.2	−2.6	−1.8
Government spending (% 1989 GNP)	49.7	32.9	60.1	36.1

Source: OECD (1991a: 184)

ODA. By the 1980s their aid programs had become complex institutionally and far-flung geographically. To varying degrees, they generally adhered to agreed-upon norms of ODA behavior and took an active role within the coalescing ODA regime.

In each case, a very different story may be told. These donors confronted foreign affairs from very different vantage points, reflecting their resources, societal traditions, political institutions, and broader relations with other industrialized and developing states. Their ODA programs both reflected these differences and served as extensions of them, thus providing evidence of the linkage between national interest and foreign aid.

Notes

1. Private financial flows of $90.5 billion exceeded foreign aid ($67.2 billion) for the first time in 1992. International bank lending more than tripled between 1991 and 1992, from $11 billion to $37.7 billion (OECD, 1994a: 65). Only six years earlier, official development finance, of which ODA is the primary component, represented more than twice the total amount of private investment and commercial loans transferred to developing countries.

2. The most widely applied definition of an international regime was articulated by Krasner (1982: 186) as follows:

> Regimes can be defined as sets of implicit or explicit principles, norms, rules, and decision-making procedures around which actors' expectations converge in a given area of international relations. Principles are beliefs of fact, causation, and rectitude. Norms are standards of behavior defined in terms of rights and obligations. Rules are specific prescriptions or proscriptions for action. Decision-making procedures are prevailing practices for making and implementing collective choice.

3. Donor states pledged in 1972 to commit one quarter of ODA in grant form. Despite the absence of sanctions attached to this target, nearly every donor state has exceeded the 25 percent level of grant aid on a consistent basis. Some aid donors, including Sweden, have often reported grant elements of 100 percent; the average rate among all DAC members in the 1980s exceeded 90 percent.

4. See World Bank (1991: 33–35) for a review of the changes in development thought that accompanied the evolution of the ODA regime.

5. Packenham (1973) and Meier (1984) usefully detail the manner in which the incipient U.S. aid programs were designed to promote leaders' vision of a post-war international order.

6. Transfers ostensibly designated for Western European recipients were often redirected toward their colonial holdings, such as Indonesia (Netherlands), Indochina (France), and Malaysia (Great Britain).

7. An informative insider's account of this process is provided by Acheson (1969). See Kolko and Kolko (1972) for a critique of Truman's motivations and performance in constructing the postwar order.

8. At its peak in the early 1980s, CMEA assistance accounted for about 6 percent of global ODA flows.

9. LDC growth rates exceeded the UN goal of 5 percent during the 1960s, averaging 6.2 percent annually before slowing to 5 percent in the 1970s and declining further in the 1980s (OECD, 1985a: 263).

10. Members of the OECD include the four donor states under study, along with Australia, Austria, Belgium, Canada, Denmark, Finland, Germany, Greece, Iceland, Ireland, Italy, Luxembourg, the Netherlands, New Zealand, Norway, Portugal, Spain, Switzerland, Turkey, and the United Kingdom.

11. DAC members include all members of the OECD except Greece, Iceland, Portugal, and Turkey. The Commission of the European Communities is also part of the DAC.

12. Galtung (1991: 287) provides an informative retrospective of the NIEO movement and its experience since the 1970s.

13. See Mikesell (1983) for more details on the IBRD's early activities.

14. See Ayres (1983) for an analysis of the World Bank's involvement during the formative years of the ODA regime.

15. Until the 1980s, India was by far the world's leading ODA recipient, accounting for nearly 12 percent of aid flows (OECD, 1985a: 123). After Egypt and Israel signed the Camp David accords in 1979, however, their subsequent annual intake of U.S. ODA made them the top two recipients. In the 1982/83 fiscal year, Egypt and Israel accounted for 4.4 and 4.0 percent of global ODA receipts, respectively.

16. See the Institute for East-West Security Studies (1992) for a detailed review of aid transfers to Eastern European states in the years immediately following their severance from the Warsaw Pact.

17. See also Hancock (1989), Hellinger, Hellinger, and O'Regan (1988), McNeil (1981), Paddock and Paddock (1973), and Kaplan (1967).

18. See Shannon (1989), Thompson (1983), and Wallerstein (1979) for detailed examinations of the world-system perspective.

19. For elaborations of this view, see Chilcote (1984), Cardoso (1972), and Frank (1966).

20. This diversity of views was also reflected in disagreements among political economists over the process of economic development in different settings. Some perceived a linear process of development more or less common to all economies and nation-states. Within the Cambridge School of the 1940s and 1950s, economists formulated universal models by which "inputs" of foreign technology and capital would lead, within a specified degree of variance, to greater "outputs" of LDC economic growth (Rosenstein-Rodan, 1943). Others delineated progressive stages of economic development and encouraged industrialized states to assist LDCs in their "takeoff" toward the same growth patterns they previously experienced (Rostow, 1971). Finding fault with this "deterministic" approach, other scholars (e.g., Myrdal, 1971; Prebisch, 1959) argued that LDCs, especially those recently freed from colonial rule, were fundamentally different from established industrial states. Not only were these LDCs emerging from distinct historical and cultural traditions, but their continuing economic and political subordination to industrialized countries called for a different set of development strategies. These scholars recommended that such states should pursue independent, self-sufficient routes to economic development, with emphasis on meeting basic human needs and minimizing their dependence on industrialized countries. In the area of trade, seen as inherently biased in favor of the wealthy states, this led to support for assertive state intervention in economic development, import-substitution strategies designed to promote self-sufficiency, and the protection of LDCs from foreign competitors.

PART 2

Country Studies

3
French ODA:
The Projection of Grandeur

All my life I have thought of France in a certain way. This is inspired by sentiment as much as by reason. The emotional side of me tends to imagine France, like the princess in the fairy stories, or the Madonna in frescos, as dedicated to an exalted and exceptional destiny. Instinctively, I have the feeling that Providence has created her either for complete successes or for exemplary misfortunes. If, in spite of this, mediocrity shows in her acts and deeds, it strikes me as an absurd anomaly, to be imputed to the faults of Frenchmen, not to the genius of the land. But the positive side of my mind also assures me that France is not really herself unless in the front rank; that only vast enterprises are capable of counterbalancing the ferments of dispersal which are inherent in her people; that our country, as it is, surrounded by the others, as they are, must aim high and hold itself straight, on pain of mortal danger. In short, to my mind, France cannot be France without greatness.

—President Charles de Gaulle

Having recovered from two world wars and foreign occupations in three decades, the French government reemerged during the 1950s as a forceful and independent actor in world politics. De Gaulle, primary architect of the Fifth Republic's constitution, paved a "third way" between the two hemispheric blocs of the postwar era, resisting both U.S. and Soviet overtures and projecting France as a bridge between the industrial countries of the North and the developing states of the South. His successors continued de Gaulle's assertive approach to foreign affairs. In addition to restoring France's social cohesion and domestic infrastructure, they pursued the objectives of *détente, entente, et coopération* with foreign countries to renew France's prestige as one of the great powers.

France's expanding foreign-aid program served as an integral component in this effort to regain the "front-rank" status in world politics that it lost during a seventy-five-year span stretching from the Franco-Prussian War through World War II. Combined with other resources of the Fifth Republic, the foreign-assistance program served as an agent of France's "cultural nationalism" (Grosser, 1967). De Gaulle (1964: 78) declared France's "historic vocation" to assist in the "ascension of all peoples to modern civilization" and articulated these goals as being consistent with the "human

47

and universal" aspirations of French citizens. "In the midst of world alarms you can see . . . what weight France's will can have again."[1]

The Contours of French Foreign Policy

France's characteristic ambition to be a member of the geopolitical elite dates back several centuries, persisting despite the country's turbulent and often tragic experiences in foreign affairs. Having suffered severe losses in the wars of Louis XIV and in the Seven Years' War, France subsequently endured the cataclysms of the French Revolution and Napoleonic wars, annexations by Germany in the Franco-Prussian War, German occupation during two world wars, and the breakdown of colonial control in Indochina, Madagascar, and Algeria. Far from suppressing France's global aspirations, these setbacks only strengthened its resolve. During the Cold War, French leaders struggled for global influence ever more tenaciously, exhibiting a "discrepancy between ambition and power [that was] the most spectacular trait of French policy and strategy" (Macridis, 1992: 50). Although France was given one of five permanent seats on the UN Security Council, its leaders were excluded from most major-power deliberations at the close of World War II, including the Yalta and Potsdam conferences. This treatment, particularly France's exclusion from Franklin Roosevelt's proposed "Four Policemen," antagonized de Gaulle, who resisted the division of Europe and the bipolar balance of global power that served to marginalize the continent's role, along with that of France, in world politics.

Postwar France's foreign policy may thus be seen as a legacy of its traditional preoccupation with protecting and projecting its influence—political, economic, and cultural—within a hostile international setting. Dating back to the celebrated heroism of Joan of Arc and Charlemagne, this evangelical strain of French political culture inspired the romantic universalism of Descartes and Rousseau and found ultimate expression in the ideals and terrors of the French Revolution. Paradoxically, the universalist themes of *liberté, egalité, et fraternité* were affixed to the particularism of French nationhood and personified by a succession of French leaders. In attempting to impose French designs on his European neighbors from Madrid to Moscow, Napoleon revealed the extremes to which such idealism could be applied with public support. The power of charismatic authority was embodied in the immediate post–World War II period by de Gaulle, who was so dominant that in the 1980s and 1990s his "long shadow . . . still falls over the French political terrain" (Hoffmann, 1984–1985: 38).

In the making of foreign policy, the enduring consequences of Gaullism included the primacy of the president vis-à-vis the French legislature.[2] Foreign policy was *le domaine réservé* of the president, who served a seven-year term and was the ultimate guardian of France's security and prestige.[3] Despite their preeminence in foreign policy, however,

French presidents under the Fifth Republic generally conformed to a limited range of actions that were largely determined by and consistent with those of their predecessors. Incoming French presidents often vowed to alter relations with the superpowers, shift development strategies, or pursue other departures in foreign policy, but inevitably they retreated to previously established positions: "Whereas the internal reforms have been swift, far-reaching, and innovative, so foreign policy appears characterized by continuity" (Smouts, 1983: 155).

By the mid-1960s, de Gaulle had effectively reasserted the French presence in world politics, staking out an independent role vis-à-vis the Cold War rivals as well as among his alliance partners in NATO and the European Community. De Gaulle initially promoted an active French role within NATO, but he soured on the alliance after his proposals for a tripartite "directorate" over Western security (with the United States and Great Britain) were rejected. This rebuff led to the construction of an independent French nuclear program (the *force de frappe*) and the country's 1966 withdrawal from the command structure of NATO. De Gaulle (1964: 77) declared that within the "living reality" of the Atlantic Alliance, "France must have her own role in it, and her own personality. . . . Her destiny, although associated with that of her allies, must remain in her own hands."

A related objective of French leaders during the post–World War II period was to restore French social and cultural cohesion at home. For de Gaulle, holding together the chronically polarized segments of French domestic society was just as important as flexing French muscle in the international arena. This preoccupation, a by-product of the geographical and economic cleavages within the country, had long been a critical one in French domestic policy. De Gaulle accepted the entrenched divisions between farmers and manufacturers, socialists and nationalists, Parisians and residents of the "periphery." But, looking to foreign affairs, he overcame these rifts and effectively rallied the French population around his overseas initiatives. By the 1990s his long-term objective of "consensual cohabitation" among rival political parties was largely achieved. In this manner, the domestic tensions in French politics were "counterbalanced by an assertive foreign policy" (DePorte, 1984: 156).

In the post–de Gaulle era, several consistent strains were evident in French foreign policy that reflected enduring national interests, or, in the words of former foreign minister Claude Cheysson, "continuity that goes beyond majorities." Politics in this respect stopped at the water's edge; France's continuing penchant for domestic divisiveness would contrast with its united front toward the outside world. This aspect of French foreign policy preceded the Cold War and reinforced the implicit presumption that France's regional status and world role, regarded as given and therefore unalterable, dictated its foreign-policy initiatives rather than the reverse. As Martin observed, "There is no doubt that an autonomous and permanent policy exists, transcending the traditional political cleavages, the various regimes and individual political leaders" (1985: 190). The main priorities of postwar French foreign policy included the promotion of French nationalism as a means to secure domestic support and project regional influence; the maintenance of strong, independent military defenses, including the independent possession of nuclear weapons with a triad of air-, land-, and sea-based launching systems;[4] support for regional integration in Europe, with France as a powerful actor within the European Community (renamed the European Union in 1993) and other regional organizations;[5] and support for Third World states, particularly former French colonies, in their efforts to improve domestic living standards and resist de facto subjugation to other major powers. Whereas U.S. presidents throughout the Cold War interpreted Third World instability as Soviet-inspired, French leaders consistently argued that "it is poverty, oppression, and injustice which clear a path for the Soviet Union" (Smouts, 1983: 166).

After de Gaulle's departure in 1969, his successors adapted foreign policy—and aid strategy—to rapidly changing global conditions. Georges Pompidou, who served from 1969 until his death in 1974, was more receptive to European integration than de Gaulle, and he worked actively to bring about the entry of Great Britain into the European Community in 1973. But his continuation of nuclear testing in the Pacific in the face of regional protests, and his criticism of U.S.-Soviet détente as superpower "condominium," reflected de Gaulle's contentious approach.[6] The initiatives of President Valéry Giscard d'Estaing between 1974 and 1981 included the granting of independence to Djibouti (one of the last French possessions in Africa), rapprochement with the United States, and stepped-up efforts to promote regional and global arms control. He was equally determined, however, to modernize French conventional and nuclear forces in the late 1970s.

After his election in 1981, François Mitterrand emphasized social justice and economic equality, while drawing closer to the United States as the Soviet Union weakened and ultimately collapsed.[7] In addition to furthering the progress of European integration, whose early pioneers included Frenchmen Jean Monnet and Robert Schuman, Mitterrand worked to bring Germany more closely into a Western European system of collective security.[8] Previously the leader of a socialist-communist coalition in the National Assembly, Mitterrand concentrated on domestic reforms, adopting a pragmatic approach to foreign affairs. Of the 110 policy "propositions" advanced by Mitterrand during his 1980 campaign for the French presidency, only 19 covered foreign-policy issues.

Many of these initiatives, however, called for a greater French role in North-South relations. Mitterrand, who previously served as minister for overseas territories, proposed an ambitious agenda for France's relations with developing countries. He pledged French support for the New International Economic Order, which had been proposed in the 1970s by LDCs in the United Nations, and he vowed to double France's flows of ODA and reach the UN-prescribed 0.7 percent/GNP level by the end of his first term. Mitterrand further supported global negotiations for the redistribution of wealth from North to South, stabilization of prices for raw materials, and long-term commodity agreements as promoted by LDCs in the Group of 77. These initiatives served the twin purposes of underscoring French autonomy in foreign affairs and serving as a symbol of its goodwill toward the Third World.

Within France's multifaceted aid program, which stood as the world's third largest into the 1990s, ODA had become an important tool in reviving the country's status abroad. French leaders concentrated on their existing spheres of influence in the Third World, particularly in francophone Africa, the Caribbean, and the Pacific. In addition, they lent support to several Arab states in North Africa and the Middle East. These LDCs provided a much-needed outlet for France's global aspirations.

In many issue areas, Mitterrand departed from the foreign policies of Pompidou and Giscard, whom he criticized for subordinating French national interests to ideological posturing. Mitterrand sought and found a strange bedfellow in Ronald Reagan, elected to office in the same year. United by their opposition to the Soviet Union's intervention in Afghanistan, its ongoing hegemony in Eastern Europe, and its new nuclear weapons deployments in the region, Mitterrand and Reagan agreed that Soviet militarization demanded a Western response to achieve a balance of strategic power on the continent. Mitterrand successfully achieved an 18 percent increase in the French defense budget during his first year in office and won approval for an expansion of the country's nuclear naval fleet and the development of a mobile ballistic missile system. Though skeptical of the U.S. strategic doctrine of extended deterrence, Mitterrand gradually accommodated French policy to that of the United States and NATO. This adaptation was in part due to Mitterrand's perception of a weakening Atlantic Alliance in the 1980s, which led to a heightened commitment by France after its years of detachment from NATO. In other areas, however, Mitterrand remained true to the tradition of French autonomy in foreign policy. Many foreign-policy initiatives, for example, were directed toward the U.S. sphere of influence in Latin America: the recognition of El Salvador's Revolutionary Democratic Front as a "representative political force," the sale of arms to Nicaragua's Sandinista government, a bilateral pact with Mexico, and a personal appearance at the October 1981 Cancún Conference to discuss aid and security in Central America.

French foreign ambitions became more modest in the late 1980s and early 1990s, as the combined effects of European integration and the end of the Cold War inflamed many of the divisive aspects of French politics. One consequence was a deepening tension between de Gaulle's goal of independence and the growth of interdependence as a salient force in international relations of the period. France's persistence in a number of domestically driven economic issues, such as its opposition to a Common Agricultural Policy (CAP) injurious to French farmers, often clashed with pressures for transnational coordination. Its accommodation to these pressures did not, however, undermine France's long-standing national interest in great-power status, nor did it discourage the country's bridge building between North and South.

The Evolution of French Foreign Assistance

As they shored up their colonial holdings immediately after World War II, French leaders also converted Marshall Plan assistance into their own rapid economic development efforts. With nearly $3 billion in U.S. economic aid, the Fifth Republic reconstructed its manufacturing base and reemerged as a prominent economic power on the European mainland. De Gaulle cited rapid industrialization as a pillar of his postwar strategy and was largely successful in this goal. Closely related to this effort was the integration of the economies of France and francophone Africa. Under the terms of the Marshall Plan, French leaders were allowed to transfer a portion of U.S. aid to their colonies in Africa to stimulate regional economic growth and develop mineral resources of value to France. Though the political status of these new recipients was transformed after their independence between 1958 and 1962, their economic relationship to the French *metropole* remained functionally intact.

This aspect of French rule was first seen in its North American settlements during the eighteenth century. Subsequently, through the post-Napoleonic "long peace," imperial rivalries were replaced by a global division of colonial spoils, and France actively incorporated widely dispersed territories into its empire: first the trans-Atlantic outposts in the Caribbean; then the former Ottoman territories in Algeria and Tunisia; Indochina in the 1860s; and, in the 1890s, many parts of Africa. The "scramble for Africa" culminated in the continent's subjugation to European powers. Belgium, Germany, Italy, Portugal, and Spain obtained smaller territories in Africa, as France and Great Britain became the preeminent colonial powers.

For France, this effort led to control over sixteen African colonies covering 1.8 million square miles. Whereas the British decolonization process gave Third World dependencies relative autonomy from London, French leaders strove to incorporate subjugated regions into a Greater French Federation. They extended the reach of the French language into these areas, along with French methods of political administration. "Local leaders could express their demands effectively only in a foreigner's tongue, forcing upon them a significant break with their past," noted

Weiskel (1988: 113). As this process unfolded, the French sought to integrate the postcolonial economies, with Paris serving as their financial hub. French officials cited their desire to "Francify" the colonial populations as justification for their imposition of French customs and institutions.

At the 1944 Brazzaville Conference, convened by de Gaulle, leaders of French colonies were granted new political freedoms but informed that their futures would still be tied to that of a Greater France. Economic and political assimilation rather than outright independence would be acceptable to French colonial rulers. This effort was institutionalized politically, as 63 of the 600 seats of France's 1946 National Assembly were reserved for colonial representatives. (This representation was illusory in many cases, as voting rights were often limited to French inhabitants.) Electoral rules varied widely among France's colonies, but national political leaders ensured the preservation of the French Empire. France's postwar colonial development plan was known by the acronym FIDES, Latin for "fidelity," carefully chosen to reflect its effort "to reinforce the bond between France and her colonies" (Manning, 1988: 126).

Just a generation after they were created, the French federations in Africa rapidly disintegrated. At the same time, France's besieged army in Indochina was withdrawn after its 1954 defeat at Dien Bien Phu (with the burden of the ongoing regional conflict being fatefully bestowed upon the United States). The following year France relinquished its hold on Tunisia and Morocco, and in 1956 the National Assembly approved the *loi cadre* ("framework law"), by which the president could grant colonial independence by executive order. By 1960 de Gaulle had accepted the independence of most French colonies throughout Africa and successfully incorporated the emerging nation-states in a Franc Zone through bilateral "cooperation agreements." (It took de Gaulle until 1962, however, to end the debilitating struggle against Algeria and accept its independence.)

After returning to power in 1958, de Gaulle declared his mission "to renew France's substance and power, to restore her influence abroad, and to have her play as independent and active a role on the world stage as the world and French resources allowed" (Hoffmann, 1974: 283). Drawing on the examples of Richelieu and Louis XIV, he emphasized the importance of French national interests as a guidepost for foreign policy, one interest being the continuing French presence in Third World economic development. In this respect he displayed a "constant, almost paternal solicitude for the economic suffering of the poorer countries" (Willis, 1982: 7). De Gaulle retained close relations with selected LDCs after their liberation from colonial rule as a central part of his geopolitical strategy of offsetting U.S. and Soviet preponderance. He used the carrot of ODA to encourage Third World leaders, including Egypt's Gamal Abdul Nasser and Indonesia's Achem Sukarno, to avoid superpower alignments during the 1960s. Other recipients of French ODA, struggling with economic development and state-building efforts, were unable to establish sustained growth and remained dependent upon France for support.

One of the government's most thorough examinations of the French aid program, the 1964 *Jeanneney Report,* argued for a benevolent approach to foreign aid: "Even if France thought the poverty of others threatened neither her own development nor her security, she would have to assist them, simply because it would be intolerable for her to ignore their fate." Cold War considerations should be explicitly proscribed in future ODA deliberations. The Jeanneney Commission would only concede that "it was theoretically possible that, in the far distant future, aid might produce a few strategic, political, or economic advantages."[9] The report also recommended that far-flung and inefficient aid bureaucracies be centralized and that future flows be geographically diversified to include recipients beyond the Franc Zone. The French government responded to these recommendations by creating the Ministry of Cooperation and Development to oversee the aid program to former French colonies. By the early 1980s this ministry controlled the activities of more than 10,000 French citizens working in recipient countries. In addition, the government created a second organization, the Central Bank for Economic Development, to oversee the distribution of ODA loans. For other LDCs receiving French aid, the Ministry of Economy provided concessional loans and food aid, whereas the Ministry of Foreign Affairs administered technical assistance programs.

Though Mitterrand departed from his predecessors' approach to the Cold War adversaries, he maintained their close ties to developing states, particularly former French colonies. This effort persisted despite growing opposition to Mitterrand's domestic agenda, which intensified under worsening economic conditions in France, Western Europe, the United States, and much of the Third World. By the early 1990s this opposition included a growing nationalist movement and the election of a prime minister from the rival Conservative Party. France remained a champion of Third World interests throughout this period, often supporting LDCs in the United Nations when they clashed with the United States and other industrialized states.

Mission Civilisatrice and Foreign Aid

Unlike the colonial undertakings of other European powers, French involvement in Third World countries was implicitly, and often explicitly, directed toward "enlightening" their inhabitants as to republican rule, egalitarian order, and the rewards of modernity. Leaders in Paris found widespread public support for these efforts, especially as the country recovered from the traumas of world war, foreign occupation, and economic disarray. "Cultural imperialism, as opposed to military or economic imperialism, is something of which the French are not ashamed," asserted Hayter (1966: 9). During the decolonization period, former European rulers adopted differing postures toward their liberated subjects: Whereas England effectively withdrew and pursued other foreign-policy goals, France maintained its close economic, political, and cultural ties, largely through the vehicle of foreign assistance. By the early 1980s it was apparent that

> France still swaggers in Africa. Twenty years after freeing its colonies, it is the only colonial master who never went home. . . . French civil servants manage African government ministries. French businessmen are building the skyscrapers, the ports, the industry. It is possible in a dozen African cities to sit in a cafe on a boulevard named de Gaulle and scan a copy of *Le Monde.* (Kronholz, 1981: 1)

From their inception, transfers of ODA were explicitly designed to promote the distinctive characteristics of French culture, thus contributing to its self-proclaimed *mission civilisatrice.* One aid official observed in 1962 that French assistance does not serve economic or military interests; instead, "we have a responsibility before History." Among a broad cross-section of French political elites, "the dissemination of the French way of life and language was conceived as an important instrument for enlarging political influence and advancing economic interests abroad" (Kolodziej, 1974: 479). Other public statements demonstrated how foreign assistance would be predicated on "the belief that France has something uniquely valuable to contribute to the world as a whole. . . . [The program reflects] a strong proselytizing compulsion that demands from the educated Frenchman that he acquaint the barbarians with the achievements of his country's thought and culture" (Tint, 1972: 164). Mitterrand, despite his more detached foreign-policy style, generally "shared de Gaulle's faith in France's special mission in the world" (Moisi, 1981–1982: 347; see also Willis, 1982). This sense of French exceptionalism informed both the pragmatism of de Gaulle and Mitterrand and the more idealistic policies of Pompidou and Giscard.

In addition to its aid relationships, France retained broad and deep economic contacts with former colonies; it remained by far the primary market for their exports and their primary source of finished goods. Rice and rubber were imported from Indochina on a massive scale. African peanut and palm oil were widely used in the manufacture of French lubricants, fuels, and soaps. In the 1980s, France continued to import much of its strategic mineral supply from Africa, including 50 percent of its uranium and most of its precious metals.[10] It agreed in February 1982 to increase oil imports from Algeria, even at prices more than 10 percent above the world rate.[11] In return, French manufacturers exported heavy equipment and other finished goods to Third World markets, whereas other firms provided engineering services, construction management, and other expertise.[12]

In extending ODA, French leaders generally relied upon bilateral flows, a noteworthy pattern given the growing proportion of multilateral aid within the global ODA regime. While president, Pompidou defended this practice as an extension of the overall effort to extend French cultural influence: "It remains true that multilateral aid, in the way it is handled in the big international organisations, ends up reinforcing the English language. And I repeat we, as Frenchmen, feel a kind of need to maintain the French language. This is a fundamental reason for maintaining bilateral aid."[13] Pompidou also argued that multilateral assistance was generally more inefficient than bilateral assistance because it involved multiple bureaucracies, often with clashing priorities. Contrary to conventional wisdom, he believed that the involvement of transnational actors rendered multilateral aid even more political than ODA transferred bilaterally between donors and recipients.

The concentration of French ODA among its former colonies was reflected in the administration of French assistance, which oversaw separate programs for the major "ambit" recipients and other LDCs.[14] The Ministry of Cooperation and Development, later regrouped under the External Relations Ministry, coordinated assistance to the thirty recipients in sub-Saharan Africa and seven Caribbean states, which collectively received between 60 and 80 percent of French development assistance. In the 1980s, as France participated in the OECD's Concerted Plan of Action for the Development of Africa (CADA), this regional concentration increased. Table 3.1 illustrates the geographical concentration of French ODA in its former colonies and *Départments d'Outre-Mer/Territoires d'Outre-Mer* (Overseas Departments and Territories, or DOM/TOM). One-third of French ODA was transferred to these recipients in the mid-1980s (OECD, 1987a: 119). The DOM/TOM recipients constituted five of the top six beneficiaries of French ODA; if they were excluded, eight of the remaining top ten recipients were in francophone Africa. Meanwhile, the share of aid flows to other regions remained stable or fell, with Latin America and the Muslim states of North Africa and the Middle East experiencing the greatest reductions in French ODA.

Francophone Africa served a predictably vital role for France, given its geographic proximity and historic ties to Paris. The general absence of other external influences within the region, at a time when much of the Third World was enmeshed in Cold War competition, further facilitated the French strategy. France's sphere of influence was largely unchallenged by the superpowers, thus providing Paris with "a right of entry to the club of world powers" (Staniland, 1987: 56). These francophone states established their own system of regional economic coordination during this period, including the formation of the African and Malagasy Common Organization

Table 3.1   Top Ten Recipients of French ODA, 1970–1990

1970–1971	1980–1981	1989–1990 A	1989–1990 B
Réunion	Réunion	Réunion	Côte d'Ivoire
Algeria	Martinique	Martinique	Senegal
Martinique	New Caledonia	Côte d'Ivoire	Morocco
Guadeloupe	French Polynesia	New Caledonia	Cameroon
New Caledonia	Morocco	French Polynesia	Madagascar
Morocco	Senegal	Guadeloupe	Zaire
Côte d'Ivoire	Côte d'Ivoire	Senegal	China
Tunisia	Guiana	Morocco	Indonesia
Madagascar	Cameroon	Cameroon	Mali
Guiana	Algeria	Madagascar	Gabon

Source: OECD (1991b: 220)
Note: Fourth column (year 1989–1990B) excludes French Overseas Departments and Territories (DOM/TOM).

of 1965. Members consistently attempted to increase commerce with other industrialized countries, including the United States, West Germany, the former Soviet Union, Japan, and China, but their intimate ties to Paris were carefully preserved.

In addition to providing political and economic support, France stationed troops in six francophone states, including the Central African Republic, Chad, Côte d'Ivoire, Djibouti, Gabon, and Senegal. French troops were engaged in support roles in Cameroon, Gabon, and the Central African Republic during the 1960s and subsequently in Zaire and Chad. France also provided civil administrators (*coopérants*) to the francophone states and to those in the Maghreb region of North Africa, including Morocco, Tunisia, and Algeria. Although crucial to France from a strategic perspective, the francophone states were characterized by relatively small sizes and sparse populations. They were among the poorest of African states, with half of them falling into the World Bank's category of LLDCs. The region depended almost entirely upon agriculture or mining; only in Senegal, Burkina Faso, and Côte d'Ivoire did manufacturing account for more than 10 percent of gross national product.

However, these recipients offered various advantages to France, including reliable destinations for exports and sources of raw materials. Under the guidelines of the Franc Zone, France served as a supranational central bank through which a common currency was tied to the French franc and guaranteed by the French treasury. By wedding its own fiscal policy to that of the Franc Zone, France attempted to preserve monetary stability throughout the region. Concurrently, it coordinated financial flows within the region; regulated the members' banking, credit, and fiscal policies; provided emergency credit when necessary; subsidized private investments to Franc Zone members; and offered tax breaks to private companies doing business in the region. For their part, member states were required to hold at least 65 percent of their monetary reserves in the French central bank. In addition, their monetary stability was linked to the often volatile exchange rates of the franc on world markets. And given the critical functions they granted to France, the African nation-states effectively sacrificed a degree of autonomy over domestic macroeconomic policy, with uncertain consequences and implications.[15]

In terms of its impact on total economic activity, trade between France and its African clients was far more significant for the latter. Trade with Africa amounted to less than 3 percent of France's total commerce during the decade, and the region absorbed less than 20 percent of French foreign investment to LDCs. As for the members of the Franc Zone, however, trade with France made up about 50 percent of their total. France consistently ran a surplus in excess of 10 billion francs with these partners, of whom three—Cameroon, Côte d'Ivoire, and Gabon—were involved in a preponderant share of Franco-African trade. Thus, paradoxically, commercial ties between the two regions affected the economies of Africa more significantly than that of France, but "the benefits of these interchanges [were] asymmetrical, helping the French more than the Africans" (Boyd, 1982: 46).[16] As some critics and the *Jeanneney Report* concluded, French postwar aid policy was self-limiting and needed to extend beyond francophone Africa if France were to become a champion of North-South cooperation on a global scale. Thus, efforts were made to diversify the recipients of ODA, resulting in larger transfers to Latin America, India, and Pakistan. But the geographical concentration and social-cultural orientation remained largely intact.

French ODA in Practice

Let us now review the empirical record of French ODA during the 1980s and consider its relationship to the country's broader foreign-policy goals. As previously noted, French leaders accelerated their ODA efforts during the decade. After its share of global ODA flows had fallen between 1970 and 1980, French aid expanded steadily during the ensuing ten years. The 4.9 percent growth rate of French ODA, in fact, was the fourth highest among DAC members during the period (OECD, 1991a: 139), propelling France to the front rank of aid donors (see Table 3.2). Aggregate French ODA transfers during fiscal year 1989/90 were twice the 1970 level and represented a 60 percent increase from the level at the beginning of the 1980s. Its 1989–1990 ODA flows of $7.6 billion exceeded those of other European donors, including Germany ($5.1 billion), Italy ($3.2 billion), Great Britain ($2.4 billion), the Netherlands ($2.1 billion), and Sweden ($1.7 billion).[17]

As noted previously, the sustained growth of France's aid program during the decade, in absolute as well as relative terms, reflected Mitterrand's desire to play a more active role in North-South relations, particularly at the regional level. Domestically, France's more assertive approach to ODA was evident during a period in which it suffered from a negative balance of payments and sluggish annual economic growth.[18] France experienced the lowest per capita GNP levels and the highest unemployment rates of the four donor states under review in this study (see Chapter 2). Thus, its ODA activism placed a heavier burden on its population relative to that of other donor states.

As a percentage of French GNP, ODA outlays reached their highest level in the final year under review, a pattern that applied to both categories of French aid—i.e., including or excluding the DOM/TOM recipients, which annually received disproportionate volumes of French aid. If aid to the DOM/TOM recipients was excluded (the preferred approach for most analysts of French ODA), the ODA/GNP proportion rose 58 percent during the decade. This pattern was also evident with regard to the proportion of global ODA represented by French flows. In this case, the French share of ODA to non-DOM/TOM recipients increased by 28 percent during the 1980s, returning France to the level maintained into the 1970s of approximately 10 percent of global ODA. When DOM/TOM recipients were included, the level during the final year of the 1980s approached but did not reach the 14.8 percent peak of 1970–1971.

Figure 3.1 illustrates the disproportionate share of French ODA transferred to recipients in francophone Africa during the 1980s. Not only did the region receive the largest share of French ODA (more than 50 percent in 1990), aggregate flows during the decade steadily increased, whereas those to other regions (particularly Latin America) remained static or declined.

Table 3.2   French ODA Transfers, 1970–1990

	ODA Commitment[a]	Percent GNP	Share of World ODA
1970–1971	3,782 (2,405)[b]	0.68 (0.43)	14.8 (9.4)
1980–1981	5,261 (3,326)	0.67 (0.43)	9.5 (6.0)
1989–1990	7,614 (5,305)	0.78 (0.55)	13.6 (9.5)

Source: OECD (1991a)
Notes: a. ODA commitment in millions of current U.S. dollars
b. Aid flows excluding those to Overseas Departments and Territories (DOM/TOM) listed in parentheses

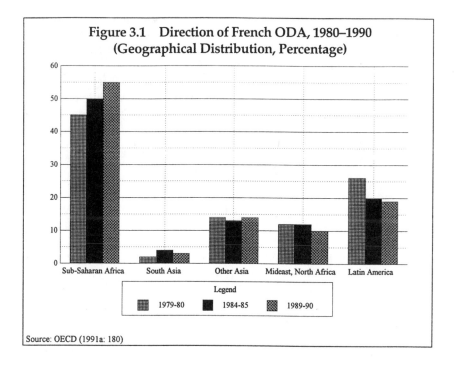

Figure 3.1   Direction of French ODA, 1980–1990 (Geographical Distribution, Percentage)

Source: OECD (1991a: 180)

When we consider the purposes to which French aid was directed, we find that technical assistance in support of political infrastructure was utilized most often during the 1980s (see Figure 3.2). The 40 percent level in 1988–1989 was the highest percentage of any DAC member for such purposes, which included engineering and construction of schools, government buildings, and other public facilities. Support for economic infrastructure (21 percent of ODA in 1988–1989) represented the secondary function of French aid, whereas efforts to promote industry and agriculture received less than 10 percent of bilateral ODA outlays and direct food aid just 1 percent. The concentration of assistance in the area of political infrastructure clearly illustrates the French government's emphasis on state building within the francophone countries; such assistance often involved the direct participation of French *coopérants,* 10,000 of whom fulfilled their obligatory national service in these projects annually during the 1980s.[19]

As noted previously, actors within the global ODA regime monitored not only the quantity of assistance transfers but also their "quality," or the degree to which they directly addressed the basic human needs of LDC populations. Throughout the 1980s, the French government declared its intention to improve its aid quality, pledging at the 1981 UN Conference on the Least Developed Countries that it would target increasing shares of

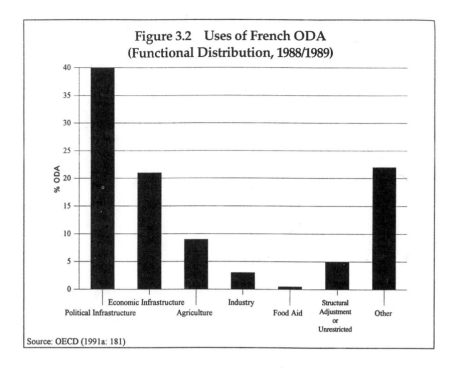

**Figure 3.2 Uses of French ODA
(Functional Distribution, 1988/1989)**

Source: OECD (1991a: 181)

ODA to the poorest of societies. In three of the four categories of ODA quality, however, French flows at the end of the decade generally ranked below the DAC average (see Table 3.3). Whereas most DAC members generally improved demonstrable aid quality during the 1980s, the ten-year pattern of French flows reflected a relatively static pattern.

In terms of the relative grant element of ODA outlays, as opposed to low-interest loans, French aid flows began the 1980s above the DAC average but fell below it in the latter half of the decade. Whereas the grant element of DAC flows increased throughout the period to a peak of 93 percent at decade's end, the grant element of French flows actually decreased between 1980 and 1986 before rising in the final three years. Even then, however, France's grant element fell short of the DAC average. In another closely watched qualitative area, the proportion of untied French development aid remained consistent during the period, averaging about 41 percent. Viewed another way, approximately 60 percent of French ODA was tied to the acquisition of French goods or services in the 1980s. This consistency was unusual among DAC members in general, whose proportion of untied ODA fell dramatically in the latter half of the decade, marking an exception to the general rule of increasing ODA quality during the period.

Table 3.3   Quality of French ODA, 1980–1989

	Grant Element (% ODA)	Untied Aid (% ODA)	Multilateral Aid (% ODA)	Aid to LLDCs (% ODA)
1980	80.9	42.7	15.3	16.0
	(75.2)[a]	(50.3)	(28.5)	(21.6)
1983	79.0	40.3	15.0	18.1
	(78.8)	(45.9)	(31.3)	(21.8)
1986	78.2	42.2	18.4	18.2
	(87.0)	(33.4)	(28.1)	(23.4)
1989	90.2	40.2	17.0	18.0
	(92.8)	(36.5)	(27.2)	(22.4)

Sources: OECD (1982b, 1985b, 1988b, 1991b)
Note: a. Figures in parentheses are DAC averages

For France, as in other areas of ODA behavior, the tying of aid was marked by a two-track policy. Whereas its leaders generally did not tie ODA transfers to Franc Zone recipients, flows to other recipients were more often linked to reciprocal obligations. Although aid to members of the Franc Zone was often *formally* untied, the web of fiscal, monetary, and commercial linkages between the two regions effectively tied their aid relationships. France's preoccupation with its overseas territories and Franc Zone recipients was also manifested in its relatively low levels of multilateral ODA during the 1980s. French multilateral transfers, though rising slightly during the period, remained below the 20 percent level, whereas the DAC average stood consistently in the range of 27 to 31 percent. As we have seen, multilateral ODA is generally viewed as less political than bilateral flows, with recipients subjected to less pressure or coercion by their ODA benefactors.

Finally, French ODA flows to the LLDCs were consistently lower than the DAC average throughout the period under study. France's contribution to these "Fourth World" recipients did not exceed 18.2 percent of its total ODA, whereas the DAC average did not fall below 21 percent. French officials, however, softened the terms of aid to LLDCs, which became subject to separate qualitative standards within the aid regime. Additionally, French aid to LLDCs was transferred entirely in grant form by the end of the decade. And in 1989, France announced it would cancel nearly $3 billion in outstanding debts incurred by the poorest recipients in sub-Saharan Africa.

In shifting our attention to the regression matrix (see Table 3.4), we observe most clearly the strong indication of French economic interest in its ODA relationships. French bilateral trade co-varied with aid flows at a statistically significant level in eight of the ten years under study. This statistical pattern of French aid following French trade provides further evidence of the economic nexus through the 1980s.

France's trading partners during this period were primarily other members of the European Community, with West Germany, Italy, Belgium, and the United Kingdom serving as the major recipients of French exports (International Monetary Fund, 1991).[20] Among developing regions, Africa conducted the greatest volume of trade with France. Morocco, Côte d'Ivoire, Cameroon, Senegal, and Gabon—all among the top ten recipients of French development assistance—were also its most active Third World trading partners. Réunion, which received the largest volumes of French ODA between 1970 and 1990, was also a major importer of French goods; its total imports amounted to $470 million in 1985 and $1 billion in 1989. French trade with Asia and Latin America, by comparision, remained relatively modest until the end of the decade, when the French government approved large-scale export agreements with Asian countries. France in 1989 exported approximately $1 billion worth of goods to China, India, Hong Kong, Singapore, South Korea, and Saudi Arabia. Among these countries, only China was a major recipient of French ODA. Also in that year, France recorded greatly increased exports to its Latin American territories of Guadeloupe ($938 million) and Martinique ($858 million), each of which received large transfers of ODA.

A negative statistical relationship between French ODA transfers and recipient life-expectancy in eight of the ten years suggests that France's economic interests were compatible with a concurrent humanitarian interest served by ODA transfers to non-DOM/TOM recipients. French aid was directed toward states with relatively low per capita life expectancies, a pattern that persisted even after other possible considerations were controlled for. The average life expectancy for the top ten recipients of French ODA was 54.6 years in 1988, much lower than the worldwide average of 64 years (World Bank, 1990: 178). Life expectancies within this group of recipients ranged from 47 in the case of Zaire to 70 in the case of China.

This relationship is far weaker, however, when DOM/TOM nations are added to the set of primary French ODA recipients. The average life expectancy in this case was 62.8 years, closer to the worldwide average. Within this group, inhabitants of Martinique lived an average of 75 years, Guadeloupe 74 years, French Polynesia 72 years, Réunion 71 years, and New Caledonia 68 years.[21] Thus, the relationship between French ODA and the humanitarian needs of recipients is far different when DOM/TOM countries are accounted for. This discrepancy has been a source of contention between the French government, which prefers to exclude the DOM/TOM recipients from its aid statistics, and the OECD, which documents overall French aid.

Table 3.4   French ODA and Recipient Characteristics: Multivariate Relationships
(Figures indicate standardized slope coefficients)

	1980	1981	1982	1983	1984	1985	1986	1987	1988	1989
	Humanitarian-Interest Variables									
Life expectancy	−.40[a]	−.46	−.41	−.41	−.27	−.58	−.29	−.42	−.53	−.51
Caloric consumption	.22	.17	.14	.28	.03	.35	.06	.32	.33	.18
	Security-Interest Variables									
Military spending	−.19	.17	−.09	.15	−.13	−.01	.20	.05	.61	.26
Conscripted population	−.17	−.01	−.10	−.20	−.06	−.09	−.20	−.22	−.30	−.22
	Economic-Interest Variables									
GNP	.16	.23	.16	−.23	.10	.05	.01	−.12	−.20	.01
Trade with France	.58	.36	.42	.44	.35	.24	.34	.34	.25	.42
Total R^2	.51	.34	.35	.36	.19	.26	.26	.26	.53	.41

Sources: U.S. ACDA (security-interest variables); IMF (trade variable); OECD (aid transfers [dependent variables]); World Bank (all other variables)

Note: a. Underlined figures indicate significance at .05 level; double-underlined figures indicate significance at .01 level

Among the non-DOM/TOM recipients, daily per capita consumption averaged 2,441 calories in 1989, about 11 percent below the worldwide average rate of 2,711 calories. Two of France's primary recipients, Morocco (3,020) and Indonesia (2,750), exceeded the worldwide average, whereas two others, Côte d'Ivoire (2,577) and China (2,639), exceeded the average per capita consumption of low-income countries as defined by the World Bank. As reflected in the statistical analysis, this measure of recipient need did not relate significantly to France's distribution of development assistance in the decade under study.

Statistical analysis reveals no direct link between security interests and French ODA flows. Aid transfers were not disproportionately directed to recipients with large conscription rates or levels of military spending. Among the ten leading recipients of French ODA in 1989–1990 (excluding the DOM/TOM recipients), conscription rates averaged 3.1 per 1,000 citizens during the 1980s, far below the worldwide average of 5.9 per 1,000. The conscription rates ranged from 0.9 in the case of Côte d'Ivoire to 8 in the case of Gabon. In terms of absolute levels of military spending, most of these recipients spent less than $200 million annually on defense; the obvious exception to this pattern was China, which averaged $23 billion in military spending during the ten-year period.[22]

The general absence of a relationship between French ODA and recipient militarization is understandable given the geographical concentration of French ODA among states within France's sphere of influence in francophone Africa. As part of its broader embrace of the region, France provided for the security of these states, either indirectly through security guarantees or directly through the presence of French troops. Unlike primary recipients of U.S. ODA, which were often located on the front lines of regional conflicts, France's primary recipients remained generally sheltered from military engagements.

Importantly, humanitarian and economic linkages to foreign assistance were explicitly sought by French leaders during the early stages of French involvement in the ODA regime. As the 1975 *Abelin Report* (quoted in Evans, 1989: 136) stated,

> Our aim is one of mutual benefit; we must affirm in frankness and without any sense of guilt that France intends to develop its commercial and cultural relations with those regions of the world whose human development it wishes to foster, not only by reason of their raw materials but also of their human resources, their geographical importance and their historical echoes.

In this sense, French behavior in transferring development assistance during the 1980s was consistent with the stated objectives of its leaders, who openly equated French national interests with those of its aid recipients and tailored aid flows to serve these collective interests. French leaders generally acknowledged the geographic and functional concentrations of ODA as well as its crucial role in furthering France's self-interests.

Summary

As illustrated in this chapter, France's preoccupation with domestic cultural traditions, a common and long-standing national characteristic, reemerged with the country's physical vitality in the first decade after World War II. These "politics of grandeur" (Cerny, 1980) found expression in the French language and within France's political, economic, educational, and religious institutions. More specifically, they found expression in France's program of supporting impoverished countries through ODA. As Smouts observed, "Development aid policy and the pursuit of a more equitable international economic order represent the extension onto the outside world of the policy of social justice proclaimed at home" (1983: 164).

Among its most important objectives, the Fifth Republic sought to secure France's prominence among the great powers through the pursuit of an independent foreign policy. France's nuclear *force de frappe* (and its refusal to abolish nuclear testing or sign the nonproliferation treaty), de Gaulle's appeals to French nationalism in Quebec and other outposts, his early challenges to U.S. and NATO strategic doctrine, and French leaders' public criticism of Soviet hegemony in Eastern Europe and Afghanistan all attest to the autonomous strain in French foreign policy. With regard to the Third World, France pursued a two-track aid strategy based upon its traditional interests. Its leaders actively supported French overseas territories, many of which did not suffer living standards as low as those found in other LDCs, and they transferred much of their remaining ODA resources to francophone states in Africa with long-standing cultural and socioeconomic ties to Paris. In both cases, economic relationships between donor and recipient remained close, extending beyond aid to bilateral trade, to the purchase of French goods and services, and to French coordination in their social and political development. Observed Boyd, "Whether aid of this sort is designed to help the people of the Third World more than it helps French firms and nationals is a debatable point, but that the French use their aid and investment policies to keep their cultural, political, and economic ties with the Third World viable is a certainty" (1982: 51).

Whereas de Gaulle exhibited a paternalistic attitude toward the states of sub-Saharan Africa, never personally venturing south of the Maghreb region after 1958, his successors visited francophone states on a regular basis and convened annual Franco-African summit meetings to discuss matters of mutual concern. French attention to its regional sphere of influence remained a central element of its foreign policy after the Cold War ended and a new era of world politics emerged.[23] To Kissinger (1994), this behavior reflected a well-established historical pattern:

> France's penchant for associating with countries ready to accept its leadership has been a constant factor in French foreign policy since the Crimean War. Unable to dominate an alliance with Great Britain, Germany, Russia, or the United States, and considering junior status incompatible with its notions of national *grandeur* and its messianic role in the world, France has sought leadership in pacts with lesser powers.

From de Gaulle to Mitterrand, four French heads of state consistently applied ODA to a discernible and enduring set of national interests. In the 1980s, French ODA assumed an especially vital role in the pursuit of those interests, responding to needs among French clients for assistance during a time of growing economic instability in both North and South. As France continued to focus on francophone Africa in its ODA policies, newly unified Germany became the primary donor of concessional development assistance to Russia and other incipient nation-states in Eastern Europe. Whether a long-term division of ODA resources will form along these geographical lines and what its implications will be for European foreign relations are compelling questions in the 1990s.

Notes

1. Like his predecessors, de Gaulle saw France as "the central source of European intellectual inspiration" and consequently viewed his diplomatic corps as "leaders and guides" of the world, not "masters or aspirants to mastery" (DePorte, 1984: 150).

2. The prime minister, although not formally granted substantial foreign-policy powers, is encouraged to speak out "in order to enhance his standing as a presidential candidate" (Clark, 1987: 135). Thus, although the general direction of foreign policy is not usually contested, specific issues (e.g., treaties, military appropriations, UN positions) are openly debated in the parliament.

3. The primacy of the French president in foreign affairs was reaffirmed in 1986 in an agreement between Mitterrand and Prime Minister Jacques Chirac. The two differed on a wide variety of issues, but Mitterrand's authority in foreign policy was a primary reason for his reelection to the presidency in 1988.

4. Toward that end, France in 1985 launched its sixth nuclear submarine, the *L'Inflexible*, which was equipped with multiple nuclear warheads. The aerial component of the triad was enhanced by a new generation of Mirage jets, and the ground-based component was scheduled for modernization in the early 1990s.

5. De Gaulle's repeated vision of a united Europe "from the Atlantic to the Urals" was a guiding force behind this effort.

6. Pompidou's observance of an arms embargo against Israel and his approval of a sale of Mirage fighter jets to Libya in 1970 further antagonized the United States during this period. Mitterrand's sale of Mirage 2000 jets to India had the same effect in the 1980s.

7. Mitterrand's rise to power included a brief tenure as minister for overseas territories between 1950 and 1951.

8. An extension of this effort was a Franco-German military brigade that was proposed as a complement to NATO in the post–Cold War period. Joint Franco-German military maneuvers took place in September 1989 as the two countries began discussions regarding collaboration in military construction. "These agreements and the deepening Franco-German cooperation strengthened both the FRG and France individually; they strengthened them both within the Atlantic Alliance and strengthened the Alliance itself" (Macridis, 1992: 60).

9. See Berthelot (1973) and Hayter (1966) for detailed elaborations of this report and its long-term impact on French foreign assistance.

10. France imported much of these strategic minerals from South Africa, even as it opposed its system of racial apartheid. By the mid-1980s, "Economic pragmatism is clearly prevailing over idealism and all idea of 'sanctions' has disappeared from official pronouncements" (Smouts, 1983: 167).

11. The Algerian gas agreement "is first and foremost political and sets the seal on a process of reconciliation with a country which France considers central to any Mediterranean policy" (Smouts, 1983: 165).

12. Like other colonial and postcolonial powers, France was prone to sometimes brutal exploitation of subject populations. Forced labor, a "head tax" that drew from the meager incomes of African workers, and summary justice were common features in French colonies. But the colonization of African nations, the future beneficiaries of French foreign aid, was cloaked in the rhetoric of cultural salvation.

13. See Tint (1972: 185) for an elaboration.

14. The ambit states included Benin, Burkina Faso, Comoros, Central African Republic, Chad, Congo, Côte d'Ivoire, Djibouti, Gabon, Guinea, Madagascar,

Mali, Mauritania, Niger, and Senegal. Cameroon and Togo had been administered by France as UN trust territories, and Burundi, Rwanda, and Zaire had been Belgian territories before becoming part of francophone Africa.

15. Two regional banks operated through the French treasury to serve these functions. A West African central bank regulated the currencies of Benin, Côte d'Ivoire, Niger, Senegal, and Upper Volta. A second central bank provided the same services for Franc Zone members in equatorial Africa, including Cameroon, the Central African Republic, Chad, Congo, and Gabon.

16. During the 1980s, French trade with Africa become increasingly oriented toward energy resources. France and oil-rich Algeria, in a step toward reconciliation after many years of animosity, signed a Charter of Economic Cooperation in June of 1982. As part of this agreement, France would be assured of Algerian oil, albeit at a price more than 13 percent above the world market cost.

17. Eleven other members of the DAC contributed less than $1 billion each in 1989–1990. Among non-DAC members, Saudi Arabia transferred $2.2 billion and the former Soviet Union $2.3 billion in development aid during this period (OECD, 1991a: 172).

18. French monetary problems worsened as the franc was devalued in June 1982 to make it more competitive against other currencies, particularly the German mark.

19. France increased its proportion of ODA allotted to program assistance, largely devoted to recipient debt relief, budget support, and structural adjustment. The impetus for this increase in program assistance (to about 5 percent) was a deepening fiscal crisis in many African states; although not on the scale of the debt crisis confronting several Latin American states during the decade, it limited the African recipients' abilities to function adequately and encouraged internal social and political unrest throughout the region. In conjunction with funds for political infrastructure, program assistance was designed to promote ongoing state-building efforts by the recipients, often with direct guidance and oversight by French *coopérants*.

20. The United States imported $11.3 billion worth of French goods in 1989, less than West Germany ($27.6 billion), Italy ($20 billion), the United Kingdom ($16.5 billion), and Belgium ($15.3 billion).

21. Other social and economic figures for these recipients were not compiled by the World Bank because of their small populations (less than 1 million); military statistics were not provided by the U.S. Arms Control and Disarmament Agency given their status as territories of France.

22. Estimates of Chinese military spending are relatively crude given the difficulty in converting its spending to U.S. dollars.

23. After more than 500,000 Rwandans were killed in an ethnically inspired war in the spring of 1994, for example, the French government took a lead role in building a multinational peacekeeping effort in the French-speaking former Belgian colony. French troops had previously intervened in Rwanda in October 1990.

4

The Geoeconomics
of Japanese ODA

Like France, Japan was decimated by World War II in almost every respect and spent the first postwar decade undergoing economic and political reconstruction. Both countries received massive amounts of U.S. economic assistance during this period, and both were gradually integrated within the U.S.-led Bretton Woods regime. As their economies recovered and their new governments achieved stability and some measure of legitimacy at home and abroad, both states hastened their emergence as great powers through integration with their regional neighbors and through the selective use of foreign assistance to promote their regional interests.

Japan's ascension from military defeat and global estrangement to the status of an economic superpower occurred in a forty-year period during which economic wealth became comparable to military might as a national power resource. Japanese leaders increasingly utilized ODA, among other instruments of "geoeconomics" (Luttwak, 1990), to promote their national interests (*kokueki*) by stimulating the economic development of regional LDCs, subsidizing their own industries, and attracting goodwill from other members of the ODA regime. In 1989 Japan surpassed the United States to become the world's leading ODA donor (a distinction the United States reclaimed in 1991). Japanese officials effectively tripled aid flows between 1970 and 1990 and continued to increase aid transfers above the $10 billion level into the 1990s. Whereas in 1970 Japan was the primary donor to six recipient nation-states, it filled that role for thirty-one states in 1991.

The resurgence of Japan was among the most portentous developments in world politics between World War II and the end of the Cold War. Large-scale military rearmament was precluded by Japan's U.S.-imposed constitution, which limited defense spending to 1 percent of GNP, so its revival as a world power was based almost exclusively on economic growth. Japan's GNP during the 1980s grew from about $1 trillion to nearly $3 trillion; its per capita income approached $24,000; and its foreign trade grew to nearly $500 billion, with an annual trade surplus of more than $50 billion. Along the way, both the unemployment and inflation rates were kept below 5 percent. Japanese elites "conceived a vision of economic power without military power" (Vogel, 1986: 755) and concluded that their principal enterprise, and their primary contribution to regional and global stability, would be in stimulating economic and technological development. As they pursued these tasks, Japanese leaders generally deferred in regional military deliberations to the United States, whose "security umbrella" covered Japan during the Cold War. As a result, "the role played by Japan in world politics has lagged far behind its evolution as an economic superpower" (Soroos, 1988: 21).

Whereas the central government in Japan adopted a low profile in foreign affairs, its approach to economic development directly involved the public sector. Wrote Scalapino, "Japanese foreign policy is strongly geared toward using economic instruments on behalf of perceived national interests" (1992: 207). Toward this end, Japanese leaders pursued a strategy of "guided capitalism" by which political and corporate leaders cooperatively targeted the most promising sectors of the economy and supported them through research and development subsidies, trade protection, the promotion of national savings versus consumption, and export-led growth strategies. As James Fallows put it, "The Japanese government famously intervenes at countless levels of society, applying formal and informal controls to everything from bank-lending policy to the number of non-Japanese teachers allowed in universities and schools" (1993: 4).

The pervasive public role in Japan's economic development prompted repeated charges of neomercantilism by scholarly and U.S. government critics along with overseas economic competitors, who argued that the Japanese government violated widely accepted norms of the liberal economic order that emerged after World War II.[1] Among foreign countries, the United States most vigorously protested Japan's industrial policies, which restricted the flow of goods and services into Japan (particularly in the automotive sector) and thus contributed to massive U.S. trade deficits.[2] Japan's largely successful attempt to restore its prewar economic influence, facilitated by domestic sacrifices and overseas trade, "adds up to a situation in which Japan is viewed in a hostile fashion from all sources. The ASEAN [Association of Southeast Asian Nations] states have feared that the prewar goals of establishing a Greater East-Asian Co-prosperity Sphere remain, with economic tools replacing military weapons as the means for achievement" (Farnsworth, 1982: 181).

As in the case of France, a succession of Japanese leaders identified and pursued a consistent set of objectives during the postwar period. In the latter case, these included the preservation and promotion of cultural integrity; the restoration of economic vitality and sustained economic growth to minimize the country's dependence on external support; the promotion of regional economic integration along the Pacific Rim, with Japan serving as a model and catalyst for regional development; and the maintenance of military security through a bilateral alliance with the United States. In some cases, these interests reflected extensions of long-term priorities: The objectives of preserving cultural integrity and economic self-sufficiency, for example, were central tenets of Japanese domestic and foreign policy prior to the U.S. "opening" of Japan in 1853 and the Meiji Restoration of 1868. In other respects the postwar objectives and the attendant strategies employed to achieve them represented a departure from the past: Japan's externally imposed pacifism followed a fifty-year period during which it defeated China (1895) and Russia (1905), annexed Korea (1910), and began its quest for regional hegemony with the 1931 invasion of Manchuria and the subsequent occupation of much of East Asia. After World War II, Japanese expansionism was replaced by the dismantling of the country's armed forces and its subordination to U.S. hegemony in the Pacific region.

Like Sweden, but under clearly different circumstances, Japan converted geographical detachment and nonmilitarism into power resources in the late twentieth century. Under the protection of the U.S.-Japanese Mutual Security Treaty, approved in 1952 upon Japan's independence, its leaders enjoyed unusual freedom to pursue economic revitalization; they were among the first to reconstitute national security in largely economic terms.[3] Along the way, the consensual basis of Japanese society, based upon its Shinto-Buddhist cultural traditions, was preserved and defended against foreign (particularly Western) encroachments. Political stability was assured by the tenets of its new constitution, by the constraints of its parliamentary government, and, most importantly, by the enduring domination of its Liberal Democratic Party.

Japan's industrial policy was applied to its growing foreign-aid program, which became a central element in its effort to reestablish regional economic ties that had been severed immediately after World War II. Like France, Japan concentrated its aid flows among neighboring LDCs, which maintained close ties to Tokyo in other areas (see Table 4.1). Aid transfers were designed to complement Japanese foreign investments and trade policies, particularly with respect to states that possessed raw materials critical to Japan's economic development. Thus, Japanese aid was "explicitly regarded as a legitimate arm of national policy" (Rix, 1980: 268). ODA flows, often tied to Japanese goods and services, stimulated domestic production and fueled the economies of regional LDCs seen as integral to Japan's long-term prosperity. Furthermore, ODA directed national attention toward economic relations rather than the military concerns that prevailed during the years preceding World War II. The Japanese parliament (Diet) and foreign ministry identified potential ODA recipients whose economic growth would benefit Japan's industries and banks through overseas loans, direct investment, and growing markets. Their application of ODA thus served as an additional forum for close macroeconomic coordination between the public and private sectors.

As Japanese officials were quick to emphasize, their utilization of ODA was also instigated by foreign pressure. Leaders of other industrialized states, LDCs, and international organizations (most prominently, the

Table 4.1   Top Ten Recipients of Japanese ODA, 1970–1990

1970–1971	1980–1981	1989–1990
Indonesia	Indonesia	Indonesia
South Korea	South Korea	China
India	Thailand	Philippines
Pakistan	Bangladesh	Thailand
Philippines	Philippines	Bangladesh
Burma	Burma	Malaysia
Thailand	Pakistan	India
Taiwan	Egypt	Pakistan
Iran	Malaysia	South Korea
Sri Lanka	India	Turkey

Source: OECD (1991a)

OECD and the UN's development agencies) considered Japan a potential source of relief during a period of prolonged economic stagnation in other donor countries. Japanese leaders responded to this pressure in the 1980s by rapidly increasing the size and scope of their aid programs as part of a broader campaign for increased "burden sharing." They found ODA particularly attractive given its proven role in stimulating Third World development and given Japan's own "graduation" from the status of LDC (and aid recipient) during its seven years under its U.S. occupation after World War II. In addition, Japanese political leaders welcomed the credibility they attracted by taking an aggressive role in ODA: "Since Japan has become awash in cash, it has felt that aid is one way in which it can be seen to fulfill its international responsibilities without having to make awkward choices about foreign policy or military spending" (Emmott, 1989: 229). Japan's growing wealth and its expanding involvement in North-South development issues led to its active role in the aid regime during the "lost decade" of Third World development.

Japanese Aid: Origin and Evolution

Only since the 1970s has Japan been a leading donor of foreign assistance, and only since the 1980s has its aid been disbursed beyond geographically and functionally restricted boundaries. As noted above, the restoration of the country's physical and socioeconomic vitality became the central objective of its leaders and those of the United States, which occupied Japan after the war. As part of their effort to stimulate the regional economy (and, secondarily, to counter the expansion of communism in East Asia), U.S. policymakers sought to establish a self-sufficient, market-oriented Japanese economy. In addition to providing Marshall Plan funding to

Western Europe, the United States transferred large sums of development assistance to Japan—$947 million in grants and $273 million in loans between 1949 and 1952. The United States disbursed an additional $999 million to Japan between 1953 and 1961 under the Mutual Security Act, along with $675 million in military assistance (USAID, 1991: 76).

Japanese foreign aid first took the form of delayed reparation payments (*baisho*) to regional neighbors, including Burma (1955), the Philippines (1956), and Indonesia (1958). Other reparation agreements were reached with Laos, Malaysia, Singapore, South Vietnam, South Korea, and Thailand. Formal Japanese recognition of the People's Republic of China in 1972 was granted in exchange for Chinese concessions on reparations payments. These transfers, mostly in the form of services and capital goods, established the pattern of geographical concentration in Asia, which continue to characterize Japanese aid into the 1990s. Japan extended its first concessional yen loan in 1958 to India, utilizing a form of foreign assistance that would become commonplace in the following decades. In 1959, the Japanese government extended cash grants to Laos and Cambodia, an exception in an aid program built largely around concessional loans.

After formally regaining sovereignty in 1952, Japanese leaders expressed a willingness to contribute to regional and global development efforts. Its representatives attended the Colombo conference, along with members of the British Commonwealth and the United States, which resulted in a multilateral program of expanded aid flows. Japan joined the United Nations in 1956 and later became active in the UN Conference on Trade and Development.

The 1960s marked the graduation of Japan from net ODA recipient to donor. Its government established the Overseas Economic Cooperation Fund (OECF) in 1961 to serve as a conduit for bilateral aid. In 1963, Japan was a founding member of the OECD's Development Assistance Committee. In 1964, it joined the International Monetary Fund and two years later helped establish the Asian Development Bank as a regional conduit for concessional financing.[4] Japan's involvement was closely monitored by the DAC, which permitted member states to pursue independent aid strategies but encouraged them to adhere to its guidelines for "quality" ODA policies.[5]

Japan's emergence as a major aid donor occurred as John F. Kennedy launched the Alliance for Progress in the early 1960s, designed to promote greater cooperation between the United States and LDCs. The United States focused its development efforts on Latin America (and later, Indochina), whereas France, the second-ranking aid donor among Western states, established large-scale aid programs in francophone Africa (see Chapter 3). Thus, a global division of labor emerged among the primary ODA donors, with Japan being accorded a primary role in the Pacific Rim region and Great Britain concentrating its aid among its former colonies in anglophone Africa and South Asia.

In addition to seeking domestic support for their development programs, Kennedy and his successor, Lyndon Johnson, encouraged leaders in Japan and other industrialized states to increase their annual commitments of ODA. Citing the U.S. military protection of Japan through the bilateral defense treaty, Kennedy and Johnson argued that increased economic assistance was something Japan could afford and should make available in large volumes. Japanese leaders were generally receptive to these appeals and announced a series of explicit timetables to enlarge their aid allocations. In this sense, the country's foreign-aid program was viewed as the price of U.S. military protection and a form of reimbursement for prior U.S. assistance to Japan.

As it broadened its aid effort, the Japanese government established the Overseas Technical Cooperation Fund (OTCF) to administer the provision of technical assistance (such as training in civil engineering for recipients). These programs, which directly involved Japanese officials in the recipients' state-building efforts, were consolidated in 1974 within the Japanese International Cooperation Agency (JICA). Development aid became a central concern for the most influential ministries in the Japanese government, including finance, foreign affairs, and the Ministry of International Trade and Industry (MITI). Their divergent interests, reflecting differing domestic constituencies and international priorities, created occasional tensions within the Japanese government. But such friction, evident in most donor states, was eased by a relatively strong societal consensus on Japan's national interests and the opportunities presented by ODA to achieve them.

Japan's economy, like those of other industrialized countries, was strained by the twin oil-price shocks of the 1970s. Given Japan's dependence on foreign oil and its vulnerability to higher petroleum prices, the oil crises slowed national economic growth and threatened Japan's industrial expansion. Among their responses, Japanese leaders approved expanded ODA transfers to LDCs in the Middle East, marking a departure from their regional concentration in East Asia. Japan by 1980 had become the primary ODA donor to such Persian Gulf states as Iran, Saudi Arabia, and the United Arab Emirates. This redirection of ODA resources also entailed a diplomatic transfer of Japanese loyalties in many issue areas toward Islamic countries and away from Israel, a shift that elicited protests from the U.S. government and served to symbolize Japan's use of ODA as an instrument to promote its national security, narrowly defined in this case as reliable access to petroleum. Even after this shift of aid, however, Japan retained its emphasis on East Asian recipients. In the late 1970s aid officials adopted a medium-term distribution plan by which fixed portions of Japanese ODA would be disbursed to Asian recipients (approximately two-thirds), with smaller shares going in roughly equal amounts to the

Mideast, Africa, and Latin America. Even after being identified as a relatively low priority for Japanese ODA planners, however, many LDCs received greatly increased resources in absolute terms. Sub-Saharan Africa, for example, received twice its 1980 share of Japanese ODA by the end of the decade.[6]

The Japanese government further used the energy crisis to its advantage by expanding its automobile industry and concentrating on the manufacture of small, fuel-efficient vehicles, a strategy of critical importance in Japan's economic resurgence. The success of Honda, Toyota, and other Japanese automakers was reflected in their rapidly growing market share vis-à-vis the United States, which responded more slowly to the shift in consumer demand. By 1980, Japan's market share in the global automotive industry (including both vehicles and parts) had more than doubled, in large part because of its penetration of the North American market. Its inroads in the consumer electronics sector, based upon technological innovations and relatively low labor costs, also contributed to Japan's rise as an industrial power. Whereas the contrasting policies of import substitution were widely embraced in other developing regions during the 1970s, Japan's export-led expansion became an example to be emulated by other states in East Asia. The pervasive role of the Japanese government in subsidizing selected industries and protecting them from foreign competition also was widely copied by neighboring states.

Responding to widespread appeals for ODA as well as a need to "recycle" capital generated by large annual trade surpluses, Japanese officials announced a series of doubling plans for the periods 1977–1980, 1981–1985, and 1985–1992, identifying specific short- and medium-term funding targets that would collectively amount to $40 billion in ODA commitments. A fifth medium-term target was announced in 1993 for the period through 1997, in which Japan pledged to transfer more than $70 billion and to increase its share of GNP devoted to development aid (Japanese Government, 1993b: 24). As Japanese ODA grew both in absolute terms and as a percentage of global ODA outlays, its leaders repeatedly promised to confront qualitative issues regarding the types and terms of ODA transfers.

The Japanese government also responded to appeals by the United States to make its ODA strategies compatible with U.S. security efforts in the Pacific region. Thus, in the pursuit of "comprehensive security," large aid packages were made available to "countries bordering on areas of conflict," such as Pakistan, Thailand, and Turkey. In 1981, Prime Minister Zenko Suzuki recognized this new aid mission by directing ODA to "those areas which are important to the maintenance of the peace and stability of the world." Large transfers were approved for the Republic of Korea and the Philippines, among other Pacific states, despite their relatively high per capita incomes and rapid rates of economic growth. To some, this effort contradicted the spirit of Japan's nonmilitaristic foreign policy during the postwar era. But to Japanese leaders, the broadened scope of its aid effort was a necessary concession to allied pressure that Japan compensate for its perceived "free-rider" status in the collective security system.

ODA and the "MITI Economy"

Unlike many DAC members, into the 1990s Japan did not assign ultimate responsibility over ODA to a single government agency. Although JICA coordinated much of the ODA effort, authority over its scope and direction fell within the purview of many ministries and specialized agencies. In addition, several private economic interests openly influenced government policy, both as independent economic actors and as members of public-private consortia. In this additional respect, the structure of Japan's ODA served as a microcosm of its broader approach to political economy.

Among the numerous governmental organizations with interests in foreign aid, three ministries were most closely involved with ODA during the postwar period. The Ministry of International Trade and Investment, a symbol of the Japanese model of industrial policy, became highly influential throughout the period in directing aid flows. MITI officials traditionally looked to aid as a vehicle for stimulating overseas markets, boosting domestic production and exports, "recycling" surplus capital, and developing reliable sources of natural resources and raw materials. MITI generally approached ODA from the perspective of private business and promoted increased flows on the basis of long-term trade or investment opportunities. (Tellingly, aid policy within MITI was formulated by the International Trade Policy Bureau.) Unlike other industrialized states, which tend to segregate corporate leaders and government officials, Japan openly integrated business interests within the state apparatus.

Whereas MITI epitomized the Japanese model of political economy, the Ministry of Foreign Affairs (MOFA) adopted a more traditional role in the area of economic assistance. MOFA was responsible for identifying prospective recipients (often with help from officials in foreign embassies) and evaluating requests for overseas aid. When bilateral aid packages were approved, MOFA oversaw their allocation and implementation. Members of MOFA's Economic Cooperation Bureau (roughly comparable to the U.S. Agency for International Development) generally approached ODA as a diplomatic, political, or humanitarian instrument; security concerns or possible benefits to Japan's industries were ostensibly not part of their deliberations. Thus, MOFA was responsive to pressure from other DAC members for net increases in aid, for grants versus loans, and for assistance to hard-pressed LDCs and LLDCs. As Japan became a leading global ODA donor, MOFA and the Economic Cooperation Bureau became more directly engaged in formulating and implementing aid policy. The Ministry of Finance also played a strong, if more muted role in the Japanese aid program. Finance ministers traditionally looked to the demonstrable cost-benefit dimensions of aid proposals, demanding that transfers conform to approved budgets in pursuit of tangible and realistic ends. Thus, members of the finance ministry, concerned with the overall levels of Japan's government budget, often discouraged ODA commitments despite the foreign ministry's arguments that they would bear long-term benefits through expanded markets for Japanese goods, services, and capital.[7]

As head of the government, the Japanese prime minister was empowered to set the agenda of aid policy by advocating general development strategies, visiting or receiving selected applicants, and emphasizing certain proposals in public statements. Leaders of most donor governments frequently used foreign assistance as a valuable carrot in their personal diplomacy; in Japan a tradition of "souvenir diplomacy" (*omiyage gairo*) emerged by which the prime minister's overseas baggage often included offers of ODA. But the role of the prime minister and his cabinet was eclipsed by the powerful ministries overseeing foreign affairs, fiscal policy, and commerce. Thus, as in the case of France (see Chapter 3), Japanese prime ministers rarely initiated fundamental shifts in foreign policy. True to these general features of the Japanese political-economic model, ODA policy was sufficiently broad-based to constrain the power of the prime minister.

Similarly, the Diet's role in foreign assistance was limited to approving aid budgets formally proposed by the foreign affairs ministry. The Diet's marginal involvement was partially a result of the early years of Japanese ODA, when aid was not a critical issue and legislators approved proposed budgets with little debate. They generally deferred to the expertise of the aid bureaucracy, which was largely controlled by senior government, corporate leaders, and party leaders. The Diet became more assertive in ODA policy in the 1990s after the collapse of the Liberal Democratic Party's (LDP) hold over the Japanese government. Growing economic problems in Japan and a succession of political scandals also prompted a more open dialogue about the appropriate role of the government and the future of Japan's development programs.

Prior to its fragmentation, the LDP performed an important function in the formulation and execution of ODA policy, albeit one fundamentally different from that of parties in most other industrialized states. The LDP, which controlled the government from its inception until the early 1990s, maintained its own advisory component, the Policy Affairs Research Council, which often initiated aid legislation and oversaw its passage through the Diet. Whereas in other countries interparty debate often shaped allocations of foreign aid, this debate occurred within the LDP in Japan, where contending factions often disagreed over the size and destination of proposed ODA packages. In this way, internal divisions over

Japanese ODA were shielded from public view; the major disputes were fought privately in LDP meetings, not among rival political parties in the glare of parliamentary debate.

As noted above, an array of private actors—representing industrialists, bankers, producers, and others with potential interests in ODA transfers— also exerted an important influence on aid policy. Aside from its direct involvement in public-private agencies, private industry played "perhaps the dominant role in the implementation of Japanese aid policy" (Ensign, 1992: 22). Industry leaders promoted aid packages tied to exports of their products; banking officials lobbied for ODA transfers with the greatest returns; and engineering firms saw to it that their services were utilized in executing development projects. This involvement of the private sector, which resulted in the widespread tying of ODA to Japanese goods and services, was, of course, not unique to Japan. The difference was rather one of degree; whereas other donor states publicly diminished the influence of domestic industry in ODA calculations, Japan openly acknowledged it. In addition to ODA "cooperation" between donor and recipient, domestic cooperation between the public and private sectors was also strongly encouraged, and the collective benefits to Japanese merchants, engineers, and bankers—indeed, to the overall economy—were sought alongside the welfare of LDCs.

The general public in Japan has been relatively uninvolved in aid deliberations and decisions, as in other areas of foreign policy. Given the multiple power centers (public and private) in the ODA network, and in keeping with the overall pattern of Japanese central government, much of this work was conducted behind the scenes and without public debate. ODA programs generally received widespread public support, however— much more so than in the United States, where foreign assistance continually ranked among the most unpopular government enterprises. Japanese leaders exploited this persistent consensus regarding the virtues of ODA, which were borne out by aid's demonstrable role in stimulating LDC economies as well as Japan's.

The growth of Japan's ODA programs was not without internal discord, however. As it grew in size during the 1970s and 1980s, the decentralized bureaucratic structures underlying Japanese ODA produced numerous contradictions in practice. The lack of central control hindered the coherent mapping of aid policy, and the fundamental differences among ministers overseeing ODA transfers confounded aid recipients and other donors alike (Kotani, 1985). "Aid policies and measures have not always been well-coordinated due to conflicting views and interests of the government ministries and agencies," explained Hasegawa (1975: 149). For their part, Japanese officials frequently cited a shortage of skilled administrators to oversee the implementation of aid programs, as well as recipients' inability to "absorb" continued transfers and their frequent failure to meet the terms of prior aid packages.[8] Regardless of the causes of these problems, their consequences included a pattern of gradual, incremental change in the program, a common result of bureaucratic inertia. As Orr (1990: 12) concluded,

> Japanese policy formulation for aid is largely made within the government bureaucracy. It tends to be "routine" rather than "crisis" or "innovative" policymaking and, as such, produces few surprises, and little drama. In short, battles are fought, bargains negotiated, compromises made, and decisions reached largely within the framework of the administrative structure.

Despite well-publicized efforts to satisfy detractors, into the 1980s the perception remained that among the DAC members "Japanese ODA has been most deeply tilted toward reaping selfish benefits" (Shinsuke, 1982: 34). Although the quantity of Japanese ODA expanded, its widely perceived qualitative shortcomings remained a contentious issue. In contrast to most other donors' ODA programs, Japan's was characterized by loans at near-market interest rates and repayment terms, by aid directed toward relatively affluent LDCs, and by aid tied to the acquisition of Japanese products or services. Critics also pointed to the concentration of Japan's aid among its regional trading partners as evidence of this self-interested basis. At the regional level, "deep-rooted suspicions among Asian politicians, intellectuals, and businessmen [held] that Japan's economic cooperation, far from being altruistic, is guided primarily by self-interest" (Stirling, 1981: 359).

Of additional concern to ODA analysts was the persistence of Japanese aid transfers to recipients that violated the human or political rights of their citizens. Key examples included large, long-term aid transfers to Indonesia, South Korea, and the Philippines despite the presence of repressive dictatorships in these countries. Large aid packages to the communist government in the People's Republic of China (PRC), even after its crackdown on prodemocracy demonstrators in 1989, served as an additional case in point, as did significant ODA transfers to repressive Middle Eastern states in the wake of the oil shocks of the 1970s. Japanese ODA behavior in this respect differed from that of many other major donors; a potential recipient's "ideological stripes [were] much less important to Japanese decisionmakers than they [were] to aid planners in the United States" (Orr, 1990: 58).

Japanese leaders rejected these charges and advanced an alternative conception of ODA that emphasized recipient "responsibility." They sought to encourage attributes and patterns of behavior in recipients that were conducive to long-term development. For example, ODA funds would be transferred largely on the basis of low-interest loans rather than grants, a practice that was contrary to the ODA regime's preference for the latter. As Economic Officer Kenko Sone (Japanese Government, 1994) argued in an interview,

> We believe aid quality has more than one meaning. In our view, lending money enforces some discipline on the recipients and encourages them to use the resources more productively than if we just gave them away. Countries sometimes get used to simply taking money. Receiving loans often makes them work harder and become more efficient. In this sense we often consider loans as of greater quality than grants, particularly since through emphasizing loans we can make more money available to developing countries.

Although Japanese leaders advanced an alternative conception of ODA in this and other respects, they pledged to adhere to most international standards of aid quality. They acknowledged the fundamental norm among industrialized states that a substantial share of their country's gross national product (in absolute if not relative terms) should be directed toward the economic development of LDCs. Inescapably, the memories of Japan's subjugation of the Pacific Rim during World War II lingered and infused the aid question; countries that suffered under Japanese domination sought ongoing compensation long after the formal period of reparations ended.

The rhetoric of global obligation, not uncommon among aid donors of longer standing, was frequently evident in the public statements of Japanese officials on foreign assistance. In 1967, the Ministry of Foreign Affairs released a mission statement suggesting that Japanese foreign assistance would increase "in the belief that such efforts will contribute to the ultimate goal of establishing prosperity and peace throughout the world." Fifteen years later, Prime Minister Suzuki (quoted in Shinsuke, 1982: 30) told a Diet budget committee that "the economic cooperation of Japan, in principle, is intended to help the recipient countries stabilize the livelihood, and improve the welfare, of their people. We cannot extend military aid to any country." And another decade later, the Japanese government (1993a: 23) proclaimed, "The stability and sustained growth of developing countries are essential to the creation of a post–Cold War framework for peace and security."

For many Japanese officials, the enhanced credibility their nation gained through ODA was especially valuable when combined with its broader role in promoting Japan as a vital "bridge" between LDCs and the industrialized North. Given Japan's location and its status as a recently modernized state, it emerged as a developmental model for regional LDCs and newly industrialized countries (NICs). Despite occasional concerns about the Japanese government's interference in the market, many recipients saw its aid flows as a relief from their previous dependence on the United States. Japan's model of economic development, based upon export-led industrialization and the collaboration of government and industry, was applied in other states in East Asia during the 1980s, including Hong Kong, Indonesia, Malaysia, Singapore, and Taiwan, all of which experienced accelerating rates of economic growth.[9]

Japan's complex administrative structure associated with ODA reflected its leaders' broader approach to political economy and to the pursuit of perceived national interests. A societal consensus on the centrality of Japanese economic growth versus other concerns, foreign or domestic, anchored ODA policy for much of its history. Such growth was seen as a prerequisite for political stability in Japan, for the restoration of societal cohesion, and for the revival of Japan as an important regional and global actor. ODA proved to be a vehicle for three of Japan's most important postwar objectives: restoring the domestic economy, generating economic growth and integration within the Pacific Rim, and regaining credibility among industrialized states in North America and Western Europe.

Japanese leaders openly acknowledged that their approach to Third World development differed from that of their Western contemporaries, arguing that Japan's expanding economy served as an engine of growth for its neighbors. Given Japan's extraordinary reliance on foreign sources of fuels and other raw materials (a point raised frequently by Japanese leaders), preserving self-sufficiency became an ongoing preoccupation. Additionally (as U.S. leaders also argued in the face of similar criticism), Japanese officials emphasized *aggregate* aid rather than aid in proportion to GNP. Their view "reflects the difficulty which Japan's ODA has experienced for much of its history in substantially outpacing the sustained growth of GNP in spite of a very rapid rise of ODA disbursements" (OECD, 1979: 126). The Japanese government, perhaps a victim of its own success in this regard, continued to struggle with this problem throughout the 1980s and into the 1990s.

Japanese ODA in Practice

Japanese ODA during the 1980s consistently increased in every functional category, rising at an inflation-adjusted annual rate of 4.6 percent, nearly twice the average of the DAC as a whole. This expansion in ODA flows occurred alongside broader efforts by the Japanese government to invest surplus capital in foreign bond markets, real estate, and industrial joint ventures. Japan was in a particularly advantageous position to distribute ODA during the 1980s, a decade that witnessed economic stagnation in most other developed states and calamity in many developing regions, particularly sub-Saharan Africa. As noted in Chapter 2, Japan experienced the only balance-of-payments surplus of the four donor states under study (1.2 percent of GNP), the highest annual rate of economic growth (5.2 percent),

Table 4.2   Japanese ODA Transfers, 1970–1990

	ODA Commitment[a]	Percent GNP	Share of World ODA
1970–1980	2,871	0.23	11.2
1980–1981	5,863	0.30	10.6
1989–1990	9,152	0.31	16.4

Source: OECD (1991a)
Note: a. ODA commitment in millions of current U.S. dollars

a low unemployment rate (2.1 percent), exceeding only that of Sweden, per capita income ($24,000) also second only to Sweden's, and a total GNP ($2.9 trillion) second only to that of the United States.

Despite its affluence, however, Japan's relative rate of domestic government spending (32.9 percent) was the lowest of the four cases and among the lowest of any industrialized country. This fact is significant in drawing attention to the relatively small pool of public resources from which ODA funds were drawn. Whereas the government generally preferred that private capital lead the way toward economic resurgence, public funds in the form of ODA proved an effective complement to this well-coordinated effort. As its aid flows increased on an absolute level, its share of global ODA also grew (see Table 4.2).

Japan's ascension to the status of the world's leading donor of ODA was also noteworthy given its previous status as a *recipient* of U.S. assistance, the relatively young age of its ODA program, and the fact that its overall GNP remained little more than one-half that of the United States. Japan's expanding ODA flow during the 1980s was exaggerated by the heightened value of the yen relative to the U.S. dollar and other currencies during the 1980s.[10] Even after this factor is taken into account, however, the growing presence of Japan within the ODA regime and the critical role its aid donations played in furthering the country's internal economic development are instructive.

Collectively, these patterns led to a global tripolarity of ODA flows. By 1990 France, Japan, and the United States combined for nearly half of all development aid to LDCs. In addition to coordinating concessional flows through the OECD, these three donors strongly influenced the regional distribution of ODA by concentrating bilateral transfers among selected recipients of particular importance to their broader economic, political, and security interests (see Chapter 2).

Its pledges to widen its geographical distribution of ODA notwithstanding, the Japanese government continued to focus its ODA efforts on neighboring states in East Asia (see Figure 4.1). More than half of Japanese development aid flowed toward this region in 1989–1990, as opposed

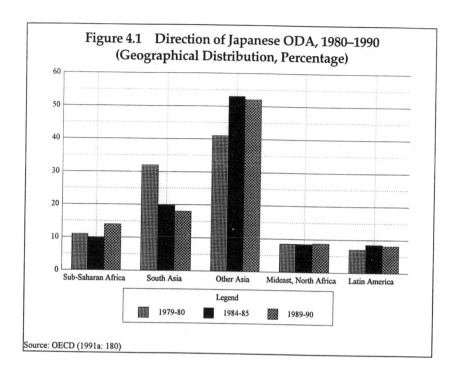

Figure 4.1   Direction of Japanese ODA, 1980–1990
(Geographical Distribution, Percentage)

Legend
1979-80   1984-85   1989-90

Source: OECD (1991a: 180)

to 41 percent a decade earlier.[11] Conversely, the share of Japanese ODA flows to South Asia fell from nearly one-third of the total to less than 20 percent during the same period. This pattern displayed remarkable continuity despite the rhetorical emphasis placed by Japanese leaders on diversifying its ODA flows during the 1980s. Although Japanese officials increased aggregate aid to other regions of the Third World, they retained their overall emphasis on Asia. Aid bound for Africa rose to 15 percent of the 1989 total, with 8 percent transferred to Latin America and 5 percent to the Mideast. Japanese ODA to the poorest states of sub-Saharan Africa, though showing a modest increase, remained a small fraction of the share directed toward its regional neighbors.

East Asia was attractive to Japanese policymakers not only because of the region's geographical proximity but also because of its rapid economic growth rates during the 1970s and 1980s, particularly as compared to those of other less developed regions. East Asia's proportion of global GNP rose from 5 to 20 percent, and its share of world manufacturing doubled to 23 percent (World Bank, 1991: 21). Its financial power grew proportionately as the region competed favorably against economic superpowers, particularly the United States, thanks in part to relatively low wage rates, the importation of international capital, and the collaborative relationship between business and government found in Japan. Foreign aid served as a catalyst for this process and figured prominently in the foreign policies of every recipient in East Asia.

Indonesia remained the greatest beneficiary of Japanese ODA throughout the period, although its share decreased from nearly one-quarter of total Japanese outlays in 1970 to about 12 percent by 1990. Prominent projects undertaken with the aid included improvements to the Jakarta water supply in 1985, construction of Bali International Airport in 1986, and support for the Jabotabek Area Railway Project in 1989.[12] Also noteworthy was the rapid increase in Japan's bilateral ODA flows to the People's Republic of China, which increased from $3 million in 1979 to nearly $400 million in 1984 and $833 million in 1989 (Quansheng, 1993). Since establishing diplomatic relations with the PRC in 1972 and signing a bilateral peace treaty six years later, Japan has emerged as the PRC's leading aid and trading partner as well as its main source of high technology and private investment capital. Japan supported other Pacific Rim states that emulated its industrial policies—including a high level of public and private coordination, the protection of key industrial sectors, an emphasis on export-led growth, and the encouragement of savings rather than domestic consumption (McCord, 1991). Japanese aid to China, like that to Indonesia, was almost entirely in the form of low-interest loans for technical assistance. Japan transferred large volumes of public resources for such projects as railway expansion and electrification, the modernization of ports, and the reconstruction of Beijing's sewage and subway systems.

Outside of East Asia, Japan transferred ODA to only three recipients at comparably high levels—India, Pakistan, and Bangladesh. Among other priorities, Japanese ODA was used for the construction of power plants and gas pipelines in India; aid to the poorer recipients of Bangladesh and Pakistan was primarily intended for agricultural programs (such as the modernization of fertilizer factories), short-term debt relief, and assistance in responding to natural disasters. In the early 1990s, Japan was an early advocate within the DAC of adding the five newly independent Central Asian states of Kazakhstan, Kirghistan, Tadzhikistan, Turkmenistan, and Uzbekistan to the committee's list of LDCs so they would become eligible for development aid.

As the cases of Indonesia and China illustrate, the preponderant share of Japanese ODA during the 1980s was directed toward the economic infrastructure of recipients, including engineering and construction of transportation and communication networks, power plants, and other facilities designed to hasten industrialization (see Figure 4.2). Through technical cooperation agreements, the Japanese government further assisted LDCs in developing work forces for such projects. To the Japanese government (1992: 34), "economic cooperation is aimed at bringing up personnel in developing countries who are technically capable of taking a positive part in the national task of economic and social development."[13] Nearly 40 percent of Japanese ODA was devoted to economic infrastructure in 1988–1989, more than twice the share devoted toward program assistance, political infrastructure, and other categories of development aid. Program assistance, mostly in the form of co-financing with the World Bank and regional development banks for recipient structural adjustment, received a modest but growing share of Japanese ODA outlays during the decade.

Although its share of Japan's ODA remained less than 10 percent, Latin America played a growing role in its aid calculations; by 1990 many South American states received more aid from Japan than from any other donor. The wide range of functions performed by Japanese ODA can be discerned by reviewing its growing role in this region during the late 1980s. Japanese funds were used to buy sports equipment for Chile's 1988 Olympic team; to provide audiovisual support for Argentina's National Cervantes Theater; and to pay for mobile libraries in Jamaica. In all three cases, the transfers were executed in grant form and were almost entirely tied to the purchase of Japanese products. Thus, they illustrate not only the widening applications of ODA but also the diverse ways in which they may promote the donor's commercial interests.[14]

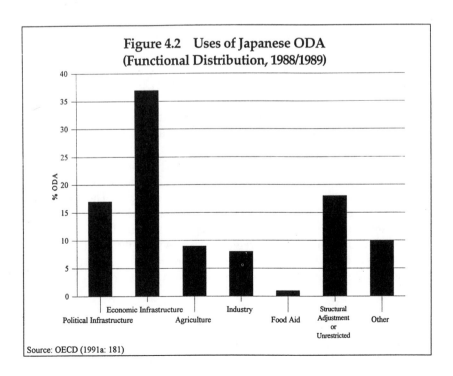

Figure 4.2   Uses of Japanese ODA
(Functional Distribution, 1988/1989)

Source: OECD (1991a: 181)

Japanese ODA, though improving in some categories, generally lagged behind that of other DAC members in terms of OECD-defined quality (see Table 4.3). A major reason for this gap was the Japanese government's rejection of many OECD standards of aid quality. As observed earlier, Tokyo considered concessional loans superior to grants because they imposed "discipline" on recipients and steered them toward long-term economic self-sufficiency. In other cases, the Japanese government acknowledged its shortcomings in the area of aid quality and pledged to improve its performance. Though defending their continuing preference for loans, Japanese officials gradually increased the proportion of grant aid. Levels of technical assistance in grant form grew rapidly in absolute terms, reaching $1.3 billion in 1989. Though Japan doubled its grant element from 40 to 81 percent of all ODA flows, it continued to fall below the DAC average, which rose to a peak of 93 percent by decade's end.[15]

In the case of Japan's largest bilateral programs, more than 90 percent of the funds were transferred in the form of low-interest loans (Japanese Government, 1993a). Whereas loans to Indonesia amounted to $842 million in 1988, for example, grant aid totaled just $143 million. The respective loan and grant figures for China were $519 million and $155 million during that year and, for the Philippines, $404 million and $131 million. Within this category, project loans constituted 63 percent of Japanese ODA loans, commodity loans 31 percent, and debt relief the remaining 6 percent (Japanese Government, 1992a: 71).

As noted earlier, Japan provided recipients with greater autonomy than most other donors with regard to the utilization of ODA transfers. Its level of untied assistance (i.e., aid that does not obligate recipients to purchase goods or services from the donor state) was higher than the DAC average throughout the period. This fact reflects the broader Japanese ODA strategy: Having constrained recipients through relatively strict terms of aid, Japan gave them considerable flexibility in their use of the concessional financing. Conversely, the proportion of Japanese ODA disbursed through multilateral organizations remained below the DAC average during most of the decade, as Japanese officials preferred to channel aid through their own ministries rather than through international agencies. The 1980s witnessed a decline in the multilateral element of Japanese ODA, reflecting a broader trend among donors toward greater reliance on bilateral aid. Japan also became more active at the regional level within the Asian Development Bank and the Inter-American Development Bank, contributing 47 percent of the former's revenue by 1989. As Yasutomo concluded, "Japan's ADB policy is a reflection of its economic aid policy, and economic aid policy is a reflection of its overall foreign policy in the late 1980s and 1990s" (1993: 332).

Finally, Japan's assistance to LLDCs, the poorest of aid recipients, also remained below the DAC average during the decade. Whereas the

Table 4.3   Quality of Japanese ODA, 1980–1989

	Grant Element (% ODA)	Untied Aid (% ODA)	Multilateral Aid (% ODA)	Aid to LLDCs (% ODA)
1980	40.0 (75.2)[a]	53.2 (50.3)	28.0 (28.5)	18.4 (21.6)
1983	41.0 (76.3)	55.3 (45.9)	26.7 (31.3)	19.1 (21.8)
1986	62.4 (87.0)	46.9 (33.4)	30.5 (28.1)	23.6 (23.4)
1989	81.4 (92.8)	59.6 (36.5)	24.8 (27.2)	17.1 (22.4)

Sources: OECD (1982b, 1985b, 1988b, 1991b)
Note: a. Figures in parentheses are DAC averages

committeewide pattern remained consistent, with the LLDC share remaining at about 22 percent, Japan approached that level before dropping to 17 percent in the final year. This trend reflected the fact that Japan's primary aid recipients—including Indonesia, China, and the Philippines—had relatively higher living standards than LDCs in sub-Saharan Africa, Latin America, and other regions. And LLDCs, unable to reimburse Japan for concessional ODA loans, were limited to generally lower aggregate levels of grant assistance.

Aside from these indicators, the net increases in Japanese ODA during the 1980s covered most functional and geographical categories and lent credibility to the proclamations of Japan's leaders regarding their expanding efforts to assist Third World development. The higher ODA levels in 1988 and 1989 were consistent with Japan's highly publicized doubling plans. However paradoxically, Japanese leaders also cited their country's rapidly increasing economy as a primary reason for their perceived failures in addressing qualitative ODA issues: The government's increases in ODA, though substantial on an absolute level, could not keep pace with the rapid growth of the national economy between 1970 and 1990. Government officials further argued that, as they placed greater emphasis on qualitative aspects of ODA in the mid-1980s, many of their major recipients had reached their "absorptive capacities"; still preoccupied with implementing development projects begun in previous years, they were unable to use further ODA flows effectively.

The overlapping presence of Japanese ODA and broader economic ties with its recipients is illustrated in the empirical record (see Table 4.4), which reveals a significant and positive relationship between Japanese ODA and bilateral trade in seven of the ten years under study. Although Japan recorded its most robust trade volumes with industrialized countries (including the United States and Western European states), Japanese exports to its neighbors in Asia rose dramatically in the late 1980s, from $46.8 billion in 1985 to $82.6 billion in 1989 (International Monetary Fund, 1991). Within this region, Japanese exports to China, the second largest recipient of Japanese ODA, averaged about $10 billion annually during this period. Other major aid recipients in the region that also imported large amounts of Japanese products included Indonesia, South Korea, the Philippines, Thailand, and Malaysia.

Linkages between Japanese ODA and recipient social-welfare conditions were not statistically significant during this period. Average 1988 life expectancy among Japan's top ten ODA recipients was 62.8 years, just a year less than the worldwide average of 64 years (World Bank, 1990: 178–179). Within this group, China, Malaysia, and South Korea each recorded average life expectancies of 70 years. The same pattern was evident in the category of daily per capita caloric consumption; the average 1989 level for Japan's ten major recipients was 2,541 calories per day, about 7 percent below the worldwide average of 2,711 calories. Four of Japan's primary ODA recipients—Turkey (3,236), South Korea (2,852), Malaysia (2,774) and Indonesia (2,750)—reported consumption rates *above* the worldwide average in 1989 (World Bank, 1992: 272–273).

Similarly, the weak relationship between Japanese ODA flows and measures of recipient militarization does not suggest a direct security orientation. Among the five major recipients of Japanese ODA in 1989–1990, conscription rates during the decade averaged 3.2 per 1,000 inhabitants, slightly more than half the worldwide average of 5.9 (U.S. Arms Control and Disarmament Agency, 1990). Significant exceptions were found in the next group of five major recipients, however, including Turkey (18.0) and South Korea (16.8). Among these recipients, absolute military spending during the 1980s varied widely, from $298 million in the case of Bangladesh to $23 billion in the case of China. If China is excluded from the group, average military spending amounted to $2.9 billion in constant 1989 dollars.

Despite the relative absence of traditional defense concerns underlying Japanese ODA, flows were often depicted as "strategic aid" (*senraku*) by policymakers, given the broader connotation of national security in postwar Japan (Yasutomo, 1986). As shall be explored in greater detail in Chapter 7, Japanese ODA behavior conformed to a strategic division of labor in which its disproportionate support for regional NICs, many of which were also seen as vital to the West's neocontainment effort, was strongly encouraged by U.S. leaders. Further, like France, Japan identified the economic development of selected neighbors as critical to its own

Table 4.4   Japanese ODA and Recipient Characteristics: Multivariate
Relationships (Figures indicate standardized slope coefficients)

	1980	1981	1982	1983	1984	1985	1986	1987	1988	1989
			Humanitarian-Interest Variables							
Life expectancy	.13	−.03	−.01	−.01	−.04	−.05	.18	−.12	.10	−.02
Caloric consumption	−.19	−.26[a]	−.12	−.05	−.09	−.08	−.20	.01	−.18	−.05
			Security-Interest Variables							
Military spending	.35	−.17	.45	.50	.07	.01	.41	−.04	.37	.24
Conscripted population	−.27	.02	−.21	−.28	−.14	−.08	−.26	−.05	−.17	−.12
			Economic-Interest Variables							
GNP	−.03	.26	−.05	−.24	.22	.33	.08	.23	.16	.08
Trade with Japan	.53	.70	.38	.55	.59	.46	.19	.45	.16	.17
Total R^2	.53	.53	.45	.53	.58	.40	.46	.32	.59	.18

Sources: U.S. ACDA (security-interest variables); IMF (trade variable); OECD (aid transfers [dependent variables]); World Bank (all other variables)
Note: a. Underlined figures indicate significance at .05 level; double-underlined figures indicate significance at .01 level

growth and channeled most aid flows to them. Both countries responded to pressures from within the ODA regime to consider recipient needs while accommodating broader political and security imperatives that prevailed during the Cold War.

Summary

Collectively, Japanese ODA behavior during the 1980s provides further evidence of the linkage between the national interests of donor states and their application of ODA policy. The empirical patterns outlined in this chapter illustrate the central role served by ODA in promoting Japan's own economic development, the primary vehicle for its reemergence as an influential political power. At the same time, growing aid flows facilitated economic expansion among Japan's neighbors in East Asia and furthered the process of regional economic integration, with Japan serving as a catalyst and a model for growth. The largest bilateral aid flows were transferred from Tokyo in the form of low-interest loans and directed toward the construction of economic infrastructure (e.g., utilities and transportation networks) within recipient states. In the process, the Japanese government worked closely with private industry in identifying possible ODA recipients and in executing aid programs. This activity, including the growing integration of the Pacific Rim region, contributed to the rapid expansion of Japan's own economy and enhanced its competitive position relative to those of industrialized states in North America and Western Europe.[16]

Within the aid regime and among outside analysts, Japanese foreign assistance remained controversial in the 1990s. Both the quantity and quality of Japanese ODA continued to attract strong criticism from abroad (an experience Japan shared with the United States) into the 1990s, despite efforts to adhere more closely to DAC-defined standards of aid quality. In the mid-1990s, Japanese leaders expressed a willingness to accommodate these and other transnational concerns within their foreign policies. To some degree, their recognition of transnational interdependence was suggestive of the broadening scope of Japan's perceived national interests. But in other respects, Japanese officials remained defiant, pointing to their rapid economic growth and to the many success stories along the Pacific Rim as testimony to the merits of their distinctive approach. Thus, although Japan continued to pledge greater adherence to the ODA regime's principles and norms, it remained determined to maintain its own standards of ODA quality and its own prerogatives in deciding the direction and form of aid packages.

Other developments in the late 1980s and early 1990s promised to keep Japan's domestic interests in the minds of its policymakers. A series of political scandals revealed a pattern of corruption at the highest levels of Japanese government. The country's economic stagnation occurred alongside growing demands by Japanese consumers for relief from the chronically high costs of living. As elsewhere in the industrialized world, these problems were accompanied by the rise of nationalist groups seeking to restore Japan's autonomy in the face of perceived incursions from abroad. In addition, the end of the Cold War raised questions, both in Tokyo and in Washington, about the continuing security relationship between the two countries. Without a Soviet threat to provide a basis for their bilateral treaty, officials in both capitals searched for a continuing rationale for defense cooperation. Moreover, Japan sought a greater role in international organizations commensurate with its economic power, including a permanent seat on the UN Security Council.

Under these growing economic strains, domestic support for foreign aid faltered in the early 1990s. Though the Japanese government continued to pledge increased aid flows and to improve the quality of ODA, it was confronted by mounting pressure to move in the opposite direction on both counts:

Questions have been raised whether aid was not being wasted . . . and whether the emphasis should not be redirected to such activities as education, medical care, and population planning. But beyond these matters, it seems likely that the average Japanese citizen will sooner or later raise the same questions brought up in the United States, where foreign aid has garnered less and less popular support. (Scalapino, 1992: 206)

Thus, the future of Japan's foreign policies, including those for ODA, was subject to conflicting influences. On the one hand, the country's leaders were asked to satisfy external demands that they assume the responsibilities of global leadership, including an improvement in their qualitative performance as members of the ODA regime. On the other hand, internal pressure mounted for Japan to place its national interests, narrowly defined, at the forefront of its domestic and foreign policies. The future of Japan's role within the aid regime—and within world politics in general—depended on its leaders' ability to reconcile these contradictory demands.

Notes

1. For example, see Steven (1990), Morse (1987), Johnson (1982), and White (1974).
2. In terms of trade volume with the United States, Japan ranked second only to Canada. More than one-third of Japanese exports went to the United States during the 1980s, and the United States was the source of nearly 20 percent of Japanese imports. Meanwhile, Japanese investments in the United States exceeded $75 billion by 1990, about half of its total foreign investment (Scalapino, 1992: 203).
3. The economic boom began less than a decade after World War II. Between 1950 and 1970, economic growth averaged about 10 percent in Japan, far above the world average.
4. Growing multilateral programs, highly publicized by Japanese officials, were exceptions to the more general rule of bilateralism in Japanese ODA.
5. This characteristic of the DAC contrasted with other international government organizations, which collected aid from donor states and made relatively autonomous decisions regarding the identification of aid recipients and the terms of aid transfers.
6. For further information on Japanese ODA to Latin America and sub-Saharan Africa, respectively, see Anderson (1993) and Inukai (1993).
7. A fourth ministry, the Economic Planning Agency (EPA), was charged with coordinating many aid programs but was vested with little functional power, its ambiguous role often attributed to the greater influence accorded other government actors with closer ties to Japanese industry.
8. Among other problems, the Japanese aid program was often plagued by corruption scandals, including the 1986 arrest of a JICA official for taking bribes in return for his support of an agricultural project in Morocco.
9. Their sharing of the Japanese "miracle," paradoxically, was often cited as one reason for the downturn in Japan's economic growth in the early 1990s.
10. Whereas in 1980 the U.S. dollar was comparable to 291.49 Japanese yen, the exchange rate in 1989 was 137.96 yen to the dollar (Japanese Government, 1992b: 93).
11. Nearly 60 percent of the 32,034 Japanese technical experts were dispatched to Asian states between 1954 and 1990. Similarly, 58.6 percent of foreign "trainees" selected by Japan to receive guidance in technical development were Asian.

12. See Japanese Government (1991) for a detailed summary of its technical assistance projects in these and other countries during this period.

13. This pattern contrasted markedly with the French case, in which the development of political infrastructure was consistently the top priority.

14. Overall, Japan became much more active in Latin American ODA during this period, serving as a member of the Partnership in Democracy and Development and in 1992 dispatching the Mission on Economic and Technical Cooperation to El Salvador and Nicaragua "to study measures to aid reconstruction and development and to promote democratization" (Japanese Government, 1993a: 4).

15. Approximately three-fourths of Japanese grant aid was transferred for general purposes during this period. Of the remaining funds, most were reserved for increased food production and support for fisheries in recipient countries. Other categories of Japanese grant aid included food aid, disaster relief, and aid for cultural activities (Japanese Government, 1992b: 13).

16. This regional focus became more pronounced as these states formed their own regional economic blocs, including the European Union and, in the 1990s, the economic integration of the U.S., Canadian, and Mexican markets under the North American Free Trade Agreement (NAFTA).

5
Swedish ODA:
The Nordic Model Under Stress

If the situation facing the developing countries, and with them the world as a whole, is to be decisively changed in a more favorable economic, social, and ecological direction, large-scale, wide-ranging, and appropriately designed development assistance is called for. . . . The basis of our assistance to those in greatest need is a conviction that all human beings are of equal worth and have an equal right to an acceptable standard of living.

—Alf Svennson, Swedish Minister for
International Development Cooperation

As a lightly populated middle power on the periphery of Europe, Sweden assumed a more modest role in world politics than most other industrialized countries during the post–World War II period. Yet the Swedish government made an exception to this rule in the case of foreign assistance. Its aggressive approach to ODA, which was shared by other Scandinavian states, served as a projection of Swedish domestic values and as a vehicle for its global designs. By the mid-1980s foreign-aid operations accounted for more than 80 percent of the Ministry of Foreign Affairs's budget. In this respect, the Nordic model of foreign assistance as applied by the Swedish government provides an illuminating contrast to other donors' pursuit of national interest through foreign aid.

Sweden's reputation as the "darling of the Third World" was reflected generally in its foreign policies of the postwar era and specifically in its approach toward foreign assistance. The emergent role of Sweden as a "benevolent neutral" in a world of partisans allowed national leaders to pursue foreign policies with a seemingly marginal connection to the country's geopolitical or economic self-interests. This role has been described in several ways, including that of "splendid isolation" from the Cold War realpolitik that dominated global politics from 1945 through the 1980s.

Sweden has sought a middle way—neutrality in war, aid to those who need it in peacetime. Abroad as well as at home, it has been determined to live up to the standards set in arriving at a middle way, though preachments on foreign policy by a small power in the north of Europe have often sounded self-righteous. Much of its policy has been concentrated

93

on the division between the industrialized West and the Third World. . . .
The cornerstone was neutrality, strict and unyielding. (Childs, 1980: 120)

Like those of its Scandinavian neighbors, Sweden's proportionate
share of ODA has traditionally been among the highest of aid donors. The
first country to reach the Development Assistance Committee's ODA/GNP
target of 0.7 percent, Sweden exceeded that level throughout the 1980s despite worsening internal economic conditions and growing internal dissension. In most categories of ODA quality, Sweden ranked among the
world's leaders throughout the postwar period. Its disbursement of ODA
almost entirely in grant form and its rejection of ODA "tied" to Swedish
goods and services set qualitative standards that no major donor was able
to match. Further, Swedish officials more actively involved the techni-
cians, engineers, and civil servants of recipient countries in development
projects funded by Swedish aid.[1]

In their general approach to foreign affairs, Sweden's Social Democratic governments pursued a discernible set of national interests founded
upon long-standing, widely shared normative principles regarding social
welfare, domestic governance, and foreign relations. At home, they acted
upon egalitarian principles in creating extensive public services, including systems of socialized medicine and child care that became models for
other industrialized states. In addition, the Swedish government adopted
fiscal policies that not only ensured its pervasive societal role but also re-
distributed wealth and produced a broad measure of economic equality.[2]
Sweden's priorities in foreign affairs, which directly informed its aid policy, also reflected these societal norms and set Sweden apart from its European neighbors, which could less easily escape the polarizing influences
of the Cold War. Its leaders consistently pursued national interests such as
strategic neutrality vis-à-vis the great powers of Western Europe, Asia, and
North America; a pacific approach to international conflict resolution emphasizing universal codes of conduct, mediation, arms control, and collective security; and the redressing of economic inequalities between North
and South through the extension of social democratic principles and programs to receptive governments in the developing world.

These interests were often cited by Swedish leaders as emanating from
their peripheral status in a system of nation-states invariably dominated by
great powers. Prime Minister Olaf Palme, the most prominent of postwar
Swedish leaders, defended Swedish autonomy as essential for a middle
power with global concerns. Palme (1982: 244–245) identified the basis of
Sweden's national interests as follows: "to secure, in all situations, and in
ways we choose ourselves, our national freedom of action in order to preserve and develop our society within our frontiers and according to our
values, politically, economically, and culturally; and in that context to
strive for international détente and a peaceful development."

Maintaining regional and global neutrality became an overriding objective of Swedish leaders upon the country's decline as an imperial power in the seventeenth century.[3] Neutrality served as "much more than a useful foreign policy instrument; it is an integral part of their political culture and strategic thinking, a way of life and the only viable political course in the international arena" (Karsh, 1988: 192). This policy led to Swedish detachment from great-power posturing in the nineteenth century, during both world wars, and throughout the Cold War. In addition, it shaped Sweden's role as an intermediary in the North-South dialogue and dictated its hands-off approach toward political integration on the European continent. Sweden was not a party to the 1957 Treaty of Rome, which established the European Economic Community, because of the pact's long-term provisions for political unification and, consequently, for the sacrifice of Swedish sovereignty.

To Swedish leaders, neutrality provided invaluable flexibility—an opportunity both to avoid foreign entanglements and, more constructively, to build bridges between rival blocs. Its neutrality did not exclude an active involvement in international affairs. To the contrary, Sweden's assertive presence in international governmental organizations and within the ODA regime led to its reputation as *The Committed Neutral* (Sundelius, 1989). Sweden was a strong supporter of the League of Nations and, after World War II, the United Nations. Its activism increased in 1953 with the appointment of Sweden's Dag Hammerskjöld as secretary-general of the United Nations. Hammerskjöld epitomized Sweden's idealism in world politics; his death on a UN peacekeeping mission to the Congo in 1961 only strengthened the Swedish public's resolve to improve North-South relations.

An exception to Sweden's nonalignment policy was the effort among Swedish leaders to bolster Nordic cooperation, primarily on economic and social issues. Palme (1982: 236) emphasized the "community of language, culture, tradition, and cohesion" that existed among Sweden and its neighbors Denmark, Finland, Iceland, and Norway. Nordic countries exploited their shared backgrounds and their detachment from the great powers to create their own model of North-South cooperation: "The designation 'Like-Minded Countries' was coined during the 1970s to depict Scandinavia, together with Holland, as Third World partners in the effort to reform the global system through multilateral negotiations in several arenas. The international stature of these small states has grown as a result of this positive record" (Sundelius and Odom, 1992: 324).

These Scandinavian countries tightened their regional links at a time when Western European states were also moving toward economic integration. For Sweden, this regional emphasis was not unprecedented; when the collective security provisions of the League of Nations disintegrated during the interwar period, the Swedish government had turned to Nordic defense against German fascism. Immediately after World War II, Sweden attempted to retain a system of Scandinavian collective security through the Scandinavian Defense Alliance, but its efforts were unsuccessful, as Denmark and Norway joined NATO and thus "took sides" in the Cold War. Swedish leaders were particularly concerned that NATO membership would rupture its tenuous but important relationships with the Soviet Union in the 1950s. The experience of neighboring Finland, which accepted Soviet hegemony but not the de facto control of Moscow, served as a constant reminder to Swedish leaders about the need to remain nonaligned and to support conciliation between the superpowers.[4]

Given the fact that exports accounted for approximately one-third of its GNP into the 1990s, Sweden's emphasis on economic aspects of its foreign policy is not surprising. Closer political ties between Sweden and the European mainland reflected their intimate economic relations: Approximately 75 percent of Swedish trade was with Western European states in 1990. (By comparison, the United States accounted for approximately 10 percent of Sweden's trade, LDCs another 10 percent.) A founding member of the European Free Trade Association (EFTA) in 1960, Sweden compensated for its isolated location by becoming a champion of open markets and transnational commerce.[5] Its government endorsed the creation of the European Economic Area and, through the EFTA, subsequently concluded free-trade agreements with Eastern European and Baltic states. Sweden was also an active supporter of open markets in successive rounds of the General Agreement on Tariffs and Trade (GATT), including the Uruguay Round, which concluded in 1994.

As they pursued this foreign-policy priority, Swedish leaders additionally promoted peaceful means of conflict resolution between military rivals. They rejected proposals from some domestic groups that Sweden develop its own nuclear deterrent and instead pressed other states in the region to form a "nuclear-free club." In addition, they encouraged détente between the United States and Soviet Union and supported efforts to reduce nuclear stockpiles in both countries and across Europe. In 1975, Sweden joined the Conference on Security and Cooperation in Europe (CSCE), which it used as a platform to advance the Helsinki accords on human rights. The CSCE adopted Sweden's conception of "common security" based on regional and global disarmament.[6] Palme's 1982 Conference on Common Security pursued these outcomes, and the 1984–1986 Stockholm Conference on Disarmament in Europe pressed further as renewed signs of East-West accommodation became evident. Swedish officials used these and other outlets to advocate restrictions on conventional arms transfers and on the development of chemical and biological weapons. In the United Nations during the 1980s and early 1990s, Sweden actively supported its growing number of peacekeeping missions.

Swedish ODA in Retrospect

Given Sweden's physical and cultural separation from continental entanglements, World War II and the Cold War served less as turning points in Swedish foreign policy than as extensions of previous patterns. In this light, Sweden's historical experience may be better viewed as one of continuity and gradual systemic adaptation than one of turbulence and abrupt change. This dimension of Swedish foreign policy, of course, contrasts sharply with the cases of France, Japan, and the United States, combatants during World War II whose international roles were largely transformed by the conflict and by the subsequent pressures of the Cold War. Sweden's Third World relations also differed from those of industrialized states in Western Europe, whose aid policies were often dictated by postcolonial commitments. From the 1800s through the 1950s, Sweden's role in the southern hemisphere was largely limited to missionary work conducted by the Lutheran Church.

Swedish leaders during the 1960s shaped the first generation of ODA flows to facilitate their progressive agenda in foreign affairs. Aid programs were premised upon a widespread antipathy toward many industrialized powers' development strategies, which were perceived by Swedish leaders as largely self-serving and tainted by Cold War preoccupations. Policymakers were strongly influenced by the writings of the Swedish economist Gunnar Myrdal (1960: 236), who argued that "a substantial increase in the bargaining power of the poor countries is necessary for attaining a new situation of world stability." With ODA as their instrument, Swedish officials pursued a "special relationship" with a relatively small number of LDCs that shared their commitment to social democracy at home and nonmilitarism abroad.

An elite and public consensus on the virtues of foreign assistance, reflecting broader societal agreement on Sweden's role in foreign affairs, ensured ODA's prominent role in postwar Swedish foreign policy. Sweden's "social homogeneity and historical tradition [produced] common political values embracing moderation and a willingness to compromise" (Hancock, 1972: 32). The public was actively involved in the formulation of government policies, and its influences were felt within the parliament (Riksdag) and the ODA bureaucracies. Vigorous debates regarding the selection of ODA recipients, the forms and terms of aid, and the function of aid as a vehicle for recipient development occurred within the context of a societal consensus that ODA could serve a constructive role in North-South relations and that Sweden was in a favorable position to provide it.

Prior to Sweden's emergence as a major ODA donor, nongovernmental organizations (NGOs) raised and disbursed foreign aid through the newly formed Central Committee for Swedish Technical Assistance to

Less-Developed Areas. Through NGOs, Swedish aid donors hoped to reach the targets of their Third World development efforts more directly. They openly mistrusted political elites in many LDCs and sought "solidarity with the poor as opposed to their governments" (Holmberg, 1989: 147). As the Swedish government assumed central control over the ODA program, bilateral transfers were approved for two recipients, Ethiopia in Africa and Pakistan in Asia. A third recipient, Ceylon (Sri Lanka), was added in the late 1950s, and many more states received bilateral assistance during the ODA "gold rush" of the early 1960s. The position of special minister for development assistance was created to manage Sweden's emerging ODA program, to consolidate public support for development assistance, and to design ongoing bilateral aid packages. These early programs largely consisted of technical assistance for aid recipients, including the construction of schools and clinics and the transfer of Swedish equipment for recipient infrastructure projects such as electrification and public health. Minister Ulla Lindstrom was largely successful in this effort, and by 1961 the Central Committee was expanded into a broader Agency for International Assistance. In 1962, the Riksdag formally articulated the aid program's long-term scope and objectives, declaring it to be "an expression of a much deeper recognition that peace, freedom, and welfare are not exclusive national concerns, but rather something increasingly universal and indivisible."[7]

General public support was obtained for the volume and direction of Swedish foreign assistance despite denunciations of the domestic policies of some aid recipients, most notably those of Ethiopia's Emperor Haile Selassie. Though many argued that recipients must adhere to democratic principles or respect human rights, others equated such requirements with the type of political interference otherwise proscribed by Swedish aid legislation. Overall, however, Sweden sought potential aid recipients that, in word or in deed, lived up to the country's model of social democracy.

Consistent with the targets articulated by the United Nations and the DAC, the Swedish government pledged to raise ODA appropriations until they reached 1 percent of Swedish national income. This target, officially adopted in 1968 and achieved in 1975–1976, became the focal point of ongoing domestic debate. (The ODA level stood at 0.1 percent of Sweden's GNP in 1960 and 0.5 percent of GNP in 1970.) Communist and Liberal Party leaders advocated a more aggressive aid program, whereas members of the Moderate and Centrist parties generally argued for more modest appropriations. No major political group, however, questioned the basic legitimacy of foreign aid as an instrument of Swedish foreign policy.

The Swedish government repeatedly pledged to separate the humanitarian aspirations of ODA from short-term domestic economic interests. If Sweden was to derive benefits from the transfers, they were to be only a "welcome side effect," not an ostensible motivation. Other steps were taken to maximize the quality of Swedish ODA. Aid was to be offered on "soft" terms, with a preponderant grant element; an emphasis on multilateral flows was designed to ensure the nonpolitical, noncoercive nature of Swedish ODA. The goals of most international organizations involved in foreign aid were "thought by many to correspond very well to a Swedish attitude of general benevolence and international solidarity, unmarred by vested interest" (Ohlin, 1973: 50). In approving the first large-scale annual ODA appropriation, the Swedish government declared that ODA would be directed toward states that were attempting

> to carry out such structural changes as will create conditions for development characterized by economic and social equalization. . . . Aid must not imply foreign economic and political interference . . . nor must questions of race and religion play any role. [Sweden must display a] positive attitude toward the cultural background and specific needs of recipient countries. (Quoted in Heppling, 1986: 22)

During its aid reorganization of the mid-1960s, Swedish officials devised a "country-programming" system by which large and sustained ODA flows would be targeted to a more limited pool of recipients. Transfers concentrated on six recipients: Ethiopia, Kenya, Tanzania, Tunisia, India, and Pakistan. Swedish officials also lent economic support to revolutionary regimes in the developing world such as North Vietnam, Cuba, and Angola. The Swedish strategy was later broadened to include seventeen "program countries," for which multifaceted, long-term plans were developed (see Table 5.1).[8] This recipient-oriented strategy allowed for more elaborate consultations between Sweden and its beneficiaries, for increased coordination among functional sectors assisted through development assistance, and for the integration of aid programs within the broader and longer-range development strategies of the selected LDCs. These states were particularly attractive to Sweden given their "equity-oriented" development policies, which broadly reflected Sweden's own societal priorities.[9]

As in the other three cases, proliferating Swedish ODA was accompanied by a proliferation of government agencies involved in the aid process. After taking over the task of foreign assistance from NGOs in 1962, the Swedish government coordinated aid flows through the Swedish Agency for International Assistance. This agency was expanded three years later and renamed the Swedish International Development Authority (SIDA), which gradually assumed oversight responsibility over most bilateral aid programs. During this period Sweden was active in creating the multinational consortium of donors within the OECD.

Other agencies important to the aid process included the Swedish Agency for International Technical and Economic Cooperation (BITS), established in 1979. Through BITS, recipients were primarily responsible for procuring and managing short-term development programs. The Special

Table 5.1   Top Ten Recipients of Swedish ODA, 1970–1990

1970–1971	1980–1981	1989–1990
Pakistan	Vietnam	India
India	Tanzania	Tanzania
Tanzania	India	Mozambique
Ethiopia	Mozambique	Nicaragua
Kenya	Zambia	Vietnam
Tunisia	Bangladesh	Ethiopia
Vietnam	Ethiopia	Angola
Turkey	Sri Lanka	China
Brazil	Kenya	Zambia
Sri Lanka	Angola	Kenya

Source: OECD (1991b: 224)

Fund for Industrial Cooperation with Developing Countries (SWED-FUND) was designed to initiate joint ventures and promote private investment in LDCs. Finally, the Swedish Agency for Research Cooperation with Developing Countries (SAREC) began its efforts in 1975 to promote research and collaboration between government and industry in LDCs.

As the organizational framework for distributing Swedish assistance overseas took shape, the Riksdag retained oversight authority over the aid programs; it consistently played a central role in determining the volume, objectives, and organization of Swedish ODA. Primary responsibility for managing the effort was placed within the Ministry of Foreign Affairs, whose minister for development cooperation authorized aid expenditures and oversaw Sweden's distribution of ODA through SIDA and multilateral channels.

As noted previously, a national consensus favoring foreign assistance was repeatedly reflected in public opinion polls and surveys. Although public support for foreign assistance fluctuated in other donor states with the ebbs and flows of their domestic economies, widespread support for Swedish ODA persisted through the prosperity of the 1950s as well as the deep economic recessions of the 1970s and 1980s. Between one-half and two-thirds of Swedish respondents consistently approved of current aid levels or supported increases (Karre and Svensson, 1989: 259). The receptiveness of Swedish citizens toward foreign assistance was largely attributable to their broad involvement in ODA policy formulation; the government enlisted the participation of many groups, including churches and charitable organizations, in researching, proposing, and implementing aid programs. Representatives of these groups, as well as those from industry and political parties, often sat on the boards of directors of aid-disbursing agencies.

Sweden's distinctive approach to ODA was modified in the 1970s and 1980s, however, after its economy was weakened by steep increases in petroleum prices and the ensuing effect on international markets. For a country so dependent on exports, Sweden was unusually vulnerable to such price shocks (an effect also observed in the case of Japan). For the first time in several decades, the Swedish government was forced to borrow money from international markets during the late 1970s. Whereas other major donors responded by diversifying aid transfers to include Mideast recipients, Swedish leaders sought to make future ODA transfers more compatible with domestic economic interests. Among such reforms, the previously scorned practice of tying Swedish aid to the purchase of Swedish goods or services or to prescribed financing arrangements became more acceptable as an element of aid policy.

The period between 1976 and 1982 also witnessed the disruption of the Social Democratic Party's control of the Swedish government, which was run by a succession of four non-Socialist coalitions. This period, regarded as a time of crisis in Swedish politics, marked the transition from the "liberal" era toward one in which economic forces, largely transnational in origin, constrained the autonomy of states and curbed their ability to effect changes through government intervention. A conservative coalition took power and immediately proposed adding commercial criteria to Swedish aid calculations. Country programming was administered on the basis of "concerned participation," which called for more active involvement on the part of donors and stricter terms for recipients (Edgren, 1986: 51).[10] In addition, Swedish officials evaluated aid programs as a condition for future assistance, shifted from capital-intensive development projects to smaller-scale ones, and promoted a steady shift from multilateral to bilateral transfers. Its efforts were consistent with those of other Nordic states that had developed large-scale aid programs of their own and eventually utilized them more than they used multilateral agencies. The segregation of Swedish development assistance from private investment also came under scrutiny during this period in response to appeals by industry that its foreign trade and expansion plans could be rendered consistent with publicly financed development objectives.

In establishing the new framework for ODA, the Riksdag declared that Swedish economic assistance would henceforth promote four specific objectives: economic growth, economic and social equality, economic and political independence, and democratic development. These goals guided more than a decade of subsequent ODA transfers until three additional goals were added in the 1980s: promoting environmentally sensitive economic development, efficiently utilizing natural resources, and integrating women in development efforts. These latter priorities were partly a response to the growing environmental movement and the recognized impact of ODA on development patterns and social relations within LDCs.

The aid debates of the 1970s and 1980s exacerbated party fragmentation, in the process exposing the divergent worldviews of Swedish elites. Sweden's multiparty system resulted in disagreement over not only the aggregate volume of aid transfers but their direction as well. Leaders of the Swedish left, for example, advocated continuing assistance to revolutionary regimes in Angola, Cuba, Nicaragua, and Vietnam.[11] The ideals of Swedish radicals often provided the ideological basis of development aid; they promoted assistance to movements of national liberation and to groups that opposed imperialism, neocolonialism, and racial oppression. Meanwhile, liberals concentrated more directly on aid to recipients on the basis of their demonstrable human needs, whereas conservatives (through the Moderate Party) sought larger transfers to states with which Sweden had established trade and investment relationships. The widening gaps between these positions in the 1980s reflected a "general process of political polarization in Sweden" (Andersson, 1986: 31).

This splintering of public opinion occurred throughout Scandinavia and in many Western European countries during the prolonged economic recession, high unemployment, and energy crises of the 1980s. The "lost decade" of Third World development aroused the left in Sweden and other countries, whose leaders "radically rejected aid policy altogether, on the grounds that it bolstered reactionary governments and allowed useless technical assistance experts to lead lives of luxury in the midst of poverty" (Ohlin, 1973: 51). Conservative groups, meanwhile, called for an end to "aid welfare," advocating that ODA be continued only if tied to domestic economic interests. Sweden did not witness the emergence of ultranationalist groups (as did France, West Germany, and other countries in Western Europe), but a growing and more assertive part of its population demanded that the country's national interests not be sacrificed in the pursuit of transnational objectives. As noted earlier, however, no significant interest group in Sweden advocated the outright abolition of development assistance; debates centered largely on the direction and terms of ODA flows rather than their legitimacy. This widespread public consensus in favor of continuing foreign aid stood in stark contrast to the skepticism felt by the U.S. public, for which the outright removal of aid from the federal budget became increasingly popular, if not likely. Broad-based support for Swedish ODA was comparable to that which prevailed in France and Japan despite the economic difficulties of the 1980s and 1990s.

As Swedish ODA diverged from its earlier "purity" and incorporated features that were compatible with domestic economic interests, critics felt the government had relinquished its status as a model of responsible behavior. To some, the penetration of private interests signaled the subordination of aid policy to the interests of Swedish capital. In this and other aspects, the Nordic model began to emulate the "OECD model" of development assistance, which for many years had openly integrated the interests of donor states with those of recipients in an attempt to promote high levels of aid flows. As Table 5.2 illustrates, the changing scope and direction of Swedish ODA flows reflected differing assumptions and objectives, which could be discerned in several aspects of aid behavior.[12]

Table 5.2   Two European Models of ODA

	Swedish	OECD
Objectives	International solidarity; socioeconomic equality	Increased donor-recipient commerce; domestic economic growth; membership in donor's bloc
Recipient role	Autonomous	Dependent on donor guidance
Terms of ODA	Untied	Tied to donor goods or services
Standard form	Grants	Concessional loans
Recipient profile	Less or least developed; radical or social democratic; nonaligned	Less developed or newly industrialized; of geopolitical or economic significance
Length of commitment	Long-term	Short or medium-term
Multilateral component	Strong	Weak or moderate
Donor self-interests	Weak	Moderate or strong

Amid this domestic debate, reforms in Swedish aid were institutionalized from the early 1980s into the 1990s. In 1981 Swedish officials implemented a new credit system under which subsequent ODA would be formally tied to Swedish exports. More elaborate guidelines were enacted that required SIDA, BITS, and SAREC to evaluate the effectiveness of aid programs. And in 1993, the Semi-Permanent Committee for the Evaluation of Swedish Development Cooperation began convening on a regular basis. These reforms did not produce net reductions in aggregate ODA; annual volumes continued to rise in most years, although the government agreed to lower the ODA/GNP ratio below the 1 percent level. Reversing earlier trends, the Swedish government turned back to NGOs for assistance in raising money and implementing aid programs. According to the Swedish government (1992), "NGOs in Sweden can contribute to the development of trade unions, co-operatives and other population movements which play a part in the growth of democratic societies. . . . NGOs are often more able than the official aid agencies to reach groups like rural laborers and the handicapped."

Swedish ODA and Global Solidarity

Regarded as among the most altruistic of DAC aid programs, Swedish ODA was "an international expression of social values that [were] widely shared with Swedish society. . . . Solidarity with the underprivileged is regarded as a moral responsibility" (Karre and Svensson, 1989: 231). Among members of the DAC, Sweden's program stood out for its ascribed commitment to the societal values of prosperity, equality, and international solidarity.

> In the case of Sweden, one is tempted to suggest that its most distinctive feature is its moralistic or even sanctimonious tone. There is a tendency, among politicians and many aid officials, to suspect the motives underlying aid policies in all other donor countries. . . . Sweden alone is thought to be acting purely in the interest of the underdeveloped countries, or at least of the deserving ones. (Ohlin, 1973: 56)

In making ODA decisions, Swedish officials looked for potential partners in their effort to convert their social democratic principles into political stability and broad-based prosperity abroad. Neither decimated nor enriched by the two world wars, Sweden served as a model to LDCs trying to avoid subordination to Cold War alignments. Sweden's marginal role in great-power politics "allowed plenty of room for indulgence in broad idealistic imperatives" (Holmberg, 1989: 124). Among primary concerns advanced by Swedish leaders was the national liberation, rapid decolonization, and progressive governmental activism in LDCs. In this manner, the Swedish government found ODA to be a valuable asset in its pursuit of "ideological imperatives" in the Third World.[13]

This aspect of Swedish policy was also reflected in government spending patterns at the domestic level. In 1989, the Swedish central government spent 40.6 percent of GNP, up from 27.9 percent in 1972 and among the highest rates of public spending in the industrialized world. Of that total expenditure, 55.9 percent was directed toward welfare programs; just 6.7 percent was spent on national defense (World Bank, 1991: 225).

In addition to promoting their own geopolitical independence, Palme and his predecessors served as champions of Third World efforts to maintain freedom from great-power hegemony. To Palme (1982: 245), "durable peace and detente are impossible as long as small states are subjected to the *Realpolitik* of great powers." Through the League of Nations, the United Nations, and other multilateral channels, Sweden opposed the imposition of the great powers' economic, military, and political hegemony and encouraged newly independent states.

To Swedish officials, political self-determination was critical for the newly independent states of Africa and South Asia. Such autonomy could not be realized, they argued, if these LDCs were subject to the economic manipulation of industrialized states. In their view, North-South cooperation would produce the additional benefits of political and economic independence. Sweden's initiatives in this regard extended well beyond ODA; it was among the earliest supporters of the movement for a New International Economic Order and of the efforts by the Group of 77 to redistribute global wealth; it encouraged revolutionary movements in Latin America and subsidized the revolt against apartheid in South Africa. In criticizing the hegemonic ambitions of both Cold War superpowers, Swedish leaders called for the political and economic autonomy of Eastern Europe as well as the liberation of Third World states from U.S.-backed dictatorships.

Swedish officials condemned the interventionism of the United States, Soviet Union, and other global powers during the Cold War, using foreign assistance to encourage LDCs to pursue social, macroeconomic, and foreign programs similar to their own. Specifically, they sought prospective recipients with nonaligned foreign policies, redistributive fiscal policies, and activist social-welfare policies. In this way, Sweden urged recipients to reproduce the Swedish welfare system within their own borders. Though they avoided conditionality in most of their aid transfers, through the country-programming approach Swedish officials engaged in an "intensified policy dialogue" with recipients that "made it possible in many cases to influence these countries' economic policies" (OECD, 1990a: 149).

This pattern, of course, was not unique to Sweden. French aid officials attempted to reconstruct the socioeconomic and cultural institutions of their *metropole,* and Japan rewarded states that emulated its model of political economy. In Sweden, a quest for hegemony was less evident than a quest for normative assimilation; the values transferred through the aid mechanism generally reflected societal principles rather than discernible material self-interest. In Sundelius's view, "The commitment to a just and equitable world order in many ways reflects the salient features of Swedish domestic life" (1990: 124).

Though widely regarded as altruistic, Sweden's approach to North-South relations was not articulated entirely in these terms. Swedish officials advanced a vision of international relations by which the equitable distribution of wealth (between North and South and within states) would promote political stability, which in turn would discourage military adventurism and thus benefit all nations, including Sweden. "Economic and social development in the developing countries is also in the interests of the industrialized nations," argued Alf Svennson (Swedish Government, 1993: 4), Sweden's minister for international development cooperation and human rights issues. "A peaceful future for the world is inconceivable if we fail to eliminate mass poverty." As a trading state shorn of geopolitical rivalries, Sweden's prevailing national interests thus centered on systemic stability. And its leaders explicitly made foreign assistance one of Sweden's primary contributions to global prosperity, equality, and stability.

Swedish ODA in Practice

As described in Chapter 2, Sweden was among the world's most affluent states during the period under study. Its per capita GNP of $26,000 in 1990 was the largest among the four donor states under study, and its unemployment rate of 1.5 percent was the lowest. Other measures of affluence, including life expectancy (74 for men, 80 for women) and infant mortality (6 per 1,000), further affirmed this dimension of Sweden's economy and society.[14] However, the country's small size and relatively low level of economic output greatly limited its impact on economic development both within its own region and among developing countries. Sweden's $188 billion GNP in 1989 was the smallest of the four by almost $700 billion, and Sweden suffered a negative balance-of-payment rate of –2.6 percent/GNP in 1990, which was the greatest such deficiency of the four donor states. Public spending accounted for more than 60 percent of Sweden's gross national product, by far the largest among the four sample states, exceeding the levels of France (49.7 percent), the United States (36.1 percent), and Japan (32.9 percent).

Among the most distinctive aspects of Sweden's ODA performance, its per capita aid flows were the highest of the four donor states under review. Sweden's per capita ODA expenditure of $150 was 50 percent greater than that of Japan as the 1980s began, three times the Japanese rate, and almost four times that of the United States. The $205 per capita level in 1989–1990 was also by far the largest, as the disparities between Sweden and the other three donors actually increased during the period.

Throughout the postwar period and including the decade under study, Sweden gradually increased its share of global ODA spending (see Table 5.3). Net disbursements in 1989–1990 exceeded $1.7 billion, a 40 percent increase above its 1980 ODA expenditures and more than 250 percent above the 1970 level. Swedish ODA also represented a larger share of its gross national product by 1990, despite ongoing internal pressures to slow or reverse its expansion. In terms of its share of global development aid flows, Sweden played a larger role by the end of the decade than it did at the outset, with its 1989–1990 contribution more than 50 percent larger than that of two decades earlier. Net disbursements actually declined slightly in 1990, both in real terms and as a percentage of Swedish GNP, because of the completion of various large-scale projects in the 1989 budget year.

An additional $628 million in Swedish development assistance was distributed through multilateral agencies during this period, primarily the European Community and organizations within the United Nations (OECD, 1991a: 233), in particular the UN Development Program. Sweden also reported spending $647 million in market-term private financial flows during the year, of which $407 million consisted of export credits and $240 million consisted of direct foreign investment (OECD, 1991a: 233). Swedish aid officials explicitly segregated foreign assistance from private economic development efforts, unlike Japan and, to a lesser extent, the United States.

In terms of geographical distribution, recipients in sub-Saharan Africa and South Asia received by far the largest share of Sweden's aid disbursements (see Figure 5.1). More than half of Swedish ODA was directed

Table 5.3   Swedish ODA Transfers, 1970–1990

	ODA Commitment[a]	Percent GNP	Share of World ODA
1970–1971	493	0.40	1.9
1980–1981	1,251	0.80	2.3
1989–1990	1,746	0.93	3.1

Source: OECD (1991a)
Note: a. ODA commitment in millions of constant U.S. dollars

toward African recipients by the mid-1980s, reflecting Sweden's effort to concentrate aid among a relatively small number of LLDCs that conformed to the basic-needs criteria established by the Swedish government and the international aid regime. Struggling African states provided an ideal forum for the globalization of Sweden's domestic values, with particular emphasis on "integration, solidarity, and equality" (Jinadu, 1984: 179).[15]

Sweden's significant long-term support of the government of India was another primary element of its aid strategy. During the decade, however, Swedish ODA flows to South Asia fell from nearly one-quarter of the total to less than one-fifth, whereas disbursements to recipients in other parts of Asia fell from 17 percent to 11 percent. Aid flows to Mideast recipients fell during the middle part of the decade before returning to their 1979–1980 levels by 1990. Meanwhile, disbursements to Latin American recipients grew from 4 percent to 11 percent of total Swedish ODA outlays. Sweden's increasing assistance to Latin American recipients was in keeping with the normative emphases underlying its larger and more longstanding aid programs for sub-Saharan Africa: "The share of bilateral assistance to Latin America [was] geared to a high degree towards democratisation and the promotion of peace in the region" (OECD, 1991a: 148).

The functions to which Swedish ODA was applied during this decade represented another aspect in which Sweden's program stood apart from most other countries' (see Figure 5.2). Nearly two-thirds of Swedish bilateral ODA was transferred to program countries, which were given a relatively free hand in allocating the resources. "The most important decision with respect to recipient-oriented assistance was the selection of the program country itself," Holmberg (1989: 138) observed. "It was assumed that the correct choice would yield results that would support the Swedish assistance goals." About one-fifth of these funds were devoted to long-term construction of social and political infrastructure, with public administration and education being the primary areas of concentration within this category. Additional Swedish ODA was directed toward emergency relief, support for nongovernmental organizations, and short-term humanitarian aid programs.

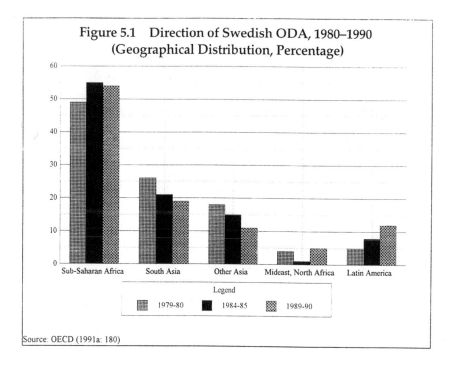

Figure 5.1   Direction of Swedish ODA, 1980–1990
(Geographical Distribution, Percentage)

Legend
1979-80   1984-85   1989-90

Source: OECD (1991a: 180)

The indicators of Swedish ODA quality listed in Table 5.4 illustrate its consistent performance above the DAC averages but also a trend toward decreased quality as the decade progressed. Only in the area of grant element versus concessional loans did Sweden's performance and that of the DAC improve. In this indicator of ODA quality, Sweden consistently ranked among the leading ODA donors; by 1989 all of its ODA was disbursed in the form of grants, with no expectations of repayment from aid recipients. In terms of the tying of Swedish ODA, the table shows a dramatic drop in untied aid during the middle of the decade, followed by a modest increase. This pattern reflected a broader movement among DAC members, which on average increased the level of tied aid by nearly one-third between 1980 and 1986. As in other categories, Swedish aid quality, though generally decreasing, remained above that of the DAC as a whole. This pattern was especially evident regarding the degree to which Swedish officials turned to multilateral assistance as a component of their ODA mix. As noted previously, multilateral aid is generally perceived as less political than bilateral flows, with fewer strings imposed upon recipients by the aid donors. Sweden consistently transferred higher-than-average levels through multilateral channels, although these levels decreased after 1983 both for Sweden and for DAC members in general. Among multilateral

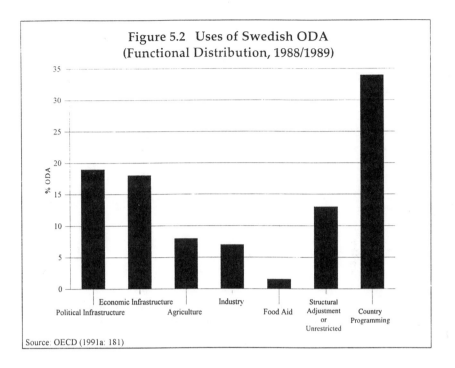

Figure 5.2   Uses of Swedish ODA
(Functional Distribution, 1988/1989)

Source: OECD (1991a: 181)

conduits of Swedish ODA, economic and social agencies within the
United Nations played the primary role. The UN Development Program
(UNDP), Children's Fund (UNICEF), Commission for Refugees, Fund for
Population Activities, World Health Organization (WHO), and World Food
and Agricultural Organization (FAO) accounted for 60 percent of Swedish
multilateral aid. The World Bank and regional development banks received
an additional 25 percent.

Finally, Swedish ODA to LLDCs also remained consistently above the
DAC average. Of the top ten recipients of Swedish ODA in the 1989–1990
fiscal year, eight (China, Ethiopia, India, Kenya, Mozambique, Tanzania,
Vietnam, and Zambia) were technically regarded by the OECD as LLDCs
(countries with per capita GNPs of less than $700); Angola ($1,130) and
Nicaragua ($850) were the exceptions. Fourteen of the seventeen program
countries that received sustained Swedish ODA were in the category of
least-developed countries.

Swedish humanitarian interests in extending development assistance
were reflected in the negative statistical relationship between aid transfers
and recipient per capita caloric consumption in each of the ten years under
study, with the relationships reaching statistical significance in five of the
ten years (see Table 5.5). The average daily intake of Sweden's top ten

Table 5.4   Quality of Swedish ODA, 1980–1989

	Grant Element (% ODA)	Untied Aid (% ODA)	Multilateral Aid (% ODA)	Aid to LLDCs (% ODA)
1980	98.6 (75.2)[a]	86.2 (50.3)	31.7 (28.5)	42.7 (35.1)
1983	99.6 (76.3)	81.2 (45.9)	36.7 (31.3)	30.4 (21.8)
1986	99.9 (87.0)	41.6 (33.4)	32.1 (28.1)	28.7 (23.4)
1989	100.0 (92.8)	49.5 (36.5)	30.2 (27.2)	32.1 (22.4)

Sources: OECD (1982b, 1985b, 1988b, 1991b)
Note: a. ODA averages listed in parentheses

recipients in 1989 was 2,097 calories, nearly 30 percent lower than the worldwide average of 2,711 calories. Only one of these recipients, China, reported per capita consumption above the 2,406 average for low-income countries. Many of these recipients, including Angola (1,807 calories), Ethiopia (1,667), and Mozambique (1,680) were among the most under-nourished LDCs by this standard, which is among the most widely utilized measures of human need (World Bank, 1992: 272–273). The average 1989 life expectancy in these recipient nations was 56.4 years, far below the worldwide average of 64 years and below the average for low-income countries of 60 years. When Sweden's ODA flows to all of its recipients are considered, however, the statistical relationship is weaker.

The growing realism that pervaded the Swedish ODA program in the 1980s was reflected in the presence of statistically significant relationships between Swedish aid flows and trade patterns during the last three years of the decade. As noted previously, Swedish political and business leaders implemented broad new measures to increase the efficiency of aid pro-grams and to make them responsive to domestic economic interests. As in the case of France, Swedish trade followed its aid in a growing number of cases, a trend that was likely to continue after Sweden announced new ini-tiatives in both trade and aid with states in Eastern and Central Europe.

Even after the growth in Swedish trade with its aid recipients is taken into account, a preponderant share of its commerce continued to be con-ducted with industrialized states, mainly in Europe. Of the $51.5 billion in Swedish exports in 1989, LDCs received $5.9 billion in Swedish goods, slightly more than 10 percent of the total (International Monetary Fund, 1990: 368–369).[16] The Swedish government traditionally segregated aid

Table 5.5 Swedish ODA and Recipient Characteristics: Multivariate
Relationships (Figures indicate standardized slope coefficients)

	1980	1981	1982	1983	1984	1985	1986	1987	1988	1989
			Humanitarian-Interest Variables							
Life expectancy	.20	−.03	.12	.09	.06	.09	−.04	.08	−.04	.04
Caloric consumption	−.28	−.41ᵃ	−.41	−.30	−.26	−.40	−.36	−.62	−.26	−.61
			Security-Interest Variables							
Military spending	−.03	.01	−.04	.07	−.00	.20	−.12	−.04	.15	.01
Conscripted population	−.02	.01	.02	−.06	−.04	.02	.10	.08	−.11	.05
			Economic-Interest Variables							
GNP	−.03	-.41	.14	−.00	.07	.20	.21	−.03	-.12	−.14
Trade with Sweden	−.03	.20	.05	.09	.08	.00	.16	.48	.44	.89
Total R^2	.06	.12	.11	.07	.06	.13	.11	.24	.21	.63

Sources: U.S. ACDA (security-interest variables): IMF (trade variable); OECD (aid transfers [dependent variables]; World Bank (all other variables)
Note: a. Underlined figures indicate significance at .05 level; double-underlined figures indicate significance at .01 level

policy from trade and investment relations; its program countries were involved in a small fraction of Sweden's bilateral trade. This pattern changed as Swedish leaders integrated aid flows into their broader macroeconomic policies. Exports to India, for example, increased from $117 million in 1985 to $550 million in 1989.

As expected, Swedish ODA flows during the 1980s were not statistically linked to either of the indicators of security interest. Conscription rates of Sweden's primary recipients averaged 6.7 persons per 1,000, which is about 14 percent above the worldwide average of 5.9 per 1,000 (U.S. Arms Control and Disarmament Agency, 1990). These averages were inflated, however, by the high levels of conscription in Nicaragua (18.2) and Vietnam (19.8); when these cases are removed the average conscription rate among Swedish aid recipients falls to 3.7 military personnel per 1,000 citizens. Military spending by these primary recipients ranged widely from $90 million in the cases of Tanzania and Mozambique to $23 billion in the case of China. When the entire pool of Swedish aid recipients is considered, the relationship between aid and military spending is statistically insignificant.[17]

These empirical trends collectively illustrate both the distinctiveness of the Swedish approach to ODA and its increasing adaptation to changes in the aid regime during the 1980s and 1990s. Swedish officials tried to keep ODA levels at or above the 1 percent/GNP level and to make ODA available exclusively in the form of grants, but they permitted the increased tying of aid projects to Swedish goods and services as well as the shift of some aid programs away from the poorest states. In the last three years of the decade, the strong connection between Swedish trade and aid flows provided further evidence of its more pragmatic approach to development assistance. More generally, it reflects the shift in Swedish foreign policy away from self-sacrificing behavior toward practices that brought some tangible benefit to Swedish citizens.

Summary

As described in the preceding pages, the Swedish government adopted an approach to foreign aid that symbolized the country's egalitarian and neutralist approach to foreign affairs. While serving as an extension of Sweden's individual character, its ODA behavior was consistent with the "Nordic model," which also was followed by Norway and Finland. In their approach to foreign affairs, Swedish and other Scandinavian leaders steadfastly avoided alignments amid often intense continental and global rivalries, exploiting their status of "splendid isolation" vis-à-vis the great powers of the late twentieth century. In so doing, they were able to focus their efforts in foreign policy (and the distribution of development aid) on normatively driven initiatives that reflected widely shared domestic values within their societies.

Sweden's overriding objective of strategic neutrality was accompanied by the pursuit of nonviolent solutions to international conflicts. Arms-control initiatives and disarmament plans were often proposed by Swedish leaders in regional and global forums. The Swedish government avoided developing a sizeable domestic military infrastructure of its own, and its leaders, most notably Prime Minister Olaf Palme, encouraged other states to pursue similar strategies. These leaders utilized their ostensible political and military disengagement as a basis for promoting egalitarian, social democratic development overseas, largely through the vehicle of foreign assistance; they projected their domestic model onto a relatively small group of LDCs and LLDCs and offered them economic support to meet their citizens' basic needs. Holmberg summarized:

> In applying its welfare principles internationally, the Swedish government has acted to expand its welfare community to include recipient countries [which were] often portrayed as extensions of Sweden's political culture during debates on the aid budget. . . . The poor countries should not only receive welfare inputs from Sweden, but should—as much as possible—*reproduce the Swedish welfare system within their*

own borders. This extension provides an external legitimation for Sweden's domestic welfare system. (1989: 128–129; emphasis in original)

As the record during the 1980s indicates, Sweden maintained its reputation for high-quality development assistance throughout the period, especially when its performance is compared to that of other major donor states. Sweden consistently directed aid toward the world's poorest people on terms requiring the least amount of reciprocal sacrifice. Its aid patterns, however, reflected the adaptation of Swedish aid to a troubled period in the global political economy. Whether Sweden could exploit the opportunities posed by the transformed systemic environment, anticipated with relish by its leaders for half a century, remained dubious given the persistence of economic strains at the regional and global levels. As the 1990s began, Sweden's ability to preserve its isolation was challenged by the pressures of an interdependent world economy. Sweden responded to these challenges by becoming more actively engaged in regional economic activity. With the end of the Cold War, Swedish officials found conditions more favorable for involvement in the European Community (renamed the European Union). With EU membership no longer considered a breach of Sweden's neutrality, its government applied for admission in July 1991 and placed the question of EU membership before the population in a 1994 referendum. At the same time, the government pledged to work closely with countries in Eastern and Central Europe in establishing stable diplomatic, security, and economic relations.

As the Cold War ended and a nebulous new order emerged in the early 1990s, Sweden's aid program underwent fundamental reforms. In response to growing concerns about the efficiency of Swedish ODA and its relationship to the country's broader program of economic development, the once formidable wall between Swedish aid and private enterprise began to erode. In the government's proposals for the 1993 ODA program, explicit objectives included "aid effectiveness" and "the development of a market economy" as well as the more traditional Swedish concerns for "human rights, democracy, and equal opportunities." In addition, the concentration of ODA among the seventeen program countries was further reduced by Sweden's commitments to provide concessional funding for Russia, Poland, and the newly independent Baltic states. The Swedish government agreed in 1990 to divert 1 billion Swedish crowns (approximately $180 million) from traditional spending categories to support these recently liberated states.

As this shift in the tenor of Sweden's aid program continued, many liberals feared it would undermine the normative values that had been a source of Swedish pride and prestige in previous years. These sentiments clashed with economic interests, which during the 1980s attempted to render Sweden's ODA program more compatible with domestic economic concerns. Conservative critics cited the perceived failures of government intervention in various sectors of Sweden's economy, including health care, as well as the failure of many "progressive" LDCs to establish market economies and promote social democracy. A polarizing debate occurred across the country, as parties from both left and right found fault with the conduct of Swedish ODA policy, often for different reasons.[18]

As the Swedish variant of the Nordic ODA model lost some of its distinctive characteristics, it appeared likely that Swedish development aid would enter "a period of quantitative stagnation and qualitative adaptation to what is most often called economic realities" (Rudebeck, 1984). Without a Cold War to mediate, in the absence of the intense ideological rivalries that had provided an opportunity to promote an alternative model, and in the midst of a prolonged economic slump, Sweden faced new challenges and a reformulation of its national interests in the 1990s. Though it appeared certain that development assistance would continue to play a central role in promoting those interests, the specific contours of that role remained ambiguous and, as always, a subject of lively debate in Stockholm.

Notes

1. Only the Netherlands, Norway, and some OPEC donors in the early 1980s contributed more aid funds on a per capita basis during this period.

2. Swedish ODA represented 2.5 percent of the government's budget in the mid-1980s.

3. See Dohlman (1989) for an elaboration of Sweden's neutralist policy and its historical applications.

4 .The Swedish government maintained a modern defense force throughout this period, spending an average of 7.5 percent of its budget on military security in the 1980s. "Considerable investment has been made in a mobile air force and advanced means of intelligence collection" (Sundelius and Odom, 1992: 313).

5. Other founding members of the EFTA included Great Britain, Switzerland, Austria, Portugal, and the other Scandinavian states.

6. In these areas, the CSCE took on greater significance after the Cold War as Western European leaders looked for alternatives to NATO in pursuing regional security.

7. See Swedish Government (1962) for the full text of this bill, which is often regarded as the "bible" of Swedish ODA. In this sense it is comparable to the *Jeanneney Report* in France, published during the same period, which outlined the long-term structure and objectives of French aid.

8. Socialist program countries received an average of 55 percent of Swedish ODA between 1976 and 1986 (Karre and Svensson, 1989: 253).

9. The program countries, which received renewable three-year disbursements from Sweden, were Angola, Bangladesh, Botswana, Ethiopia, Guinea-Bissau, India, Cape Verde, Kenya, Laos, Lesotho, Mozambique, Nicaragua, Sri Lanka, Tanzania, Vietnam, Zambia, and Zimbabwe. Cuba, Pakistan, and Tunisia were dropped as program countries in the mid-1970s for economic and political reasons.

10. Though still the major focus of Swedish ODA, the share of aid expenditures directed toward program countries fell between 1975 and 1985 from 74 percent to 61 percent.

11. These groups also advocated large volumes of economic support for frontline states surrounding South Africa and for nongovernmental organizations such as the African National Congress in South Africa and the South West African Peoples' Organization in Namibia.

12. Karre and Svensson (1989: 271) acknowledged the convergence of the Swedish and OECD models but concluded that "the aid constituency in Sweden has been comparatively successful in defending genuine development co-operation. There is still a 'Swedish model,' and this model is being shared and sometimes bettered by some other donors."

13. In addition to participating in UN agencies, Sweden played an active role in regional efforts such as the Southern Africa Development Coordination Conference, a cooperative effort among Nordic countries to improve living standards in the region. These efforts further reflected the "multilateralist ethic" in Swedish foreign policy during the 1960s and early 1970s.

14. See Milner (1989) for a detailed summary of Sweden's economic performance during this decade.

15. Samuelson (1975: 335) identified the following six values that informed Sweden's welfare policies: humanitarianism or mercy, resocialization or rehabilitation, integration, solidarity, equality and justice, and social security.

16. Sweden's primary trading partners during the 1980s were, in order, West Germany, the United Kingdom, Norway, Denmark, Finland, and France. Swedish exports to Asian states doubled between 1985 and 1989 to $2.4 billion, as Swedish firms greatly expanded exports to China, Taiwan, Singapore, and South Korea. Swedish exports to African states, conversely, remained much smaller; the $614 million in 1989 exports represented slightly more than 1 percent of total Swedish exports.

17. In other cases, including Angola, Nicaragua, and Vietnam, military spending figures were not available during all or part of the 1980s.

18. The failure of many capital-intensive aid programs was acknowledged by observers across Sweden's political spectrum. Primary examples were the Bai Bang pulp and paper mill in Vietnam, the Mufundi paper mill in Tanzania, and the Kotmale dam project in Sri Lanka.

6

The Geopolitics of U.S. ODA

We must embark on a bold new program for making the benefits of our
scientific advances and industrial progress available for the improvement
and growth of underdeveloped areas. . . . The United States is pre-emi-
nent among nations in the development of industrial and scientific techniques. . . . Democracy alone can supply the vitalizing force to stir the
peoples of the world into triumphant action, not only against their human
oppressors, but also against their ancient enemies—hunger, misery, and
despair.

—*President Harry S Truman*

When American forces sought outside assistance in the Revolutionary War
against England, they turned to the French government for support. French
economic and military assistance tipped the balance in the Americans'
favor, providing an early illustration of the value of foreign aid. Given this
historical precedent, it should not be surprising that the United States became a prolific aid donor in the late twentieth century.

The French precedent is illustrative in a second respect. French military assistance was quite obviously not provided for altruistic reasons, the
rhetoric of its leaders regarding the need to support liberty notwithstanding. The termination of Britain's hegemony in North America, which had
strengthened after the Seven Years' War (1756–1763), and the disruption
of its control of Atlantic shipping lanes were long-standing geopolitical
objectives of the French monarchy, objectives that were served by the
colonial challenge. Thus, the role of foreign aid in promoting donor interests, even as it benefited its recipients, was clear for all to see.

As noted in Chapter 2, the U.S. government was the primary force behind the creation of the liberal international economic order that emerged
after World War II. Through the three pillars of the Bretton Woods system—the World Bank, the International Monetary Fund, and the General
Agreement on Tariffs and Trade—the United States took advantage of its
postwar predominance to recast much of the global economy in its image.
And through extensive programs of bilateral economic and military assistance,
the United States supported almost every country outside of the Soviet
Union's sphere of influence. By 1990, the U.S. government had transferred

$374 billion in loans and grants to more than 100 LDCs, $233 billion in the form of economic assistance. The U.S. Agency for International Development (USAID), with approximately 4,300 employees in 1990, maintained permanent offices in ninety countries. U.S. ODA extended to much of the former Second World in the mid-1990s to recipients that had previously been adversaries in the Cold War.

As in the other cases, a continuous tension existed between the humanitarian functions of U.S. foreign aid in improving social welfare conditions in LDCs and the narrower imperatives of U.S. self-interests. At one level, generosity by the United States toward impoverished peoples was consistent with its historical self-image as a messianic "city on the hill."[1] At another level, however, U.S. aid was inconsistent with the self-help principles of many Americans, as reflected in their traditional distrust of government and their dislike of social welfare programs. In order to garner support for foreign aid from a skeptical public, the U.S. government consistently identified national interest as a primary rationale for transferring public resources to the Third World. As Undersecretary of State William Clayton argued in 1947, "Let us admit right off that our objective has its background in the needs and interests of the people of the United States. We need markets—big markets—in which to buy and sell." Almost half a century later, USAID (1992: 1), in a report entitled *Why Foreign Aid?* answered this question bluntly: "Because it is in the United States' own interest."

Whereas early U.S. aid efforts in the post–World War II period focused on the reconstruction of industrialized states and the establishment of a global alliance of anticommunist states, beginning in the 1960s the social and economic aspects of decolonization and Third World state building were also cited as major reasons. As a result, the "objectives of official U.S. foreign assistance have gradually blurred" (USAID, 1989: 1). With the end of the Cold War, and in the midst of a reassessment of the U.S. role in world politics (a recurrent preoccupation of the U.S. government), leaders again attempted to reconcile national interests with the foreign-aid program, calling for continued aid flows as an instrument of "preventive diplomacy."

USAID officials launched this effort as the United States was suffering from chronic budget and trade deficits; a skyrocketing national debt; faltering education, welfare, and health care systems; and a crime rate that was among the highest in the world. Under the leadership of Bill Clinton, who admitted to being relatively disinterested in foreign affairs when he took office in January 1993, the U.S. public appeared less inclined than ever to support new initiatives in foreign aid. Thus, the level of U.S. ODA as a percentage of its GNP, already one of the lowest in the world, was likely to slip even lower in the mid-1990s.

National Interest in U.S. Foreign Policy

The U.S. foreign-aid program reflects the tension between the competing strains of idealism and realism that has coexisted uneasily through much of its history, defining the "American style of foreign policy" (Spanier and Hook, 1995). As noted in Chapter 1, these traditions were reflected in the cyclical shifts between parochial and universal conceptions of national interest. Whereas one or the other of these conceptions generally prevailed at any given time or place, both were present to a great degree in the United States.

Early U.S. leaders acknowledged the centrality of self-interest in guiding behavior. To George Washington, "A small knowledge of human nature will convince us that, with far the greatest part of mankind, interest is the governing principle." Alexander Hamilton extended this argument to the policies of governments, drawing a moral line between individual and state action: "An individual may, on numerous occasions, meritoriously indulge the emotions of generosity and benevolence, not only without an eye to, but even at the expense of, his own interest. But a government can rarely, if at all, be justifiable in pursuing a similar course." In Federal Paper 10, James Madison (1938 [1787]: 56) noted that competing interests are "sewn in the nature of man" and recommended that the federal government be based upon "the regulation of these various and interfering interests."[2] These principles were applied to the early formulation and conduct of U.S. foreign policy. Leaders of the United States believed its geographic position, abundant natural resources, and cultural values delineated a set of national interests that, if defended consistently, would protect the country during its infancy. "Europe has a set of primary interests which to us have none or a very remote relation," Washington (quoted in Rappaport, 1966: 29) observed in his farewell address of 1796. "Our detached and distant situation invites and enables us to pursue a different course."

Throughout the nineteenth century, U.S. foreign policy reflected this resistance to "overseas entanglements." Successive administrations focused on internal development, both economic and political. The separation of the United States from the Old World was codified by the Monroe Doctrine of 1823, establishing the basis of U.S. hemispheric hegemony that has continued throughout the twentieth century. Continental expansion, which included the slaughter and expulsion of Native Americans and the conquest of northern Mexico, was justified on the basis of the country's "manifest destiny" to extend its cultural and political values. In these instances, policies that seemed consistent with Old World standards of realpolitik were instead attributed to idealistic motives. This was a characteristic trait of U.S. foreign policy that bemused overseas leaders, who often did not feel it necessary to cloak their pursuit of national interests in moral justifications.

After the internal cohesion of the United States was threatened but ultimately preserved in the Civil War, its previous emphasis on political and economic development and detachment from great-power politics was revived in the era of reconstruction. The rise of the United States as an industrial power coincided with the collapse of order in Europe and the convulsions of two world wars. In the aftermath of World War I, Woodrow Wilson equated U.S. interests with universal values of democracy, self-determination, and collective security (see Chapter 1). This formula was rejected by the U.S. Senate, however, and the League of Nations (absent the United States) failed to prevent or punish aggression. After the United States was again drawn into world war, both in Europe and in the Pacific, and after it prevailed on both fronts, an activist foreign policy was ensured. The ideological antagonism between the United States and the Soviet Union, which split the world into two hostile blocs and produced nearly a half-century of Cold War, served as the basis of U.S. globalism.

Postwar realists such as George Kennan and Hans Morgenthau blamed the failures of U.S. foreign policy during the interwar period on the subordination of national interests to universal moral aspirations. In the 1950s and 1960s, U.S. leaders advanced their geopolitical interests in tandem with those of its allies in all corners of the world. Richard Nixon, influenced by another prominent postwar realist, National Security Advisor Henry Kissinger, explicitly placed the concept of national interest at the fulcrum of U.S. foreign policy in the early 1970s by stating that "interests must shape our commitments, rather than the other way around." This approach led Nixon to pursue détente with the Soviet Union and to normalize relations with the People's Republic of China despite continuing ideological divisions between East and West.

Given its transformed role in the international system, the United States pursued a broader range of interests in the postwar period. These included the preservation and dissemination of cultural values such as limited but representative government, respect for individual political liberties, and religious tolerance; the promotion of economic growth through market-oriented development and support for a liberal international trading system; and the protection of U.S. territory and the security of its allies through the establishment of military defenses, bilateral and multilateral security arrangements, and selective intervention in overseas conflicts. Reflecting this expanded scope, as well as the moralism that animated previous conceptions of U.S. national interest, Rostow (1960: 543) observed, "It is the American interest to maintain a world environment for the United States within which American society can continue to develop in conformity with the humanistic principles which are its foundation." Throughout the Cold War, all of these goals were intimately associated with the effort by the United States to contain communist expansion, a central preoccupation that was applied to all aspects of U.S. foreign policy, including the allocation of development assistance.

U.S. Aid as an Agent of Containment

 Prior to the Cold War, U.S. foreign aid generally "consisted of admonition and was consequently neither expensive nor effective" (O'Leary, 1967: 5). Examples of early U.S. initiatives included its disbursement of private funds to assist Santo Domingan refugees in 1793, security assistance for Greek nationalists in the 1820s, and disaster aid for victims of Ireland's famine in the 1840s. In the early stages of World War II, the flow of U.S. military hardware to Great Britain, Russia, and other allies bolstered the collective defense against Nazi Germany. But it was after this war that the U.S. aid program assumed global proportions. Through the Marshall Plan, "the high-water mark of U.S. foreign aid" (USAID, 1989: 17), the United States helped rebuild decimated states in Western Europe and Asia.[3] And through the military aid programs that derived from the Truman Doctrine, the United States utilized a second form of foreign assistance in the pursuit of its transformed national interests.

Western European states received most Marshall Plan funding ($13.6 billion in economic and $7.8 billion in military assistance). Among these recipients, France ($5.9 billion) received the largest share, followed by Great Britain ($3.8 billion), West Germany ($2.9 billion), Italy ($2.4 billion), and the Netherlands ($1.8 billion).[4] At the same time, the United States transferred large volumes of aid to other regions. East Asian states received $3.9 billion in both types of assistance, and states in the Near East and South Asia received $2.5 billion (USAID, 1990: 7, 69).[5]

After the completion of the Marshall Plan, U.S. foreign assistance was redirected toward the geopolitical objective of communist containment. Aid flows were coordinated with other efforts by the U.S. government to support LDCs along the periphery of the Soviet Union and China, many of which (including the Philippines, South Korea, Pakistan, and Turkey) joined the United States in anticommunist security alliances. Under the 1951 Mutual Security Act, subsequent U.S. aid flows were dominated by military rather than economic transfers. Many LDCs reached aid agreements with the Soviet Union and China, thus initiating an "aid rivalry" among the superpowers that would intensify in subsequent years. Yet in urging Congress to increase aid flows to the Third World, Eisenhower (quoted in Treverton, 1987: 73) continued to frame his proposals in humanitarian language: "The purposes of this great work would be: To help other peoples to develop the underdeveloped areas of the world, to stimulate profitable and fair world trade, to assist all peoples to know the blessings of productive freedom."

During the ten-year life of the Mutual Security Act, the United States transferred about 50 percent more foreign assistance than it had under the Marshall Plan. The Eisenhower administration directed aid flows to strategic allies in the Third World, many of which were not among the most impoverished, and allowed "market forces" to dictate support for economic development. Rather than emphasizing development aid in these latter efforts, Eisenhower relied on multinational corporations and bilateral trade agreements to promote capitalism (Cingranelli, 1993: 138).[6]

In the early 1960s, Kennedy redirected U.S. ODA toward broader developmental goals. The Foreign Assistance Act of 1961, the Alliance for Progress, the Peace Corps, and other initiatives were aimed at promoting political and socioeconomic development in LDCs, particularly in Latin America. U.S. aid flows extended beyond the Soviet periphery and were accompanied by direct guidance in public works, agricultural techniques, and the establishment of stable, nominally democratic governments. In the revised calculations of aid officials, the peaceful and prosperous development of LDCs was ultimately tied to that of the United States. Thus, for the Kennedy administration, which vowed to fight communism as vigorously as it championed the cause of North-South cooperation, the seemingly distinct motivations of humanitarianism and self-interest were rendered complementary in the "decade of development." Analyses of U.S. foreign aid were often infused with idealistic language about its potential to hasten the liberation of LDC populations. To Cropsey (1963: 130), "Our duty to lighten the load of human misery is derivative from, indeed it is the reflex of our duty to bear ourselves as a great nation."

After Lyndon Johnson succeeded Kennedy, U.S. ODA was again diverted toward Cold War imperatives, this time in Southeast Asia. The central themes of Kennedy's Alliance for Progress—long-term development, nation building, an emphasis on LDCs and LLDCs—were largely discarded as the United States became mired in the Vietnam War. A preponderant share of resources, more than $20 billion in mostly military grants, was transferred to South Vietnam to support its efforts against the Viet Minh. By the late 1960s, Vietnam received nearly half of U.S. ODA and most of its military assistance (USAID, 1991: 85). U.S. aid to Southeast Asia continued after the United States withdrew its forces in keeping with Richard Nixon's "Vietnamization" strategy of shifting the onus of political stability and military defense to recipients.

After U.S. military involvement in Indochina ended in the mid-1970s, the U.S. aid program underwent new shifts in geographic distribution, content, and bureaucratic structure. Under the New Directions initiative, officials attempted to make USAID more responsive to rapidly changing conditions and basic needs in LDCs. Congress responded to the appeals for such reforms, including an amendment to the 1973 Foreign Assistance Act that redirected future ODA to "give the highest priority to undertakings submitted by host governments which directly improve the lives of the poorest of their people and their capacity to participate in the development of their countries." Whereas previous aid programs had emphasized capital-intensive projects such as dams and power plants, those under the New Directions mandate focused instead on small-scale farming, nutrition, literacy, and population planning.

Jimmy Carter emerged in the late 1970s as a strong proponent of U.S. ODA, which he regarded first as a tool to promote Third World development and observance of human rights, later as a means to protect U.S. interests in the face of heightened competition from the Soviet Union, and finally as an instrument to maintain stability in the Middle East. Among the recommendations of Carter's Development Coordinating Committee was a renewed emphasis on human-needs concerns in U.S. aid allocations and the formation of an International Development Cooperation Agency (IDCA) to coordinate the multifaceted U.S. program.[7] But as before, the tidal fluctuations in U.S. aid policy revealed themselves. Like the Alliance for Progress, the effort by the Carter administration to lessen the security dimension of U.S. foreign aid was curtailed in the late 1970s under the strains of renewed Cold War tensions. Carter responded to the Soviet Union's invasion of Afghanistan and other developments by requesting increases in U.S. defense spending and the restoration of many military-assistance programs he had previously suspended. His decisions marked the abandonment of his earlier foreign-policy goals, which had included the shift of emphasis from East-West relations to those between North and South (see Rosati, 1987).

Meanwhile, Carter was sympathetic to arguments that the peaceful coexistence of Egypt and Israel would require ongoing, large-scale financial support from the United States. The result was an annual U.S. commitment of $5 billion to the two countries. This aspect of the Camp David accords contributed to stability along the Israeli-Egyptian frontier, but it overshadowed U.S. aid practices in other areas. Aid to Israel served a variety of domestic and global U.S interests, including the protection of an ally in the Middle East—a region viewed as a "vital" U.S. interest since the Eisenhower administration. As for Egypt, U.S. aid flows served less apparent interests and were hence more controversial. Among the objectives cited was the need for an ongoing U.S. presence in the Arab world and the weaning of Egypt from Soviet economic and political influence. Neither recipient fit the profile of an LDC, so aid on such a massive scale could not be justified on a human-needs basis; thus, Carter and subsequent presidents were forced to defend the aid flows on other grounds.

With Ronald Reagan's election to the U.S. presidency in 1980, the renewed Cold War was reflected in aid policy. Though constrained by the massive aid commitments to Israel and Egypt, Reagan directed additional funds toward states pivotal in his neocontainment strategy, many of which were in Central America (see Table 6.1). As for recipients not facing an imminent threat of communist takeover, Reagan (1981: 1185) advocated linking aid to free-market economic reforms: "History demonstrates that time and time again, in place after place, economic growth and human progress make their greatest strides in countries that encourage economic freedom." During this period, Secretary of State George Schultz (1984: 17) argued that international stability founded on economic development

would be a primary objective of the administration and that "threats to stability impede development."

More so than other presidents, Reagan attempted to influence the for-
eign-policy behavior of aid recipients. Like previous administrations, the
Reagan team attempted to get U.S. clients during the Cold War to support
U.S. military initiatives and U.S. positions in international organizations.
During his second term, Reagan attempted to tie assistance transfers to the
voting behavior of recipients in the United Nations, where adherence to
U.S. policy positions had fallen steadily during the previous three decades.
This effort failed, however, as aid recipients continued to vote against the
United States on most resolutions in the UN General Assembly. It is re-
vealing that U.S. aid to these recipients generally continued at previous
levels or was increased (see Kegley and Hook, 1991).

For this and other reasons, Reagan's foreign-aid program was scruti-
nized by Congress, which threatened to reduce development aid flows to
recipients that could not demonstrate sufficient levels of human need. Reagan responded by appointing the Carlucci Commission on Security and
Economic Assistance. Like groups that had previously examined the aid
program, the Carlucci Commission called for a structural reorganization of
USAID. Its proposal for a Mutual Development and Security Administration designed to integrate the aid programs more efficiently was not acted
upon by Congress. This and other recommendations were greeted with
tepid enthusiasm within USAID and other aid-dispensing agencies, where
"there was a tendency to view the initiative as just the latest of the 'development fads' which emerge at the beginning of each new administration"
(McGuire and Ruttan, 1990: 142).[8]

Reagan's effort to press U.S. ODA into the service of the Cold War
was exemplified by his support for the government of El Salvador despite
widely reported instances of human rights violations in that Central American country. Congress required the administration to verify that the Sal-
vadoran government was making progress in protecting human rights
before new ODA funds were approved; although atrocities continued, sufficient support for aid existed in Congress to keep the funds flowing. Further, the administration's support for antigovernment rebels in Nicaragua,
another aspect of its neocontainment effort, produced a major political
scandal after it was revealed that funding for the insurgents, prohibited by
Congress under strong domestic opposition, had been continued with prof-
its from the secret sale of weapons to Iran in exchange for the release of
U.S. hostages. The scandal was among the only drains on Reagan's otherwise strong level of public support.

George Bush largely maintained Reagan's ODA policies during a period in which Congress and the U.S. public grew increasingly skeptical
about the aid program. Growing budget and trade deficits and a prolonged
economic recession exacerbated these concerns. Under Bush, USAID

Table 6.1   Top Ten Recipients of U.S. ODA, 1970–1990

1970–1971	1980–1981	1989–1990
India	Egypt	Egypt
Vietnam	Israel	Israel
Indonesia	India	Pakistan
Pakistan	Turkey	El Salvador
South Korea	Bangladesh	Philippines
Brazil	Indonesia	Honduras
Turkey	Pakistan	Bangladesh
Colombia	El Salvador	India
Israel	Peru	Sudan
Laos	Portugal	Costa Rica

Source: OECD (1991b: 225)

encouraged aid recipients to abandon statist macroeconomic strategies—including the nationalization of key industries, subsidies and price supports, and the pursuit of import-substitution trade strategies—and to establish market-driven programs for accelerating economic growth. The demise of the Cold War between 1989 and 1991 further deprived many bilateral aid programs—and U.S. foreign policy in general—of their previously stated rationales. Containing communism could no longer serve as the guiding principle behind U.S. policy; thus, new doubts arose about many established ODA programs. Moreover, the developmental needs of the former Soviet Union and its Eastern European clients imposed new demands on the aid resources of the United States and other members of the ODA regime.

Under the Clinton administration, USAID rapidly aligned its objectives with those of the United Nations and other international organizations, pledging to use future aid flows to promote sustainable development and democracy in the developing world. As they frequently had in the past, USAID officials proposed to redefine the agency's mission; in addition, they announced plans to curtail aid flows to repressive Third World regimes and to shift the most security-oriented ODA programs, including those for Egypt and Israel, to other funding categories (see Chapter 7). The overall effort was designed to reflect the changing basis of U.S. national interests in the post–Cold War period and to render ODA programs more consistent with emerging transnational interests.

U.S. Foreign Aid: The Security Dimension

Although this study is directed toward better understanding development assistance as an instrument of donors' national interests, the U.S. government's

extension of military assistance to LDCs must also be considered. As Table
6.2 illustrates, the United States transferred foreign military assistance to
each of its major ODA recipients between 1962 and 1989, the period in
which the United States allocated development aid as part of the contemporary aid regime.

Overall, the United States transferred $104 billion worth of military
assistance to more than 100 foreign countries during the twenty-seven-year
period, compared to the $175 billion in economic assistance allocated by
the U.S. government. Of this total, $66 billion in military aid was provided
in grant form; the additional assistance was extended in the form of low-
interest loans. The military-assistance figures do not include government-
sanctioned sales of U.S. military hardware at market prices, many of
which were made to middle- or low-income recipients (see Klare, 1987;
and Pierre, 1982). Recipients in the Near East–South Asia region, which
includes the Middle East, received more than half ($58 billion) of U.S.
military assistance. The United States provided $32 billion in military as-
sistance to recipients in East Asia, half of which went to South Vietnam
during the 1960s and early 1970s. Another $3.5 billion was transferred to
Latin American states, $3.1 billion to those in Africa (particularly Morocco
and Tunisia), and $4.7 million to European recipients (particularly Portu-
gal and Spain), many of which received continuing U.S. ODA after the
Marshall Plan period.

The largest proportion of military grant aid was provided through the
Military Assistance Program (MAP) and used for military equipment, supplies, and support services. Twenty-seven nations received MAP funding
in 1989. Although MAP grants represented the largest dollar volume of
any U.S. military-assistance initiative, most countries received U.S. support through the International Military Education and Training (IMET)
program. In 1989, the United States provided assistance to eighty-six
countries through IMET, which provided "grants of instruction and training services to military and related civilian personnel of friendly countries" (USAID, 1993a: 4). In most cases, including the primary U.S. ODA
recipients of Bangladesh, India, Sudan, and Costa Rica, these aid flows
amounted to less than $1 million, but they still provided for a U.S. pres-
ence in each of the recipient states.[9]

U.S. military assistance was generally provided for explicit security
reasons related to its leading role in containing communism during the Cold
War; thus, the ambiguities regarding its intent did not pertain as in the case
of development aid. It is instructive to note, however, that most ODA recipients were simultaneously receiving annual disbursements of U.S. military assistance during much of the post–World War II period. The other
three ODA donor states reviewed in this study did not provide substantial
volumes of military assistance; only France provided such aid, as part of its
effort to provide protection to many of its allies in francophone Africa.[10]

Table 6.2   U.S. Military Assistance to Major ODA Recipients

Major ODA Recipient (1989–1990)	U.S. Military Assistance, 1962–1988[a]	U.S. Military Assistance, 1989[a]
Egypt	10,674	1,301
Israel	25,834	1,800
Pakistan	1,983	231
El Salvador	869	81
Philippines	1,206	128
Honduras	428	41
Bangladesh	3	0.3
India	147	0.3
Sudan	328	0.9
Costa Rica	39	0.2

Source: USAID (1993)
Note: a. Figures represent millions of current U.S. dollars

In these respects, U.S. ODA must not be considered in isolation from its broader foreign relations with LDCs; development and security assistance may be viewed as two sides of the same coin. More broadly, foreign aid represented one element of a broad pattern throughout the Cold War of U.S. intervention in LDCs where successive presidents claimed vital national interests to be at stake (see Schraeder, 1992). As the empirical patterns below indicate, even within the narrow spectrum of U.S. development assistance, the pursuit of security interests was evident.

U.S. ODA and Domestic Politics

When security and economic assistance programs are both taken into account, the U.S. aid effort during the post–World War II period was by far the largest in the world. Given its steadily increasing scope, it is not surprising that the U.S. aid program produced a large and complex institutional framework that exerted its own impact on the volume, direction, and terms of aid flows. Among the consequences of this bureaucratization was ongoing confusion over the objectives of the myriad programs and constant clashes between federal agencies in planning, implementing, and monitoring aid. In this respect, the U.S. ODA program was widely viewed as "a by-product of the American political system, a highly bureaucratized network of actors that clash over resources and the authority (or turf) to influence policy. . . . The making and execution of foreign aid policy has been characterized by intense confusion over both objectives and evaluative criteria" (Guess, 1987: 2).

This pattern was evident early in the evolution of the U.S. ODA program, when Montgomery (1962: 197) noted, "The survival of foreign aid is the result of a series of uncertain political compromises." This pattern led in sucessive administrations to a growing detachment of U.S. ODA flows from stated foreign-policy goals, many of which extended beyond the containment of communism. U.S. aid programs became increasingly vulnerable to intragovernmental conflicts and compromises. In the mid-1970s, amid great uncertainty over the future of U.S. foreign assistance in the post-Vietnam era, USAID continued to be "subject to the slings and arrows of the rest of the government to which it belongs" (Tendler, 1975: 4).

This bureaucratic tangle must be appreciated in any assessment of U.S. ODA. In addition to USAID, other federal agencies with a role in foreign assistance included the Export-Import Bank, the Overseas Private Investment Corporation, the Trade Development Program, the U.S. Information Agency, and the Office of the U.S. Trade Representative. Among cabinet-level agencies, the Agriculture Department managed Food for Peace and other programs involving the transfer of farm surpluses; the Commerce Department coordinated U.S. aid relationships with other donor-recipient economic ties; the Defense Department managed the transfer of military assistance and many forms of economic aid; the State Department oversaw the activities of USAID; and the Treasury Department played a key role in formulating U.S. policy toward multilateral banks and in coordinating the debt schedules of aid recipients (see Baker, 1984; and Demongeot, 1984). The problem of coordinating the far-flung foreign-assistance programs in the 1980s prompted USAID (1989: 9) to ask rhetorically, "Is it possible to even talk about a unified development strategy when assistance is routed through so many independent, and often competing, government departments and agencies?"

Coordination of U.S. aid was complicated not only by the involvement of several executive-branch agencies but also by conflict between these agencies and Congress. Given its constitutional "power of the purse," Congress exercised a critical role in the granting of foreign assistance, making this one of few issue areas in which the legislative branch could compete with the White House. Although overall aid levels consistently increased throughout the postwar period, frequent debates between Congress and the executive branch centered on the specific uses of development aid. "With rare exceptions, debate is acrimonious, final action is usually not taken until the session is nearing adjournment, and program cuts are the rule," observed Lewis (1984: 28). This contentious relationship hindered efforts by USAID to implement aid programs, but effectiveness was hampered even further by the constantly shifting aid mandates that originated from new presidential administrations and congressional majorities.[11]

Within Congress, the complexity of foreign assistance was illustrated by the numerous committees with a voice in decisions over aid transfers.

The Senate Foreign Relations Committee and the House Foreign Affairs Committee exercised primary jurisdiction over bilateral ODA; the agriculture committees of both houses, along with the House Foreign Affairs Committee, supervised food aid; and the House Banking Committee considered multilateral packages in consultation with the Senate Foreign Relations Committee. Within and between these congressional bodies there were frequent disagreements over the shape of U.S. foreign assistance (Gimlin, 1988: 472).

As a result of this diffusion of ODA authority, members of Congress often were able to achieve approval of particular aid projects by "earmarking" appropriation bills. These projects were often of as much interest to politician's constituents, who provided the goods or services that were made available to recipient countries, as they were to the LDCs themselves. In this manner the 535 members of Congress pursued "multiple goals and detailed spending mandates that frequently conflict" (Doherty, 1992: 1356).[12] Congress further encouraged this pattern by passing foreign-aid bills with little or no debate in the form of continuing resolutions.

As U.S. aid programs were refined and expanded throughout the postwar era, one pattern remained constant: the lack of public enthusiasm about them. "In few areas of American public life is there so little national consensus on purposes as in foreign aid," Montgomery argued (1962: 197). These problems had not subsided a decade later, when Huntington (1970–1971: 162) noted: "The continuing quest for a rationale for foreign aid is one of its distinguishing characteristics as an area of public policy." In public opinion surveys conducted in the late 1970s, nearly 70 percent of respondents felt the U.S. government was spending too much on foreign assistance, whereas less than 4 percent believed aid levels were insufficient. The two most prevalent reasons for this view were: (1) "We have problems of our own here at home and should spend the money here instead of overseas"; and (2) "Most of the economic aid we provide never gets to the people who need it" (Roper, 1979: 650–653).

Public disdain for foreign assistance intensified in the late 1980s as growing budget and trade deficits were accompanied by slow economic growth and high unemployment. By the late 1980s the political popularity of foreign aid had fallen even below the chronically low levels of earlier periods.[13] Aside from their support for specific measures that were of value to their districts or states, members of Congress often granted foreign aid the lowest priority in their spending preferences. "It is the program their constituents most want to see cut," explained Obey and Lancaster (1988: 146).[14]

The debilitating intragovernment struggles led to ever-worsening morale among USAID administrators, who were often unable to propose innovative projects for fear of further arousing public and congressional criticism. According to the U.S. General Accounting Office (1983: 5), "the

Agency's sensitivity to this situation has resulted in an operating style that is excessively cautious to the point of hindering the achievement of U.S. objectives." In the 1980s, these criticisms only diminished the Reagan administration's already low regard for the foreign-aid program and further inflamed public opposition. A congressional task force chaired by Representative Lee Hamilton reviewed the country's foreign-aid programs and concluded that "it is time to start anew" (U.S. House of Representatives, 1989: 29).

U.S. ODA in Practice

As noted above, the United States played an important but diminishing role in the global ODA regime during the 1980s. Whereas in the 1950s and 1960s the United States disbursed between 60 and 90 percent of all foreign-aid flows, the U.S. contribution represented less than one-sixth of world ODA by 1989, the year in which Japan, with a GNP roughly half that of the United States, had a higher net aid commitment.

On an absolute level, U.S. ODA rose marginally between 1970 and 1990, but as a percentage of U.S. GNP aid flows decreased throughout the post–World War II era (see Table 6.3). Whereas foreign aid accounted for 3.2 percent of U.S. GNP in 1949, it represented less than 0.2 percent of U.S. GNP in the late 1980s, among the lowest relative ODA commitments of the world's major donors. Ironically, it was about the time that the UN and OECD identified the 0.7 percent ODA/GNP level as the benchmark of aid quality that the U.S. share fell below that level.

The United States was the world's leading donor on an absolute level during the 1980s, and it retained this status in the early 1990s. The decreasing relative U.S. contribution was attributed by officials to the country's disproportionate burden in regional and global defense efforts, to the disappointing results of past development projects, and to the need to address domestic priorities during an extended period of stagnant economic growth. Under the Reagan administration, military rather than economic assistance became the preferred means of transferring resources abroad, and nearly half of the ODA budget was claimed by Egypt and Israel as a result of the Camp David accords. The remaining funds for Third World development were largely directed toward strategic allies whose compliance the U.S. sought in the revived Cold War of the 1980s.

The United States possessed by far the world's largest GNP through the 1980s, amounting to more than $5 trillion in 1989. Although the U.S. economy expanded consistently throughout the decade, per capita U.S. GNP fell below that of many other industrialized states in Western Europe and East Asia, including Sweden and Japan. As its productivity and economic growth stagnated, the U.S. government steadily amassed a

Table 6.3   U.S. ODA Transfers, 1970–1990

	ODA Commitment[a]	Percent GNP	Share of World ODA
1970–1971	8,618	0.30	33.7
1980–1981	9,128	0.23	16.5
1989–1990	9,292	0.18	16.6

Source: OECD (1991a)
Note: a. ODA commitment in millions of current U.S dollars

balance-of-payments deficit (–1.8 percent/GNP in 1990) that rendered interest payments the fastest-growing element of the federal budget.

During the 1980s, the largest segment of U.S. ODA was directed toward recipients in the Middle East–North Africa region, particularly Egypt and Israel (see Figure 6.1). Total ODA to this region accounted for approximately half of U.S. transfers. Having brokered the agreement that created peaceful coexistence between Israel and Egypt, the United States was committed to nurturing the peace by providing billions of dollars annually to both states. Recipients in Latin America received the second largest share of U.S. ODA disbursements during this period. As noted above, the Reagan administration identified Central America as a key strategic interest in the 1980s and reshaped the ODA program to accommodate that interest (see Robinson, 1991; and Blachman, Leogrande, and Sharpe, 1987). Among South Asian recipients, Pakistan rose to become the third greatest beneficiary of U.S. ODA in the world, eclipsing India and Bangladesh.[15] African countries (not including Egypt), of which more than forty were U.S. ODA recipients during the period, received much smaller amounts. Only in 1989–1990 did an African LDC, Sudan, rank among the top ten U.S. ODA recipients.

Among the functional applications of U.S. development aid, the largest single category during the 1980s was that of unrestricted assistance (Figure 6.2). This category, in which the U.S. share was twice the average of Development Assistance Committee members, represented to a large degree the flows transferred through the Economic Support Fund (ESF) to strategically important states, who were given direct control over the spending of these resources (see OECD, 1991a: 152).[16] This was the form taken by most bilateral transfers to Egypt and Israel. These funds, most often transferred in cash, were also used to ease immediate balance-of-payment problems faced by LDCs and, to a growing degree, middle-income countries (MICs) such as Mexico, Brazil, and Argentina. The second largest share of U.S. ODA was directed toward the development of political

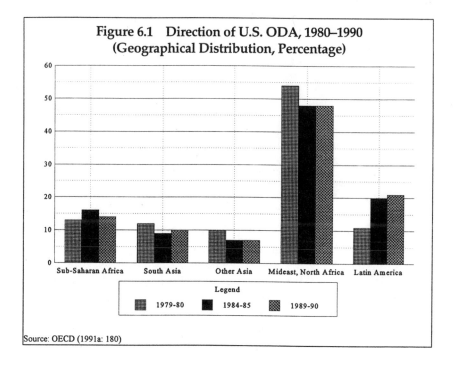

Figure 6.1   Direction of U.S. ODA, 1980–1990
(Geographical Distribution, Percentage)

Source: OECD (1991a: 180)

infrastructure of recipient states, who often used U.S. resources to construct civil and administrative facilities in unstable settings.

In three of the four categories of ODA quality, the United States fell below DAC averages, with overall qualitative indicators in 1989 lower than those at the beginning of the decade (see Table 6.4). Only in the category of proportionate grant aid did the United States improve, and only in this category did it exceed DAC averages during the 1980s. About half of U.S. ODA consisted of grants in the 1960s, but that proportion rose to above 90 percent by 1989. This shift, consistent with a trend among all DAC donors, brought praise from the United Nations and other international organizations, which had consistently urged aid donors to provide assistance on the softest terms possible. According to Wood, "No issue has been more prominent in the debate on foreign aid than the loan-grant controversy" (1986: 67).

The relative increase in U.S. grant aid was partly a response to the debt crisis of the late 1980s, which hampered the ability of aid recipients to reimburse the U.S. government for medium- and long-term concessional loans. Many aid recipients had also accrued large debts to international organizations and commercial banks, exacerbating the debt crisis and prompting the Baker and Brady plans, which rescheduled or "forgave"

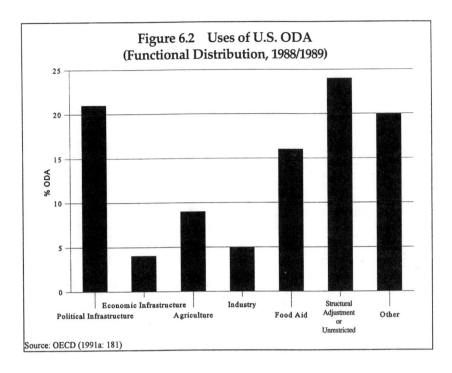

**Figure 6.2   Uses of U.S. ODA
(Functional Distribution, 1988/1989)**

Source: OECD (1991a: 181)

much of the Third World debt. A consensus on the U.S. response to this crisis emerged: "Both Congress and the executive branch supported the view that foreign aid should not add to the already existing debt burden carried by these countries" (Congressional Research Service, 1992: 11).

The United States continued to tie a higher-than-DAC-average proportion of ODA transfers to the acquisition of goods and services, one closely watched indicator of aid quality. The country's 1989 level of untied ODA (30.9 percent) represented a significant decrease from the 1980 level and mirrored an overall growth in tying of aid among DAC donors during the decade. In the United States, the tying of aid packages was viewed as essential for the continuation of programs in the face of growing political opposition. In "selling" foreign assistance to a wary public, U.S. officials often emphasized the fact that most aid packages were tied to the procurement U.S. goods and services (Congressional Research Service, 1992: 9). About 90 percent of military aid was used to purchase U.S. military equipment and training, and about one-half of bilateral ODA was spent in the United States.[17]

As noted elsewhere, donor states generally utilize bilateral transfers to promote their foreign-policy interests, so a high proportion of multilateral aid is often regarded as evidence of a high-quality aid program. The United

Table 6.4   Quality of U.S. ODA, 1980–1989

	Grant Element (% ODA)	Untied Aid (% ODA)	Multilateral Aid (% ODA)	Aid to LLDCs (% ODA)
1980	72.6	38.8	25.6	40.7
	(75.2)[a]	(50.3)	(28.5)	(35.1)
1983	81.6	36.8	35.0	17.4
	(76.3)	(45.9)	(31.3)	(21.8)
1986	97.0	26.3	21.1	15.4
	(87.0)	(33.4)	(28.1)	(23.4)\
1989	92.5	30.9	20.2	15.5
	(88.9)	(36.5)	(27.2)	(22.4)

Sources: OECD (1982b, 1985b, 1988b, 1991b)
Note: a. DAC averages listed in parentheses

States allocated a diminishing share of its ODA flows to multilateral agencies during the 1980s, with the proportion in the final year falling to about one-fifth. U.S. officials justified the increase in bilateral flows on grounds of efficiency. As former Secretary of State Alexander Haig (1981: 21) observed, "It has been our experience that we achieve greater precision and greater value to the American taxpayers if we emphasize bilateral assistance." Testifying before Congress, Deputy Secretary of State Clifton Wharton (1993: 528) reiterated Haig's contention that bilateral aid serves U.S. national interests better than multilateral aid: "USAID provides a direct linkage between U.S. foreign policy goals in our bilateral relations. Multilateral agencies do not necessarily reflect U.S. foreign policy in their programs and activities."

Finally, the share of U.S. ODA allocated to the poorest of recipient states, or LLDCs, fell by more than half during the decade, from about 41 percent to 16 percent. As in the other categories of quality, the U.S. pattern was consistent with that of DAC members in general, who dramatically decreased the proportion of ODA flows to the poorest recipient states. Especially in this category, overall patterns were skewed by U.S. ODA flows to Egypt and Israel, given their status as middle-income states. With such a large share of U.S. funds designated for those two recipients, remaining funds for poorer populations were limited. Consequently, in 1989 five of the top ten recipients of U.S. ODA were designated by the World Bank (1991) as lower-middle-income states, whereas four were in the low-income category and one, Israel, was considered an upper-middle income state.[18]

U.S. ODA flows were statistically linked to both security-interest variables during much of this period (see Table 6.5). U.S. ODA transfers were related to levels of recipient military spending in six of the ten years under study and to relative militarization—the proportion of recipient population enlisted in the armed forces—in five of the ten years. These patterns illustrate the centrality of security concerns within the ODA program, quite apart from the military-aid relationships the United States had established with many of the same LDCs.

As in many aspects of the U.S. ODA program, the preponderance of U.S. assistance transferred to Israel and Egypt skewed this relationship between aid flows and levels of recipient militarization. With an average rate of 48.5 military personnel per 1,000 citizens and an average annual defense expenditure of $6.3 billion during the 1980s, Israel was among the world's most heavily militarized countries. Egypt's average conscription rate of 9.6 per 1,000 was also above the world average, and higher than those of the other top ten recipients of U.S. ODA in the 1988–1989 fiscal year. The Egyptian government spent an annual average of $6.3 billion on defense during the 1980s, one of the highest net spending rates among developing countries (U.S. ACDA, 1991).

Both countries spent much of their ODA funds on U.S.-made military equipment and on civilian goods and services tied to aid transferred through the Economic Support Fund. During the five-year period from 1985 through 1989, Israel purchased $6.1 billion in U.S. military equipment,

Table 6.5   U.S. ODA and Recipient Characteristics: Multivariate Relationships
(Figures indicate standardized slope coefficients)

	1980	1981	1982	1983	1984	1985	1986	1987	1988	1989
Humanitarian-Interest Variables										
Life expectancy	−.13	−.13	.19	−.07	−.06	.12	.02	.02	−.04	.07
Caloric consumption	.17	.08	.04	−.09	.04	−.19	−.08	−.17	.03	−.06
Security-Interest Variables										
Military spending	.24	.35	.27	.39a	.55	.97	.60	.14	.46	.71
% population in military	.14	.32	.33	.48	.22	−.02	.30	−.44	.27	.19
Economic-Interest Variables										
GNP	−.10	−.26	−.16	−.28	−.44	−.42	−.57	−.16	−.38	−.60
Trade with USA	.01	.07	.01	.07	.10	−.05	.20	.13	.06	.04
Total R^2	.10	.23	.19	.35	.27	.60	.34	.19	.22	.27

Sources: U.S. ACDA (security-interest variables); IMF (trade variable); OECD (aid transfers [dependent variables]); World Bank (all other variables)

Note: a. Underlined figures indicate significance at .05 level; double-underlined figures indicate significance at .01 level

Egypt an additional $2.9 billion. Pakistan, the other major ODA recipient with a concurrent status as a major customer of U.S. arms, spent $925 million during the five-year period.

Among other major recipients of U.S. ODA, India reported the third highest average rate of military spending ($7.3 billion). Aside from Pakistan, with a ten-year average of $1.8 billion, the other recipients in the top ten spent less than $700 million annually on defense. El Salvador's conscription rate of 7.8 per 1,000 citizens ranked it among the most militarized of states, but in most other cases the rates were less than half the Salvadoran average. Clearly, the disproportionate share of U.S. ODA flows to Israel and Egypt explains much of the security orientation of the U.S. program, which, as noted earlier, is a primary reason USAID has proposed disconnecting the Economic Support Fund from other, more development-oriented bilateral aid programs. Whatever budgetary form these transactions take, however, the future of concessional aid to Israel and Egypt appears secure, given these countries' centrality to U.S. interests in the Middle East.

No statistical relationship was evident between U.S. aid transfers and the social welfare conditions of recipient states. Neither life expectancy nor consumption rates in recipient countries co-varied significantly with U.S. ODA flows. In the former category, life expectancy in the top ten U.S. ODA recipients in 1989 averaged 62.4 years, slightly less than the worldwide average of 64 years (World Bank, 1990). In the latter category, inhabitants of these states consumed an average of 2,447 calories per day, compared to the worldwide average of 2,711 calories. (Israeli citizens lived an average of 76 years and consumed an average of 3,174 calories per day, placing them among the most affluent states in both categories.)

Similarly, economic factors appeared to have little relationship to aid patterns. None of the major recipients of U.S. ODA produced relatively large volumes of goods and services during the 1980s. India's 1988 GNP of $238 billion was the largest in this group; the other nine major recipients recorded a total GNP of less than $200 billion (World Bank, 1990). The United States conducted far less trade with these recipients than with industrialized states in Western Europe and Japan. It also recorded large volumes of trade with neighboring Canada and Mexico; the latter, although widely considered a developing country, received a relatively small share of U.S. ODA commitments (an average of $36 million a year during the period 1986–1989).

As noted previously, the large share of U.S. ODA flows to Egypt and Israel strongly influenced the overall relationships between the country's aid and its foreign-policy priorities. To demonstrate the impact of the disproportionate aid flows to Egypt and Israel, U.S. ODA patterns in the 1980s may be further examined by removing these recipients from the statistical sample and observing the residual relationships.

As Table 6.6 illustrates, the picture is very different when Egypt and Israel are removed from the analysis. Two major changes are evident. First, the security orientation of U.S. ODA disappears from view; the statistical relationship between aid flows and recipient militarization (both absolute and relative) is insignificant throughout the decade. Second, aid flows are more generally concentrated among recipients with lower levels of per capita caloric consumption, an indicator of social welfare needs. These patterns were evident in five of the final six years under consideration. Thus, it may be inferred that, in the absence of ODA transfers to Egypt and Israel, the U.S. development aid program was less related to security considerations and more oriented to humanitarian concerns.

This inference must be heavily qualified, however, for two primary reasons. First, as noted above, the U.S. ODA program has been intimately connected with its programs for transferring military assistance, and the fungibility of the two types of aid discounts their linkage to U.S. foreign-policy goals in isolation. Second, the commitment of such large amounts of U.S. ODA to Egypt and Israel limited available funding for other bilateral or multilateral programs, clearly reflecting U.S. foreign-policy priorities in

---

Table 6.6 U.S. ODA and Recipient Characteristics: Multivariate Relationships, Egypt and Israel Excluded
(Figures indicate standardized slope coefficients)

	1980	1981	1982	1983	1984	1985	1986	1987	1988	1989
Humanitarian-Interest Variables										
Life expectancy	.08	.13	.19	.15	.26	.40[a]	.30	.24	−.15	.34
Caloric consumption	−.17	−.22	−.16	−.31	−.35	−.60	−.38	−.39	-.28	−.51
Security-Interest Variables										
Military spending	−.47	−.16	−.17	−.11	−.09	.15	−.17	−.07	.04	−.10
Conscripted population	.16	.02	−.01	.05	.01	.03	.02	.07	.04	−.02
Economic-Interest Variables										
GNP	.76	.39	.38	.24	.23	.06	.21	.05	.03	.13
Trade with USA	−.33	−.23	−.29	−.12	−.17	−.06	−.04	−.04	−.09	−.10
Total R^2	.14	.07	.08	.07	.10	.16	.08	.08	.05	.12

Sources: U.S. ACDA (security-interest variables); IMF (trade variable); OECD (aid transfers [dependent variables]); World Bank (all other variables)

Note: a. Underlined figures indicate significance at .05 level; double-underlined figures indicate significance at .01 level

the 1980s. Such arguments cannot so easily be dismissed through statistical manipulation. In this respect, one must consider the overall record and consider its implications for foreign policy.

Summary

In the aftermath of World War II, the United States established and institutionalized a global economic order based on market principles and oriented toward the preservation of existing capitalist economies and like-minded regimes in the developing world through trade concessions and economic assistance. Concurrently, the Cold War's security emphases, including rearmament on a massive scale and the global pursuit of bilateral and multilateral alliances, led to the expansion of concessional transfers of military assistance to LDCs that supported U.S. geopolitical objectives.

As the patterns reviewed in this chapter demonstrate, the U.S. development aid program was intimately connected to the broader effort during the Cold War to contain communism and promote compliant states, primarily in Latin America, Southeast Asia, and the Near East. This geopolitical orientation, which reflected the preponderant U.S. role in advancing Western political and economic interests, differed from the three cases previously reviewed. In varying ways, leaders of France, Japan, and Sweden portrayed their states as "bridges" between North and South and their development strategies as alternatives to the subordination of LDCs to either Cold War superpower. The U.S. government, by contrast, could not use LDC solidarity in the face of superpower encroachments as a basis for extending foreign aid, and the global scope of its containment effort prevented the consistent regional focus that characterized French and Japanese ODA into the 1990s. U.S. aid flowed to virtually every LDC, though the predominant share of bilateral transfers shifted over time in response to changing circumstances in world politics.

As in the 1960s (McKinlay and Little, 1979), security interests were evident in U.S. ODA calculations through the 1980s, suggesting that the country's aid strategy displayed strong continuity during the intervening period. This static pattern transcended the periodic fluctuations in U.S. ODA policy resulting from the differing ideological postures of successive administrations. Whether the rhetorical emphasis of U.S. development aid was on encouraging development in Latin America, containing communism in Southeast Asia, promoting human rights in Africa, or securing peace between Egypt and Israel, the underlying security dimension remained extant.[19]

These findings are particularly noteworthy given the differences in the geopolitical environment of the 1980s compared to that of two decades earlier, when concerns during the "high" Cold War dominated foreign policy in general and aid policy in particular. The mid- to late 1980s witnessed rapidly diminishing tensions between the Cold War superpowers and, ultimately, the end of the conflict itself. Yet the structure and content of most U.S. aid programs remained largely intact. The slow response by the United States to the fundamental changes in the international system was typical of a government program propelled by bureaucratic inertia (Zimmerman, 1993). In the mid-1990s, the Clinton administration attempted to reformulate U.S. foreign policy—and the approach to foreign aid—in light of these developments. Future analysis will determine to what degree new geopolitical realities were reflected in the delivery of U.S. foreign aid.

Notes

1. To one such observer, "It is in the underdeveloped countries . . . that some Americans have seen the opportunity to do great things, to alter the world in great ways" (Westwood, 1966: 3).
2. See Good (1960) for a detailed examination of this principle.
3. The Marshall Plan was widely regarded as one of the most successful efforts in the history of U.S. foreign policy. To Huntington (1970–1971), the Marshall Plan was so successful because it was "(a) directed to specific and well-defined goals; (b) limited to a geographic area of vital concern to the U.S.; and (c) designed for a limited period of time."
4. U.S. officials tentatively included East European states and the Soviet Union in its postwar economic aid program. The Soviets were required to meet several requirements, however, including the removal of its troops from Eastern Europe. The collapse of these negotiations was one of several steps leading to the Cold War, which in turn served as a basis for expanding U.S. aid flows. See Paterson (1974) for a detailed examination of this period.
5. The primary recipients in East Asia were Japan, Korea, and the Philippines. In the Near East–South Asia region, recipients that received the most U.S. assistance included Greece, Turkey, and newly independent India.
6. See Rostow (1985) for an examination of the U.S. aid program under Eisenhower and Kennedy.
7. Like other aspects of the Carter presidency, however, these recommendations "foundered in interagency bureaucratic politics" (McGuire and Ruttan, 1990: 138). Although the IDCA was established in 1979, its authority overlapped almost entirely with that of USAID, and its independent role was "more apparent than real" (U.S. General Accounting Office, 1983: 15).
8. See Wilhelm and Feinstein (1984) for a transcript and elaboration of the commission's report.
9. Among recipients of U.S. foreign aid, those receiving U.S. military-training programs included every state in the Near East–South Asia region except Afghanistan, Bhutan, Cyprus, and Israel; every Latin American state except Barbados, Nicaragua, Panama, and Trinidad-Tobago; every East Asian state except Laos and Western Samoa; and every African state except Angola, Comoros, Congo, Ethiopia, Mauritius, Mozambique, South Africa, and Zambia.
10. The French government established technical military assistance conventions with twenty-five LDCs during the 1980s, which provided for French military

training and assistance through a French Rapid Action Force in the event of military conflict.

11. In 1989, USAID (1989: 25) listed thirty-one distinct interests to be served by development aid, many of which appeared contradictory.

12. See Halperin (1974) and Allison (1971) for elaborations on bureaucratic politics and foreign policy.

13. These views were expressed by most respondents in surveys conducted by the New York Public Agenda Foundation and the Chicago Council on Foreign Relations.

14. See Zahariadis, Travis, and Diehl (1990) for an analysis of public opinion and U.S. foreign assistance.

15. U.S. support for Pakistan was suspended in the early 1990s, however, because of concerns over its nuclear weapons program.

16. The Economic Support Fund, which was largely driven by U.S. security concerns, was one of three primary forms of U.S. aid considered ODA by the OECD. The other major category was that of development assistance, designed to "overcome severe constraints in such areas as agriculture, energy, health, and family planning, and in building the institutions necessary for sustainable growth." Finally, in the 1980s USAID subsidized food exports to more than sixty LDCs under the Public Law 480 program. Despite the humanitarian rhetoric surrounding this program, "the goal of establishing and maintaining commercial markets for U.S. products remains the underlying objective of the food aid program" (U.S. General Accounting Office, 1983: 16).

17. In a well-coordinated public-information campaign, USAID further demonstrated that LDCs, most of whom were aid recipients, purchased more than $125 billion worth of U.S. products in 1990.

18. Israel, with a population of 4.3 million in mid-1986, had a per capita GNP of $6,210 during that year. Life expectancy in Israel was 75 years, one of the highest in the world, and other indicators of social welfare, such as daily per capita caloric intake (3,019), were also among the world's highest (World Bank, 1988).

19. For elaborations, see McCormick and Mitchell (1989), Cingranelli and Pasquarello (1985), and Carleton and Stohl (1985).

PART 3

Patterns and Prospects

7
The Comparative Record

As the previous four chapters have demonstrated, the French, Japanese, Swedish, and U.S. governments transferred large amounts of foreign aid to developing countries in pursuit of widely varying objectives throughout the post–World War II period. The historical and political settings of their development aid programs have been reviewed in detail, along with their relationships to the donor's broader foreign policies. The direction and assigned functions of each donor's aid flows were also examined along with their performance in relation to the ODA regime's qualitative standards.

This chapter contrasts the performances of these donors from a variety of perspectives: in the context of the three potential foreign-policy interests outlined in previous chapters; in terms of the relationship between the quantity and quality of aid flows; from the standpoint of state behavior within an international regime; and from systemic and domestic levels of analysis. Each perspective provides distinct insights into the foreign-aid policies of these donors; collectively, they strengthen our understanding of the intimate relationship between national interest and foreign aid.

Donor Interests and ODA Patterns: A Summary

The basic needs of impoverished peoples ostensibly represent the basis of contemporary development assistance, as reflected in the proclamations of donor states and multilateral aid organizations. These aid providers most often emphasize the narrowing of economic disparities between the world's rich and poor, the alleviation of short-term suffering within LDCs, and the benefits derived from long-term economic, social, and political development. Within the ODA regime, aid flows have been commonly characterized as a moral obligation of the world's wealthy toward the less fortunate.

As previously observed, in an attempt to codify these humanitarian objectives, the Development Assistance Committee of the OECD has established a series of qualitative standards for aid flows. These standards involve minimum proportions of ODA flows relative to donor GNP, the appropriate recipients of aid, the mode of aid delivery, and the terms upon which aid is extended. Although OECD members have not always embraced these standards and have often acted upon their own conceptions of aid quality, the ODA norms continue to reflect widespread presumptions about the humanitarian basis of development aid.

Among the four donor states under study, the Swedish government most closely adhered to these qualitative standards during the 1980s. More so than the other three donors, Sweden distributed aid to the poorest recipients and on the terms most favorable to them (often exclusively in the form of grants). The statistical analyses revealed a consistent emphasis on humanitarian interests in Swedish ODA disbursements. France's ODA flows, which were concentrated among its former colonies and overseas territories, were also found to be related to the social welfare conditions of its recipients. In the case of Japan, no significant statistical relationship between ODA flows and social-welfare conditions within recipient states was found. The United States' aid program also lacked such a relationship when all recipients were considered; when the two primary recipients (Israel and Egypt) were eliminated from the analysis, U.S. ODA flows were found to be statistically related to humanitarian interests during five of the final six years of the decade.

In challenging the OECD's qualitative standards, leaders of major donor states often advanced alternative conceptions of recipient humanitarian interests. The emphases of their ODA programs—including regional economic development related to bilateral trade and military support in support of geopolitical goals—were seen as compatible with the long-term human needs of LDCs. In the Japanese case, for example, leaders argued that their own robust economic growth served as a model and as a catalyst for development within neighboring LDCs, who thus improved their living standards more effectively and more enduringly than they would have through the receipt of economic aid based exclusively on their social welfare needs. And in the case of the United States, the protection of allies and many LDCs from communist infiltration was expressed in humanitarian terms; the preservation of political freedoms was viewed as a moral undertaking comparable to that of promoting socioeconomic welfare in the Third World. Neither of these conceptions of humanitarian interest was maintained by most other donor states or by the ODA regime in general, which continued to emphasize more immediate responses to basic human needs as the essential imperative of development aid.

The preceding discussion relates directly to the linkages between ODA flows and donor economic interests. Significant empirical relationships between the two existed in the case of Japan and, to a lesser degree, in that of France; both countries' ODA flows were disproportionately directed toward recipients with which they maintained close bilateral trade ties. As Japanese leaders acknowledged, not only did domestic economic growth stimulate that of neighboring countries, but the process of sustained regional growth served Japan's own long-term economic interests as well. France similarly integrated its aid and trade relationships as part of an effort to enhance its own economic interests through the growth of the regional economy in francophone Africa and among its overseas territories. The trading networks were more important to LDC economies than to that of France, but collectively they provided crucial sources of raw materials and destinations for finished products and investment capital.

No such relationships were evident in the cases of Sweden or the United States. More so than other donors, Swedish officials framed aid policy in the context of transnational economic redistribution and of reducing long-standing material inequalities between the affluent North and the impoverished South. This focus could be readily observed in the concentration of Swedish ODA among a small number of Third World recipients—most of them in sub-Saharan Africa and many of them among the poorest of developing countries—with little economic connection to Stockholm.[1] U.S. leaders, meanwhile, emphasized market-driven growth strategies as the best means for LDCs to achieve prosperity and close the gap between North and South. Many influential observers of U.S. ODA (e.g., Eberstadt, 1988), reflecting the conventional wisdom of government officials, believed U.S. technical assistance should primarily be directed not toward addressing basic needs in the poorest LDCs but instead toward encouraging leaders of LDCs to stimulate private enterprise and attract foreign investment. As Baldwin (1985: 324) observed,

> American policy makers have repeatedly gone to great lengths to emphasize that economic development is primarily a matter of domestic effort and that external assistance can merely supplement such efforts. Both explicitly and implicitly American policy has reflected the belief that development must come from within and cannot be imposed from outside.

The relationship between donor states' economic interests and ODA may be illuminated further by considering aid flows in the context of the economic systems maintained by recipient countries.[2] In Africa, the region with the largest number of recipients and the only one in which all four aid donors maintained extensive bilateral ODA ties, France, Japan, and the United States directed more than 70 percent of their ODA flows to states with capitalist economies, whereas 80 percent of Swedish aid was transferred to states with Marxist or socialist economies (see Table 7.1). Although U.S. aid flows were not statistically related to trade ties with recipients, the United States distributed the highest percentage of ODA (88 percent) among the four donors to capitalist states in Africa. This fact suggests that economic interests may be expressed in various ways by donor states. In addition, it demonstrates the tendency of donors to direct aid flows to recipient countries with economic systems similar to their own.[3]

Table 7.1   Patterns of Donor ODA Flows to African Recipients, Percentage of
             Total Commitments, 1980–1989

| | Recipient Economic System | | |
Donor	Capitalist	Marxist	Socialist
France	77	13	10
Japan	71	9	20
Sweden	20	43	37
United States	88	6	6

Source: U.S. Department of State

The relationship between development aid and donor states' security interests has been rendered increasingly ambiguous given the shifting bases of security in an era of "economic statecraft." This study relied on the traditional conception of security interests, which were related to recipients' levels of militarization on a relative and absolute level. Its underlying assumption has been that selective economic support to militarized LDCs serves indirectly to project the security interests of aid donors.

Most significant in this respect was the consistent correspondence between the flow of U.S. ODA and both absolute and relative indicators of recipient militarization. This relationship was principally a by-product of the concentration of U.S. assistance to Egypt and Israel. The security emphasis, consistent with the nation's broader approach to foreign policy as one of the two Cold War superpowers, was magnified by the transfer of U.S. military assistance to many of the same LDCs that received annual infusions of U.S. ODA.

In none of the other cases were security interests significantly related to bilateral ODA transfers. France's security agreements with most of its aid recipients in francophone Africa allowed for French assistance in times of crisis but otherwise discouraged militarization within the region. Japanese militarization was proscribed by the country's U.S.-imposed constitution, and its military security was assured by its bilateral defense treaty with the United States, factors that were reflected in the absence of security considerations in its ODA policies. Finally, the Swedish government based its national security on neutrality and the pursuit of pacific resolution of international conflicts; military considerations were explicitly omitted from Swedish ODA calculations and were not evident in aid patterns during the 1980s.

Like Swedish leaders, those in France and Japan distanced traditional security objectives from their ODA calculations but acknowledged that their aid relationships enhanced their own security, more broadly defined. All three of these donors characterized themselves during the 1980s as "bridges" between the Cold War superpowers and portrayed the economic and social development of their selected aid recipients as a means to reduce the latters' dependence on either superpower. Through the development of LDCs, these donors presumed, their own security would be enhanced. As one of the superpowers, however, the United States subsumed its aid flows within a broader security orientation. Its conception of national security was most congruent with traditional standards of military preparedness, both at home and within its allies, and these norms were reflected in the flow of U.S. aid, both military and economic, to supportive LDCs throughout the world.

ODA Performance: Quantity Versus Quality

As noted above, ODA programs are generally evaluated on the basis of two criteria: first, the quantitative or aggregate volume of aid outlays; and, second, their qualitative characteristics as defined by the Development Assistance Committee. To many analysts of foreign aid, per capita aid flows, their proportion to donor GNP, and the adherence of donors to other qualitative standards serve as better reflections of the commitment of donors to Third World development than do the absolute sums of aid transferred overseas. It is for this reason that the U.S. aid program, although the largest in absolute terms throughout the Cold War, was regularly criticized for its qualitative shortcomings.

An inverse relationship between the quantity of aid flows and their quality was evident in the allocations of France, Japan, Sweden, and the United States during the 1980s and for all members of the OECD during the final year of the analysis (see Table 7.2). The major donors of ODA on an absolute level, particularly the United States and Japan, ranked among the sources of lowest-quality aid. Concurrently, those transferring lesser net amounts, such as the Netherlands, Norway, and Sweden, were among the leaders in terms of quality. These negative relationships were strongest when the top ten ODA donors were considered; the correlations were negative and significant in all four cases, particularly vis-à-vis aid to the poorest LDCs. When all eighteen members of the DAC were included the relationship between ODA flows and the top two categories of aid quality were positive but insignificant, whereas the relationship between aid and the final two categories was negative and of moderate significance. These patterns demonstrate that the tension between ODA quantity and quality extends beyond the four countries reviewed in this study and represents a general tendency among aid donors.

The discrepancy has propelled an ongoing debate within the ODA regime regarding appropriate standards of conduct in this issue area: Donors of relatively small volumes of aid routinely criticize major donors, namely the United States and Japan, for contributing less on a proportionate or per capita basis than they seemingly can afford and for violating the norms of aid quality as articulated by the DAC. Major donors, conversely, emphasize their large aggregate volumes, dismiss certain DAC qualitative standards as invalid, and point to their leadership in stimulating regional and global economic growth, providing for the military security of overseas allies, and so forth. The debate, often conducted in public forums, continued through the 1980s and into the 1990s as donor states large and small struggled with sluggish domestic growth rates, growing domestic demands for fiscal austerity, and ongoing pressure from LDCs for continued or growing amounts of development assistance.

In absolute terms, the United States consistently operated the largest ODA program during the post–World War II period; its preponderant role in global foreign aid is magnified when U.S. military assistance is taken into account. This pattern continued throughout the two decades between 1970 and 1990, during which annual U.S. ODA flows averaged about $8.5 billion (see Figure 7.1). The volume of Japanese ODA increased threefold during the same twenty-year period, from about $3 billion to more than $9 billion. Japanese ODA, which was not accompanied by military assistance, ultimately reached and exceeded U.S. levels, although its higher levels were in part a reflection of a stronger yen during the 1980s. France and Sweden reported similar growth rates, but their aggregate flows were far smaller than those of the other two donors. For the DAC as a whole, inflation-adjusted aid outlays grew from $25.5 billion in 1970–1971 to $47.6 billion two decades later, an overall increase of nearly 90 percent. This quantitative increase coincided with the expansion both of bilateral and multilateral sources of ODA and of aid recipients.[4]

Table 7.2   Quantity Versus Quality of ODA Flows, 1989–1990[a]

Measure of ODA Quality	Ten Largest OECD Economies	All OECD Economies
ODA/GNP	−.59	.13
Per-Capita ODA	−.75	.09
Percentage ODA in Grants	−.71	−.34
Percentage ODA to LLDCs	−.84	−.47

Sources: World Bank (1991), OECD (1991a)
Note: a. Figures represent Spearman's rho rank-order correlations

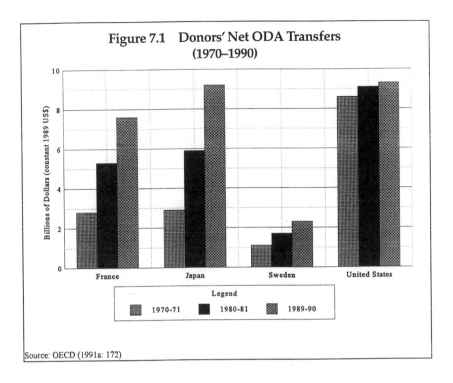

Figure 7.1 Donors' Net ODA Transfers (1970–1990)

Source: OECD (1991a: 172)

Among qualitative indicators of ODA performance, the ODA/GNP ratio is most widely considered to be indicative of a donor state's commitment to Third World social welfare and economic development. At the 1968 UNCTAD meeting, members of the DAC pledged to dispense at least 0.7 percent of their GNPs in the form of ODA. This became the accepted benchmark of aid quality. Sweden, the first country to reach and exceed this level, frequently transferred a full 1 percent of its GNP in economic assistance; its government was unable to maintain these levels in the early 1990s, however, amid continuing economic austerity and growing dissension over the direction and terms of aid flows.

In the French case, ongoing disputes over whether its overseas territories should be considered ODA recipients were closely related to its performance in this category of aid quality. Excluding these recipients, French ODA averaged about 0.55 percent of French GNP; if they were included, the average approached 0.8 percent throughout the 1980s. In the same time span, the high absolute levels of ODA from the United States and Japan contrasted with their relatively low levels of proportionate aid flows. Although the share of national product allocated to ODA rose marginally in the Japanese case, it fell in that of the United States, reflecting a long-range pattern that continued into the mid-1990s (see Figure 7.2).

Similarly, Japan and the United States contributed less ODA on a per capita basis than France or Sweden (see Figure 7.3). Per capita outlays rose during the 1980s in every case except that of the United States during the decade. The greatest proportionate increases were reported by Sweden, whose per capita flows jumped from about $150 to $205, and by France, whose per capita flows grew from $98 to $135 in 1989 dollars. Japanese per capita ODA flows increased from $50 to $74 during the decade, whereas U.S. flows declined slightly from $40 to $37. As previously observed, per capita ODA was one of the few categories in which aid quality generally improved during the 1980s. Among the eighteen DAC members, per capita aid flows increased in twelve cases, with the greatest proportional increase reported by Finland, which tripled per capita flows, from $43 to $143. Decreases were reported by Australia, Belgium, New Zealand, and the United Kingdom, along with the United States.

Another closely watched indicator of ODA quality was the degree to which resources were offered in the form of grants rather than concessional loans. Members of the contemporary ODA regime collectively increased the relative grant element during the 1980s, responding to the

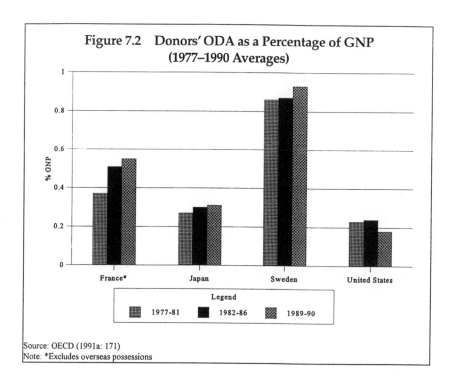

Figure 7.2   Donors' ODA as a Percentage of GNP (1977–1990 Averages)

Source: OECD (1991a: 171)
Note: *Excludes overseas possessions

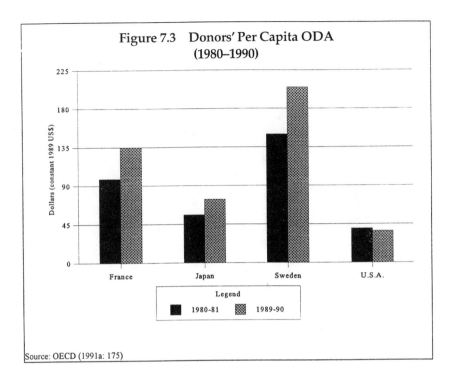

Figure 7.3   Donors' Per Capita ODA (1980–1990)

Source: OECD (1991a: 175)

emergent norm that LDC recipients should not take on reciprocal burdens in exchange for ODA. Sweden, for example, adhered to its standard of nearly 100 percent grants, and French and U.S. leaders gradually increased their grant proportions (to 85 and 99 percent, respectively). Japan, however, maintained relatively greater levels of concessional loans in the name of recipient "discipline." But even in this case, the grant level grew considerably during the decade.

Figure 7.4 further illustrates the effort by the Swedish government to conduct a high-quality ODA program. The share of Swedish ODA directed to LLDCs, which measured 33 percent of outlays in 1990, respectively, was nearly twice the 1989 French and Japanese levels (18 percent) and nearly three times the U.S. level (13 percent). Among the two major donors, the concentration of Japan's flows to newly industrialized countries along the Pacific Rim limited its contribution to LLDCs, and the disproportionate share of U.S. ODA directed to Egypt and Israel had a similar effect. Overall, DAC members reduced their relative disbursements of ODA to the poorest subset of recipients from 25 to 22 percent during the 1980s. Their performance in this regard reflected the general decrease in aid quality over the decade.

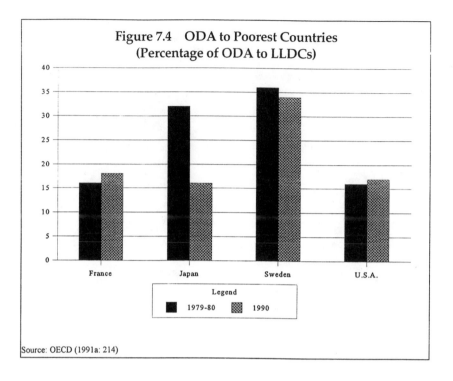

Figure 7.4   ODA to Poorest Countries
(Percentage of ODA to LLDCs)

Legend
■ 1979-80   ▨ 1990

Source: OECD (1991a: 214)

These patterns have been reviewed collectively to illustrate the wide variations in aid behavior among these few donors. Further, they have reinforced the inverse relationship between the quantity and quality of aid flows, the latter of which is monitored by the ODA regime in several categories.

Systemic Dimensions of ODA Behavior

The inverse relationship between ODA quantity and quality, which reflects the broader variation in the absolute scale of donor economies, suggests that systemic factors are closely related to their behavior in this area of foreign policy. More broadly, it calls attention to the general importance of systemic factors in influencing state actions.

In contrast to unit-level factors (incorporating both societal and governmental characteristics), systemic explanations "account for state behavior on the basis of attributes of the system as a whole" (Keohane, 1984a: 25). Such explanations are not intended to deny the importance of such unit-level factors, nor do they presume a narrowly deterministic relationship between systemic factors and state behavior. Instead, they suggest that analysis of foreign policy should begin with a look at the broader milieu of state action and its impact on the calculations of foreign policy. As opposed to deterministic models, *environmental possibilism* (Sprout and Sprout, 1969: 44) "postulates some set of limits that affect the outcomes of any attempted course of action."

Analysts of international relations have long argued that the distribution of state resources is a salient determinant of military stability within the international system. They have disagreed as to whether a bipolar (Waltz, 1964) or a multipolar (Deutsch and Singer, 1964) distribution of power is more war-prone, but they have shared the underlying presumption that "outside-in" interpretations are instructive in the study of world politics. By contrast, the systemic sources of states' foreign economic policies, in areas that include the transfer of foreign aid, have received less attention. As in the case of security issues, however, economic policies are not created in a vacuum; they reflect the relative capabilities and more general roles of each state in the international system. In this view, "the foreign economic policy of any individual country is affected both by the international economic structure . . . and by the state's position within it" (Lake, 1983: 523–524).[5]

The importance of systemic factors in influencing the volume and direction of donor aid flows begs the larger question of what systemic roles have been played by individual aid donors and how their roles have been reflected in foreign-policy behavior in general and aid policy in particular. Among early analysts of systemic roles and foreign policy, K. J. Holsti provided a typology of roles that may be usefully applied to this important dimension of world politics (see Table 7.3). Holsti (1970: 307) defined the role concept as an "analytical tool for explaining certain ranges or patterns of foreign policy decisions and actions." These systemic roles, as apprehended by political leaders and translated into political action, shape the long-term objectives of nation-states and must be considered in any comprehensive effort to understand comparative foreign-policy behavior (see Walker, 1987; and Wish, 1987).

Applying Holsti's typology to the four donor states during the 1980s, the behavior of France was most characteristic of a systemic "active independent," which is prone to "emphasize at once independence, self-determination, possible mediation functions, and active programs to extend diplomatic and commercial relations to diverse areas of the world" (Holsti, 1970: 262). A consistent relationship was evident between this systemic role and France's overall approach toward foreign affairs as well as its actions in transferring ODA. French leaders' pursuit of autonomy in foreign affairs, their identification of French interests with those of their francophone neighbors, and their active involvement in international organizations reinforced this aspect of France's systemic role. In the area of ODA, France extended concessional financing as part of an orchestrated effort

Table 7.3　Systemic Roles, National Interests, and ODA Behavior

Donor	Systemic Role	National Interests	Geographical Concentration	Significant Relationships	Functional Concentration
France	Active independent	Strategic independence; regional hegemony	Francophone Africa, overseas territories	Humanitarian, economic	Political infrastructure
Japan	Regional-subsystem collaborator	Economic development	Pacific Rim	Economic	Economic infrastructure
Sweden	Mediator	Neutralism; nonmilitarism	None	Humanitarian	"Country programming"
United States	Bloc leader	Globalism; bloc security	Near East, Central America	Security	Unrestricted (Economic Support Fund)

Source: Holsti (1970)

to serve as a bridge both between North and South and between East and West and to enhance its regional influence and prestige.

Meanwhile, Japan's foreign-policy performance was most characteristic of a "regional-subsystem collaborator," which deliberately eschews a global role and undertakes "commitments to cooperative efforts with other states to build wider communities" (Holsti, 1970: 265). As noted earlier, after World War II Japanese military rearmament was precluded under its constitution, which limited its defense spending to 1 percent of GNP, and its territorial security has been protected ever since through its bilateral treaty with the United States. Japan's narrow focus on tightening economic relations within the Pacific Rim, extending beyond ODA policy to trade and private investment, was consistent with this systemic role. Regional integration was complicated by Japan's previous imperial ambitions in East Asia, but it remained an explicit goal of Japan's leadership into the 1990s and found expression in the interrelationships between Japanese ODA flows, trade ties, and patterns of overseas private investment.

Sweden's disavowal of political and security alignments, its preference for pacific means of conflict resolution, and its promotion of like-minded LDCs exemplified the behavior of a systemic "mediator" (Holsti, 1970: 255). Such a state characteristically ventures to create an "interposition into bloc conflicts" and provides a forum for negotiated settlements and integration. Swedish leaders often emphasized both the constraints and opportunities posed by their country's role as a small power in the midst of stronger states. In this respect, Prime Minister Palme often referred to the "small-state doctrine" that guided Swedish foreign policy. This effort entailed support for other small powers, particularly those sharing Sweden's social and political values, along with the application of those instruments of foreign policy that most "equalized" the influence of states: international organizations, international law, and, if concentrated toward a few key recipients ("program countries"), development assistance. Its neutralist foreign policy entailed a defensive military capability and the avoidance of formal alliances. To Sundelius (1990: 122), these strategies exploited the natural advantages of a "committed neutral":

> By keeping a distance from both sides, the Swede indicates a commitment to impartiality in any political conflict between these sets of values. Through such reasoning, the neutral position can be justified in positive terms. It provides a foundation for a unique and valuable mediating role between two alien antagonists. *This stand is identified with a vital systemic function and is thus transformed from a strategy of political necessity to a moral imperative.* In such a perspective a neutral democracy is clearly not morally compromised. On the contrary, it represents reason and a concern for the overriding interests of the international community (emphasis added).

The United States, by contrast, assumed the role of "bloc leader" throughout this period, described by Holsti (1970: 255) as one based on ideology, systemic predominance, active resistance to perceived external threats, and the maintenance of "bloc cohesion." The U.S. preoccupation with military security, which was evident in its patterns of military and economic assistance, was typical of a great power, which attempts to establish and retain global influence in the face of perceived threats from other great powers.

These role profiles call attention to the importance of each state's broader role within the international system in shaping its foreign policies. In all four cases, the documented patterns of ODA behavior were consistent with the expectations of Holsti's analysis. The consideration of systemic roles as a source of foreign-policy behavior focuses on the relative attributes of each state and their impact on shaping policy. The question may be probed a step further by examining the relationship between a state's absolute resource base and its behavior in distributing ODA. As noted previously, states that provided the most ODA were less likely to adhere to DAC standards of aid quality; of additional interest is whether the wealthiest states, as measured by GNP, varied in their qualitative ODA behavior in a similar manner. The evidence from the year 1989–1990 suggests that they do. When the ten largest OECD economies are ranked for their performance in four areas of aid quality, the negative rank-order correlations range from −.32 to −.72. This pattern is also evident when all eighteen members of the DAC are considered, although the negative correlations are weaker in each case (see Table 7.4).

Table 7.4   **Wealth of Aid Donors Versus Quality of Aid Flows, 1989–1990[a]**

Measures of ODA Quality	Ten Largest OECD Economies	All OECD Economies
ODA/GNP	−.32	−.23
Per capita ODA	−.45	−.20
Percentage ODA in grants	−.67	−.43
Percentage ODA to LLDCs	−.72	−.61

Sources: World Bank (1991), OECD (1991a)
Note: a. Figures represent Spearman's rho rank-order correlations

Collectively, these patterns demonstrate the relationship between the size of a donor state's economy, a key aspect of its systemic role, and its behavior in providing assistance to LDCs. These findings are consistent with those advanced by Ruggie, who found that the amount of economic resources available to aid donors was inversely proportionate to the extent to which they provided aid through multilateral channels. Thus, "the condition of possessing a certain level of national resources seems to be related to a state's propensity to organize the performance of a task internationally" (Ruggie, 1972: 883). This relationship has profound implications for the future volume, direction, and quality of aid flows under the rapidly shifting systemic conditions of the 1990s. Observers of aid policy may wish to consider the emerging roles of states, based on both relative and absolute standards, in attempting to understand current aid strategies or anticipate future patterns.

Donor Behavior Within the ODA Regime

Though systemic factors have most often been related to the international system's propensity for armed conflict and to the behavior of states in matters of war and peace, they have increasingly been applied to other aspects of state behavior in economic affairs. Kindleberger (1973) and Gilpin (1975), among others, have developed and refined the theory of hegemonic stability, which argues that the preservation of a liberal international economic order is facilitated by the presence of a preponderant economic power. In this view, the absence of a global hegemon during the period between the world wars contributed to widening economic warfare and the collapse of many industrialized economies. Conversely, post–World War II

U.S. preponderance in both economic and security areas presumably sustained global economic stability. Current debates over hegemonic stability concern the prospects for a viable monetary and trading system in the absence of a hegemon. The relative decline of the United States (whose share of global GNP fell from about 50 percent in 1945 to about 22 percent in 1994) and the concurrent ascension of Japan, NICs, and members of the European Union since the 1970s have provided the impetus for these debates.

It is widely presumed that many of the economic regimes that emerged as part of the liberal international economic order (LIEO) immediately after World War II were manifestations of U.S. hegemony. Contrary to the expectations of hegemonic-stability theorists, the erosion of U.S. hegemony has not been accompanied by the breakdown of most transnational economic regimes. Many middle-income states continue to violate principles of the LIEO, "free-riding" under the economic and security protection of the United States, yet the postwar order has remained largely intact. Recent evidence for this cohesion was the conclusion in early 1994 of the Uruguay Round of the GATT talks, at which delegates agreed on many measures to further coordinate and liberalize their macroeconomic policies and to institutionalize global trade within the World Trade Organization.[6] To Keohane (1984a: 215) and others, the persistence of many regimes is due to the endurance of the norms, principles, and procedures that were established under conditions of hegemonic influence: "International regimes perform functions demanded by states having shared interests; when the regimes already exist, they can be maintained even after the original conditions for their creation have disappeared."

The foundations of the ODA regime were established during the peak of U.S. hegemony and reflected the developmental principles of GATT, the World Bank, and the International Monetary Fund. Although the current institutional framework did not take shape until after the process of decolonization had largely concluded in the early 1960s (see Chapter 2), when the decline of the relative U.S. position was well under way, the developmental models conceived in the 1940s and 1950s were largely adopted by the OECD and its Development Assistance Committee. Like other transnational regimes, that which coordinated ODA reflected the prerogatives of its most powerful members, including those providing the greatest aggregate volumes of aid. DAC members agreed upon the collective interests and broad objectives to be served by the ODA regime—to ease the suffering of the world's poor and to promote market-oriented economic growth —but their self-interests were accommodated and were evident in both their bilateral and multilateral aid flows.

In addition to being reflected in the deliberations of state leaders and their proclamations of shared interests and collective actions, international regime behavior may further be demonstrated by the coordinated activity of states in areas not immediately apparent. In distributing development assistance, for example, donor states concentrated aid flows along geographical lines; they identified Third World recipients of particular salience to their own national interests and directed a disproportionate share of aid flows to them. Recalling that the United States, Japan, and France represented the three top donors of ODA during the 1980s, their geographical concentrations effectively amounted to a division of labor in global ODA flows (see Appendix 2). France served annually as the primary source of aid to LDCs in francophone Africa; Japan played that role for its Pacific Rim neighbors (and increasingly to East Africa and South America); and the United States provided most concessional resources to Central American recipients and those in the eastern Mediterranean, particularly Egypt and Israel (and to a far lesser degree Oman and Cyprus).[7] Shifts in geographical ODA concentration reflected broader changes in the donors' foreign policies during the decade, particularly in recent years as the Cold War ended and the international system experienced a fundamental transformation.[8]

Donor states coordinated the volume and direction of ODA flows in many other respects. During the height of the Cold War, for example, the U.S. government urged Japan to supplement its own economic support for many Pacific states that were considered strategically important in the face of perceived internal challenges. "Japan's foreign aid has become inseparably incorporated into the world strategy of the United States," argued Shinsuke (1982: 32). Prominent examples of Japanese aid initiatives that were at least partially driven by Cold War concerns included aid to Indonesia following the departure of Achem Sukarno (1966), to Thailand during the Vietnam War (1968), and to the Philippines at the peak of the Ferdinand Marcos dictatorship (1969). U.S. pressure on Japanese aid policies was widely acknowledged. As Akira (1985: 141) put it, "Japan is responding to American wishes in its allocation of ODA. And in this sense the Japanese motivation in giving foreign aid lacks the basic humanism that animates most international aid organizations."

The empirical patterns outlined above are largely consistent with theoretical expectations of regime behavior under conditions of hegemony. Specifically, the security orientation of U.S. economic and military aid reflected the country's preponderant role in providing for the security of its allies throughout the Cold War. The patterns of French and Japanese ODA flows, which were statistically related to their own economic interests, were consistent with the anticipated behavior of smaller states, which, in the area of trade policy, were given to "free-riding" within the LIEO. This patterned crossnational behavior was consistent with that expected of an international economic regime, in which persistent competition among states is regulated and coordinated policy behavior ensures each participant some benefit. The global ODA division of labor thus adds empirical evidence of regime behavior in foreign assistance, a fact that is of particular merit given the limited number of international economic regimes available for study. Further, the coordination of ODA flows with broader aspects of donor foreign policies reflected the cohesion of the ODA regime in its first three decades.[9]

Domestic Sources of ODA Behavior

Although the emphasis in this discussion has been on the influence of systemic factors in shaping donor ODA policies, these policies must not be considered in isolation. In each case, internal societal values strongly influenced donor approaches to foreign aid and foreign policy in general, and the institutional mechanisms by which aid policies were implemented also exerted a powerful impact. Systemic context may be a useful starting point in cross-national analysis, but a comprehensive understanding of state behavior requires an additional assessment of the role of unit-level characteristics that bridge the gap between systemic context and observable behavior. A review of these domestic factors strengthens our understanding of donor states' behavior (see Table 7.5).

In the United States, the broad scope of its foreign-aid program led to the creation of a complex bureaucracy, giving domestic politics a prevalent role in the shaping of U.S. aid policy. Within USAID, administrators often clashed over the objectives of specific bilateral aid programs and the general strategy of achieving U.S. national interests through bilateral and multilateral aid. These debates were exacerbated by the concurrent flows of U.S. military assistance, coordinated by the Department of Defense, to many of the same LDCs receiving ODA. The arena for domestic politics further involved Congress, whose "power of the purse" provided it with strong leverage in directing the flow of foreign assistance. Congress, of course, was far from a unitary actor in this regard; its members reflected the interests of their disparate district and state constituents and advanced the prerogatives of a wide array of committees and subcommittees. The continuity in many bilateral aid programs even spanned successive presidential administrations pursuing widely varying foreign policies, reflecting the strong roles of Congress and the aid bureaucracy, which collectively served to mitigate the fundamental shifts in aid strategy proposed by the White House.

The prevalence of domestic politics in the U.S. ODA program was in large part a by-product of the absence of public support for foreign assistance. Overseas aid was consistently among the least popular federal programs, and it was far less popular in the United States than in the other three countries under review in this study. This fact was reflected in the relatively small amounts of per capita U.S. ODA, the relatively small percentage of U.S. GNP devoted to ODA, and the low level of U.S. aid quality as

Table 7.5　ODA and Domestic Politics: Crossnational Comparisons

	France	Japan	Sweden	United States
Political culture	Conflictive	Consensual	Consensual	Conflictive
Role of chief executive	Strong	Weak	Moderate	Moderate
Role of legislature	Weak	Weak	Strong	Strong
Level of public support	Moderate	High	High	Low
Role of private industry	Strong	Strong	Moderate	Moderate

defined by the DAC. Yet U.S. aid transfers, both economic and military, continued to grow throughout the period in absolute terms, and collectively they represented the largest flows of foreign aid by any single donor. The impetus for U.S. aid, therefore, must be found outside the realm of public opinion—and inside the institutional framework of the federal government.

As demonstrated in the statistical analysis, the aid programs were largely related to U.S. security interests throughout the Cold War, serving as extensions of the overall effort by the United States to maintain its leadership role as a "bloc leader." When they did appeal to the general public for support, influential political leaders justified aid programs on the basis of their contribution to the broader effort of containing communism and preserving U.S. influence in overseas regions of "vital interest." The large volume of U.S. ODA transferred to Egypt and Israel, which served many domestic constituencies as well as the U.S. interest in Middle East stability, reflected this security orientation—one that was relatively distinct from Cold War concerns.

The large Japanese ODA program was also driven by domestic politics but under very different circumstances. In contrast to their U.S. counterparts, neither the chief executive nor the legislative branch of the Japanese government played a strong role in formulating and executing aid policy. Instead, aid policy was largely driven by decentralized government ministries, many of which pursued parochial foreign-policy interests. As Orr noted, "There exists a greater degree of delegation of authority by the [Japanese] legislative branch to the administrative branch. Career government officials play a larger role in making foreign policy than do their counterparts in the United States" (1990: 11–12). This facet of Japanese politics helps to explain why successive prime ministers' frequent pledges to diversify the direction of Japanese aid flows and increase its DAC-defined quality were largely unfulfilled.

Though the general public widely supported Japanese ODA, its influence over the volume and direction of aid flows was relatively modest. Instead, its general assent provided a mandate for the rapid growth of the aid
program, whose specific applications were determined within government
ministries. These bodies, particularly the Ministry of International Trade
and Industry, comprised both political leaders and powerful economic actors. In this environment, the economic basis of Japanese postwar national
interests found expression in bilateral aid packages to LDCs that maintained strong economic relations with Tokyo in other areas, including foreign investment and the expansion of multinational corporations. Japanese
officials acknowledged the role of ODA flows in tightening their broader
economic links to regional LDCs along the Pacific Rim and in furthering
their own economy, which was viewed as an engine of regional growth. In
this respect, they differed with OECD standards of aid quality and emphasized the successful application of Japanese ODA in promoting the ascension of many aid recipients from LDC status to that of NICs.

During the postwar period, French presidents and the general public
held widely varying ideological orientations and advocated disparate national objectives, reflecting the country's conflictive political culture. This
discord existed to a lesser degree in the area of foreign policy, however; a
general consensus existed on France's role within the "front rank" of
major powers and, more specifically, on the continuing concentration of
French influence within the developing regions formerly under its colonial
control. French presidents, who maintained broad authority over foreign
policy under the political system designed by de Gaulle, shared these objectives and ensured the continuities in French foreign policy, including
the distribution of development assistance. The French legislature, though
formally empowered to approve the president's specific policy initiatives,
generally deferred to the chief executive as the "guarantor" of French national interests.

In this respect, France's cultural tradition served as a strong and consistent impetus for its relations with developing countries, which in turn
served as a primary vehicle of the country's overseas ambitions. As Cerny
put it, "French policy was always dominated by a cultural element which
put cultural values . . . before a search for either economic wealth or pure
military power" (1980: 75). In aid policy, French leaders declared their
mission civilisatrice in maintaining close relations with former African
colonies that were connected to Paris through monetary integration, trade
ties, and ongoing ODA transfers. The French government also maintained
close security relationships with many of these states, but its influence was
generally limited to providing material and logistical support in times of
crisis.

The Swedish aid program was also sustained by high levels of public
support, which, in contrast to the French case, extended to other aspects of

Swedish public policy, both foreign and domestic. The country's consensual political culture was based upon widespread and enduring social values. In domestic policy, these involved the promotion of socioeconomic equality and the observance of social democratic principles; in foreign policy, they entailed the pursuit of geopolitical neutrality and active support for peaceful conflict resolution among great powers.

As in the French case, the Swedish government endeavored to use foreign-aid relationships to project these societal values, identifying and rewarding LDCs that emulated the Swedish system of social democracy. In many cases, Sweden supported regimes that were emerging from wars of national liberation—such as Cuba, Vietnam, Angola, and Nicaragua—and that had established socialist or Marxist systems. Swedish leaders hoped their "third way" of economic and political development would provide an alternative to the dependence of these LDCs on either of the Cold War superpowers.

Given the strong societal consensus that endured in Sweden through two world wars and within the bipolar system of the late twentieth century, the executive and legislative branches played a relatively modest role in affecting Swedish foreign policy in general and aid policy in particular. The country's aid strategy epitomized the "Nordic model," founded upon explicitly humanitarian interests, support for LLDCs, the transfer of funds exclusively in the form of grants, and relatively high per capita aid and ODA/GNP ratios. The distinctive aspects of Swedish ODA policy were modified in the late 1980s, however, in response to domestic economic strains and growing preferences for greater "realism" in advancing Swedish economic interests through foreign-aid flows. These modifications were reflected in the presence of economic interests in Swedish ODA during the final three years of the decade. But the qualitative aspects of Swedish aid, and the overall thrust of Sweden's foreign policy and approach to North-South relations, were largely retained.

The relation of domestic politics to the development and pursuit of national interest is complex and, in most cases, ambiguous. As the American Federalists (Madison, 1938 [1787]: 56) acknowledged, domestic politics are invariably divisive based on the presence of contending economic factions: "a landed interest, a manufacturing interest, a mercantile interest, a moneyed interest, with many lesser interests, grow up of necessity in civilized nations." In other respects, domestic divisions are sustained along religious, linguistic, or ethnic lines. When these divisions become predominant and overwhelm the ability of central governments to reconcile them, states fall prey to civil war and disintegration. More often, and in the case of the four countries under study, a sense of holistic identity and purpose transcends parochial concerns, thus providing the basis of national interest that is expressed in foreign policy.

In all of these ways, the national interests and foreign-aid policies of these donor states were influenced by societal values and government practices. Despite their many internal differences and systemic roles, these states were influential in creating and maintaining the ODA regime for more than three decades. Their continuing involvement in transferring ODA in the 1990s—a period in which their relationships with many LDCs were reshaped by the end of the Cold War and in which economic strains placed limits on their involvement in foreign affairs—presages the endurance of the regime well into the future.

Challenges to the ODA regime continue to be expressed by its members, and long-standing disputes over aid quality and other issues remain unresolved. These tensions will be explored in the final chapter, along with the future prospects for development aid. In addition, emerging conceptions of national interest will be examined as world politics moves further away from the Cold War and toward an uncertain new millennium.

Notes

1. Another aspect in which this differing emphasis was observable was in the Swedish practice of promoting agricultural development in LDCs.

2. I acknowledge the assistance provided by Peter J. Schraeder in suggesting this avenue of inquiry and providing background information regarding the African ODA recipients.

3. These distinctions were based upon the economic systems of African states as defined by their leaders and reported by the U.S. State Department during the 1980s. Of the forty African states (excluding Egypt) documented, twenty-six maintained capitalist economies, whereas seven maintained Marxist and socialist economies. Only one state, Uganda, was reported to have changed economic systems during the decade (from capitalist to socialist in 1986). Many other states moved from Marxist or socialist to capitalist systems in the 1990s.

4. Several states established aid programs in the 1970s, particularly members of the Organization of Petroleum Exporting States (OPEC). Led by Saudi Arabia, OPEC outlays reached $12.7 billion in 1980–1981 before plummeting to about $3 billion by the end of the decade.

5. See also Lake (1988) for an elaboration of this thesis with regard to U.S. trade policy.

6. More than thirty LDCs "have notified the GATT of comprehensive tariff reform" as part of the Uruguay Round and have agreed to lower many nontariff barriers (Richards, 1992: 23).

7. France retained its primary role in transferring ODA to its former Near Eastern dependencies, Syria and Lebanon.

8. Sweden, without a regional ODA concentration, served as the primary aid donor to Angola, Mozambique, Vietnam, and Nicaragua. The German government served this role for Lesotho and Swaziland in Africa, Ecuador in South America, and India, Iran, and Yemen in Asia. Italy was the primary ODA donor to Ethiopia and Somalia in Africa and Cuba and Peru in Latin America. The United Kingdom provided the most development aid to three African LDCs: Gambia, Malawi, and

Uganda. A noteworthy exception to this geographical concentration was the status of France as the primary ODA donor to Mexico and Colombia in Latin America.

9. Paradoxically, given their neglect of many of the qualitative standards of the ODA regime, both the United States and Japan may be said to have been "free-riders." OECD members with smaller economies, presumably less capable of affording ODA outlays, accepted greater sacrifices in transferring aid. Thus, the pattern of regime behavior in the area of ODA is the reverse of that which analysts have found in the area of trade, in which the wealthier powers assumed greater sacrifices. In both cases, however, donor states rejected these qualitative standards and argued that they assumed responsibilities and served the interests of recipients in other respects.

8

National Interest and Foreign Aid: Toward the Millennium

In this book I have sought both to enhance our substantive understanding of French, Japanese, Swedish, and U.S. aid strategies and to suggest ways in which the differences among them may be reconciled. Four objectives, as outlined in the preface, were pursued. I examined national interest as an orienting principle in international relations, its multiple faces over time and across boundaries, its manifestations in the routine practice of foreign policy, and more specifically its presence in the transfer of development assistance from rich states to poor states. As demonstrated in the previous chapters, observable variations in the volume, direction, and terms of aid flows mirrored donors' national interests and general behavior in foreign affairs since World War II.

As noted in Chapter 2, development aid was by no means the primary medium of financial flows from North to South during this period. Private investment, trade, and commercial bank lending contributed more capital to many LDCs than did ODA by the early 1990s. More so than these other financial flows, however, the widespread transfer of ODA challenged long-standing assumptions about the behavior of states in a competitive global environment. Development aid served as a crucial supplement to private capital, playing an influential role in LDCs' broader relations with industrialized states. In this capacity, ODA served as an effective vehicle for the pursuit of donor national interests however they were defined. As the U.S. General Accounting Office (1983: 1) acknowledged, aid donors "consider their bilateral development assistance to be an instrument of foreign policy which takes into account political, economic, cultural, and developmental objectives of both donor and recipient countries."

This study has been directed toward moving beyond this axiom of contemporary world politics and toward identifying more concretely these donor objectives as they were revealed in practice. Along the way, this study has sought empirical support for the "pre-theoretical" assumptions of Morgenthau (1963: 88), who believed a coherent understanding of foreign assistance must presuppose a political basis:

> The problem of foreign aid is insoluble if it is considered as a self-suffi-
> cient technical enterprise of a primarily economic nature. It is soluble
> only if it is considered an integral part of the political policies of the giv-
> ing country, which must be devised in view of the political conditions,
> and for its effects on the political situation, in the receiving country.

The comparative assessment in Chapter 7 suggested that the broad normative approaches to understanding foreign policy and foreign aid, which were reviewed in the first two chapters of this book, did not adequately account for the actions of these donor states during the period under study. The observable behavior of these donors diverged in many important ways, as closer examination made evident. Foreign-aid behavior was highly contingent upon multiple internal and external factors and was therefore not amenable to interpretation through a single analytic lens. Though theoretical paradigms help us understand the differing manners in which political behavior is perceived, and though they illuminate contending visions for how political actors *ought* to behave, their application to specific cases demands attention to contextual factors that pertain to each case.[1]

This critical point may be clarified by considering the varied impact of transnational interdependence on the foreign policies of donor states. Whereas the major donors may be said to have been "situationally interdependent" on other states, largely because "improvements in others' welfare improve their own," smaller industrialized states demonstrated "empathetic interdependence" and were thus more "interested in the welfare of others for their own sake, even if this has no effect on their own material well-being or security" (Keohane, 1984a: 123). This aspect of state behavior helps explain both the inverse relationship between the quantity and quality of aid flows and the propensity of major powers to pursue security or economic interests through ODA more aggressively than other aid donors. In a similar manner, these variations reflected the levels of "sensitivity" and "vulnerability" (Keohane and Nye, 1989: 12–13)—or the relative capacities to surmount threats posed by interdependent relationships—present in each case. The behavior of aid donors was contingent upon their broader capabilities—political and economic—within the interstate system. Finally, the variations underscore the importance of placing state policy in the context of different issue areas, which "generate different coalitions, both within governments and across them, and involve different degrees of conflict" (Keohane and Nye, 1989: 25). In David Clinton's words:

> The security of a state in a self-help system, the balance between its
> power and its commitments, goes far toward delimiting its "moral oppor-
> tunity"—that is, the degree to which it is safe in trying to realize its do-
> mestic principles in its international actions. Because of their circum-
> stances, some states are safer than others and can devote more of their

resources to the promotion of their ideals. Others, in a less secure setting, may believe that they lack the luxury of participating in reformist efforts and must focus their attention solely on their material interests. (1994: 56)

Such an emphasis on the context of state action calls attention to the linkages between states' foreign-policy behavior in specific issue areas and their broader involvement in world politics. As noted in Chapter 1, the perceived national interests of states are also highly variable across time and space. In the former sense they responded to prevalent systemic conditions and norms of behavior; in the latter sense they reflected states' domestic values and institutions, their physical resources, and their broader ties to other states. Although behavior in some respects was most consistent with realist models, in other cases it affirmed the expectations of political idealism. Further, the aid patterns reinforce structuralist assumptions that international political behavior is highly contingent upon the locus of decisionmaking within the world economy, although it departs from Marxist or Leninist assumptions about the primacy of historical materialism, the internal cohesion of the "modern world system," and the inability of North-South financial flows to produce sustained economic development under some circumstances in low-income societies. Ultimately, this conclusion calls upon the analyst to contrast the relative presence of "opportunity and willingness" (Most and Starr, 1989: 17) in foreign policy and to recognize that "the *most general* questions or propositions might not hold because there are at least [some] partitioning factors that might limit their general applicability" (emphasis in original). In short, foreign aid takes the shape of its container.

The Record of Third World Development

As emphasized throughout this book, the ODA regime is a tangible by-product of the post–World War II international system. The first major flows of economic assistance originated in the United States and were distributed mainly among Western industrial states attempting to recover from the war's devastation. Within two decades, the decolonization of many Third World regions and the emergence of dozens of new nation-states recast the scope, direction, and purposes of economic assistance. North-South relations emerged during this period as an important aspect of world politics, to be tangled within the conflicted web of East-West rivalry during the Cold War. In the 1960s, the UN's "first" Development Decade, more than a dozen industrialized states coordinated ODA flows to newly decolonized LDCs to support their political stability and economic growth. This development effort achieved mixed results, substantially improving social welfare conditions in many countries but also leading to frustrations and disappointments that followed the failure of many development programs and the growing economic gaps between the most impoverished regions of the South and the industrialized regions of the North.

Among indicators of sustained economic development in the Third World, growth rates in the 1960s averaged 6.2 percent in the 1960s, well above the UN's target of 5 percent annual growth for the first Development Decade. Average life expectancy in LDCs increased rapidly between 1950 and 1980, from 43 to 59 years; average LDC literacy rates increased from 33 to 59 percent; and the rate of child mortality fell by more than two-thirds (OECD, 1985a: 270). The problem of overpopulation was widely publicized and led to rapid reductions in birthrates in many regions and the establishment of effective family-planning programs. These trends were acknowledged at the UN-sponsored Conference on Population and Development in the summer of 1994, similar in scope to the "Earth Summit" of 1992.

Progress in LDC population control and general living conditions varied widely, however, and many LDCs did not share in the economic growth that occurred elsewhere. As has been widely documented, many inhabitants of East Asia and, to a lesser extent, Latin America experienced considerable improvements in social welfare during this period, but those in sub-Saharan Africa and parts of South Asia suffered from deteriorating social and economic conditions. Furthermore, the economic growth enjoyed by many LDCs in the 1960s and 1970s slowed considerably in the 1980s, the "lost decade" of Third World development; by 1990, social welfare indicators such as life expectancy and per capita income had fallen below their levels of a decade earlier in many areas. Famines in Ethiopia, Sudan, and Somalia attracted worldwide attention in the 1980s and 1990s, but the growing overall disparity between the Third and "Fourth" Worlds was equally portentous.[2]

The ODA regime began its development efforts in the 1960s with very limited consensus and expertise in promoting economic growth and social stability in the world's poorest regions. Industrialized states, adopting prevalent assumptions of linear economic development through predictable "stages of growth," often imposed their own developmental models on Third World states. But even within those states, substantial disagreement existed regarding the most effective means available to reduce poverty and stimulate economic development in the South (see Chapter 2). With the benefit of experience, leaders and development experts in the 1980s and 1990s were able to draw upon the past and consider new ways to hasten economic growth and relieve social distress within LDCs. Their successes and failures in distributing ODA were central aspects of this assessment. In the early 1980s, the OECD (1985a) reviewed its record in coordinating ODA flows. The DAC's Expert Group on Aid Evaluation recommended that recipient populations be actively engaged in development projects and prepared to manage them permanently in the absence of advisers from donor countries; that aid projects be better suited to the varying conditions and needs of recipient communities, meaning that labor-intensive rather than capital-intensive techniques should be applied more often; and that attention be redirected to agricultural rather than industrial production given the former's immediate benefits to local populations and greater compatibility with their existing resources.[3]

In general, the DAC urged aid donors to abandon their "urban bias" in promoting large-scale, capital-intensive industrial projects. Its findings recalled those of ODA critics during the 1970s who called for greater attention to basic human needs in the Third World; they also anticipated the subsequent consensus among participants in the 1992 UN Conference on Environment and Development, who generally agreed that future ODA flows should promote "sustainable development" based upon sensitivity to local conditions and needs, population control, environmental protection, demilitarization, and democratic development (or, more generally, "good government").

The repetition of such studies, the consistency of their findings, and the widely perceived potential for industrialized states to act upon them suggested that a constructive new period in North-South relations had emerged in the mid-1990s. The disappearance of Cold War tensions, which had previously overwhelmed these relations and the internal development of many LDCs, provided a further basis for this expectation. In their place arose a growing sense of shared problems and opportunities for collective action in a variety of issue areas. Many national development programs, including that of the United States, changed emphasis to align broadly with the stated objectives of the United Nations and the OECD.

At the same time, many donors, under growing domestic economic strain, announced that they had reached their limits in making ODA available. Bilateral ODA flows by members of the OECD, which grew steadily during the 1980s, fell in 1992 by about $4 billion in real terms to $38.5 billion, and aid from non-OECD countries continued to dwindle (OECD, 1994a: 64–65). During the same period, multilateral ODA flows increased only slightly, from $15.2 billion to $16.8 billion. Of the eighteen members of the DAC, nine reported lower levels of ODA disbursements in real terms.

Though pledging to continue North-South cooperation through development assistance, leaders of donor states stated that future aid flows would also be increasingly contingent upon the ability of recipients to use the resources productively. Past abuses, in which many funds were embezzled by recipient elites or directed toward extravagant municipal projects, had often been tolerated because these aid relationships furthered donor interests during the Cold War. With the Cold War's demise, and under intensifying domestic pressures, donors were more explicit in conditioning aid resources upon the performance of recipients in redressing socioeconomic disparities and establishing sustained economic growth.

Challenges to the ODA Regime

To an unprecedented degree, major aid donors expressed widely shared concerns and expectations about global economic development in the 1990s and adopted new norms and principles for future ODA allocations. As always, however, they resisted incursions against their prerogatives as sovereign states, and they continued to fashion ODA programs to accommodate their perceived national interests. Long-standing disagreements within the ODA regime continued to fester, and the collective response of these states to the changes in the international system was inhibited in several respects. Among these, four may be identified.

First, "sustainable development" proved to be a slippery concept with a variety of meanings, both among donors and recipients. Under the terms of *Agenda 21,* the long-range development plan adopted by participants of the "Earth Summit" in Brazil, North-South relations were to be redirected toward global problems such as population control and environmental protection. Signatories to the document did not specify the costs and policy ramifications of *Agenda 21,* however; these were ultimately left to member states to interpret on their own. As a result, conditionalities attached to aid packages were often ambiguous, inconsistent, and difficult to enforce.

Second, unresolved debates over the meaning and connotations of "democratic development" were revived in the 1990s, particularly over the issue of whether social-political or economic criteria were to be paramount. As in the past, Scandinavian countries and many socialist LDCs considered socioeconomic equality a primary component of democratic society. To the United States, Japan, Great Britain, and to a lesser degree other industrialized states, civil and political liberties were given primacy; indeed, state enforcement of equality was viewed as an *infringement* on political freedom. This debate, which was an extension of a centuries-old disagreement over the basis and function of democracy, had important implications for the direction and quality of aid flows, which continued to reflect the dispositions of their donors.

In a related manner, the linkage between these largely political considerations and the economic performance of LDCs remained problematic. During the 1970s and 1980s, the countries with the most rapidly expanding economies—Japan, China, South Korea, and Taiwan—openly violated standards of "good government" as defined by the United Nations and the ODA regime. Yet to many LDCs along the Pacific Rim and beyond, and in many World Bank reports exalting the East Asian "miracle," these countries provided a blueprint for modernization and economic integration within the industrialized world. Thus, the tension between these examples and the political requirements of good government—multiple political parties, direct elections, and widespread political participation—was obvious.

To many leaders of LDCs, the benefits of economic growth out-weighed the costs of domestic political repression. In their view, such costs would only be necessary in the short term, until material affluence led to the societal stability that would enable these leaders to liberalize their political systems. In the meantime, market-oriented economic growth would not be possible in a pluralistic political environment.[4] Critics of this view questioned both its normative presumptions and its optimistic expectation that authoritarian rule would necessarily yield, in the presence of improving economic conditions, to representative government. For every case of such a transformation in the Third World, there were many more in which authoritarian rulers were incapable of stimulating broad-based economic growth, much less of relinquishing their hold on power to political opponents.

The third ongoing source of contention within the ODA regime involved the perception within many LDCs that industrialized states were hypocritical in demanding global "responsibility" of Third World states in the early stages of industrialization. Among commonly raised examples of the schism between words and deeds was the United States. Though it was the world's greatest consumer of fossil fuels, a primary source of air and water pollution, one of the most militarized societies in the world, and one of the most prolific manufacturers and exporters of lethal weaponry, the United States urged environmental and military restraint among recipients.[5] Continuing transfers of large amounts of foreign aid to resource-rich but repressive regimes (e.g., Indonesia from Japan) and strategically important, heavily militarized, relatively affluent states (e.g., Egypt and Israel from the United States) was seen as further evidence of hypocrisy among major aid donors.

Finally, disputes continued over the definition of ODA "quality." The DAC continued to advance its standards, which reflected a consensus among most of its members. As noted previously, Japanese officials questioned many of these qualitative standards, particularly the DAC's preference for grant aid rather than concessional loans. In the view of the Japanese government, loans forced a measure of fiscal discipline on recipients that was lacking when they received grants with no reciprocal obligations. As in other areas, Japan's leaders pointed to the economic growth of its recipients as evidence of the superiority of this interpretation. The United States, meanwhile, moved further below the DAC standard of 0.7 percent ODA/GNP. The anticipated shift of Economic Support Fund outlays for Egypt and Israel away from the category of ODA was expected to lower the U.S. proportion even further. The U.S. government, however, continued to draw attention to its large aggregate aid flows, its large contributions to the United Nations and other international organizations, and its continuing role in providing military security for its allies.

Dissension continued not only within the ODA regime during the 1990s but also more broadly between North and South. The ideological cleavages and regional conflicts that grew out of the Cold War produced a legacy of distrust among states, and the transparent influence of donor self-interests in past aid programs left recipients skeptical about the sincerity of current efforts. The continuing tensions between donor and recipient states were likely to make the new objectives of the ODA regime more difficult to realize. As Moore and Robinson (1994: 153) observed,

> There is confusion of various kinds, and little basis on which the donors can validly claim to have been acting ethically in implementing a policy that ultimately can only be justified in ethical terms. For the intervention by aid donors in the internal affairs of other states . . . can only be justified if the donors can reasonably argue that they are acting in good faith to enure that development aid is used for the interests of the intended beneficiaries—the poor.

Yet, importantly, none of these challenges threatened the long-term viability of the ODA regime. Under some models, systemic volatility may be a precursor to the demise of regime cohesion (see Keohane, 1980). But in the case of the ODA regime, which had demonstrated great malleability in responding to shifts in donor objectives and the developmental needs of recipients, the framework persevered amid the seismic shifts in world politics in the 1980s and early 1990s. Rather than being withheld in the face of fiscal austerity, aid flowed each year from more sources, in more forms, to more recipients. The end of the Cold War relieved many tensions but produced new strains as the foreign policies of all states were reoriented. Future analysis will determine how these strains will be manifested in aid policy.

Future Prospects

The status and future prospects of donor aid strategies may now be considered, as all four states confront a rapidly changing and volatile global environment. Systemic upheavals in the 1980s corresponded with observable shifts in the donors' ODA policies as they adapted to the new conditions. These shifts and their possible implications will be explored in each case before the study concludes with a more general assessment of the future of national interest and foreign aid.

France

As the 1990s began, François Mitterrand welcomed the end of Cold War bipolarity and the corresponding division of Europe, outcomes that French leaders had actively sought since World War II. The emerging order provided an opening for France, which had been overshadowed by the competition between the United States and Soviet Union, to reassert its influence as a global power. France's ability to exploit this situation, however, was limited by its ongoing economic problems and growing domestic fissures. The amorphous balance of power that emerged after the Cold War further raised doubts about France's role. Paradoxically, though France was no longer constrained by the superpowers, it was likewise unable to continue promoting itself to the developing world as a bridge between the ideological competitors.

France served as both a catalyst of the Euro-integration process and a potential obstacle to it because of growing nationalist sentiments among economically depressed sectors of the population. In September 1992, voters narrowly approved the Maastricht accords, which called for greater coordination among EU members in foreign policy, but the referendum revealed widespread public skepticism of the move toward greater integration. In June 1994, Mitterrand's Socialist Party made a weak showing in voting for the European Parliament, suggesting that it would not retain the French presidency in the 1995 general election (Riding, 1994: A4). French domestic politics—always divisive and polarized—appeared even more so as the Gaullist Party, the Union for French Democracy, the Rally for the Republic Party, and the rightist National Front all received strong support at the polls.

As noted previously, domestic fragmentation has traditionally not threatened the otherwise strong national consensus regarding France's foreign affairs; politics has traditionally stopped at the water's edge. But in the 1990s doubts were raised even in this regard. Many observers believed that, as a middle-sized power with chronic internal difficulties and stagnant population growth, France must moderate its global ambitions and exploit its role as a regional power.[6]

France's foreign-assistance program, however, continued to serve a vital function in the service of its perceived national interests. ODA flows increased into the 1990s; the $8.3 billion in French transfers in 1992 represented a 2.3 percent rise in real terms from the year before (OECD, 1994a). Nearly all of this increase was recorded in the category of multilateral assistance, although more than 75 percent of French ODA was disbursed directly to LDC governments. The overall growth of French ODA in the early 1990s contrasted with the decreasing aid flows from other major donors, including the United States. Beyond some marginal shifts, the three-tiered pattern of French aid remained intact, with the largest bilateral packages disbursed to overseas territories, the second largest to former colonies, and the relatively small amount of remaining funds transferred to other developing countries.

Throughout the post–World War II period, the preponderance of French aid flows to overseas territories such as Réunion, Guadeloupe, and Martinique was not lost on the OECD and other international aid agencies, which insisted that France account for these aid flows in a separate category from its other ODA commitments. This issue remained contentious into the 1990s; in response to unrest in distant New Caledonia, the French government agreed to permit a referendum on independence in 1999 but would retain control over the territory until then. In addition, French relations with francophone Africa were ruptured in early 1994 when the government, responding to growing fiscal strains within its former colonies, devalued the Franc Zone currency by 50 percent. This action served to both antagonize leaders in francophone Africa and demonstrate further their continuing dependence on Paris for sustained development.

Though French ODA increased in the early 1990s, the perceived failures of many Socialist policies, continuing domestic economic stagnation, and the ascendance of nationalist sentiments threatened to curtail flows to the Third World in the late 1990s. As in the case of the United States throughout the Cold War and in Sweden during the 1980s, "the evolution of French co-operation with developing countries may depend on the ability of governments to convince public opinion that Third World development aid is at least as important as assistance to the relatively poor regions of metropolitan France" (Evans, 1989: 143).

Of paramount importance, given the integration of the Franco-African political economies, was their combined ability to withstand a prolonged recession in the industrialized world and a fifteen-year period of low or negative economic growth in the Third World.[7] Also critical for France was its response to the rise of Islamic fundamentalism in Algeria and the impact of this trend on relations between France and the Maghreb states of North Africa (Balta, 1986). Economic stagnation and Islamic fundamentalism both exacerbated domestic tensions in France, where nationalistic sentiments gained strength during the 1980s. Meanwhile, some critics objected to the expensive modernization of French military forces initiated by Giscard and continued by Mitterrand. As Howorth (1986: 80) concluded, "France cannot afford nuclear superpower status (even of the second rank) and a meaningful contribution to the conventional defense of western Europe and a trouble-shooting world role. But its 'great-power' self-perception is so deeply rooted that it will have enormous difficulty in abandoning any of these roles."

Japan

The case of Japan further illustrates how ODA flows may be incorporated to further a state's shifting objectives. "Japan has expanded its postwar economy by utilizing to maximum effect the dual tools of finance and trade offered by economic aid," observed Shinsuke (1982: 34). Its distinctive approach to development aid, combined with its continuing economic growth during a period of global recession, incited repeated charges of aid mercantilism. Japan recorded a $40 billion trade surplus with its East Asian neighbors in the late 1980s, many of which were primary recipients of Japanese ODA. To some analysts, these statistics provided evidence of Japan's "new imperialism" (Steven, 1990). Johnson added, "Japan's not yet fully revealed goal for the end of this century appears to be the reconstitution of the Greater East Asia Co-Prosperity Sphere—but this time based on real prosperity and not created at the point of a bayonet" (1993: 27).

After a prolonged period of stability and prosperity, Japan suffered from economic recession and political crisis in the mid-1990s. The sudden halt in the country's rapid economic growth exacerbated political tensions, leading to the dislodging of the Liberal Democratic Party from the Japanese Diet for the first time since World War II and the election in 1994 of a Socialist-led government. A coalition of new leaders vowed to revive the economy and reform government ministries, whose intimate links with Japanese industry led to numerous corruption scandals, including the "Recruit" controversy that brought down Prime Minister Noboru Takeshita in 1989. And the general public, which had previously been quiescent amid the country's economic boom, became more critical of the cramped living conditions and high consumer prices in Tokyo and other large cities.

Japan in the early 1990s began to exhibit the same symptoms of "aid fatigue" experienced by Western European and U.S. donors in the 1980s. Japanese ODA flows in 1992 fell in real terms by 6 percent to $11.2 billion, and bilateral loans dropped by 22 percent to $4.6 billion (OECD, 1994a). As a percentage of Japanese GNP, aid flows slipped from 0.32 percent to 0.30 percent. The Japanese government continued to meet its medium-term targets for ODA, however, and pledged to increase aid flows again after the fiscal problems of the early 1990s were resolved. These circumstances suggested a static pattern for future Japanese flows, at least relative to the robust growth of the thirty-year period prior to 1990.

In response to ongoing criticism of their ODA program, Japan's leaders continued to pledge greater aggregate volumes and higher levels of aid quality in the mid-1990s. Their efforts reflected a continuing interest among Japanese leaders to attain recognition as a global power and to attract greater credibility within the post–Cold War ODA regime. Continuing this effort at improving the public perception of Japanese aid, the Japanese government (1992b) released an ODA "charter" on June 30, 1992, identifying its "basic philosophy" and objectives that would subsequently be pursued through ODA transfers: "It is an important mission for Japan, as a peace-loving nation, to play a role commensurate with its position in the world to maintain world peace and ensure global prosperity. . . . Such assistance is expected to further promote the existing friendly relations between Japan and all other countries, especially those in the developing world."

In announcing the charter, former prime minister Kiichi Miyazawa identified four objectives to be pursued through future ODA flows: peace, freedom, democracy, and sustainable development. New criteria regarding recipient behavior were placed alongside others that had been predominant in earlier Japanese ODA calculations, such as past performance in managing aid flows, ability to utilize future aid effectively, and long-term trade relations with Japan. Japanese leaders embraced the environmental goals of the UN Conference on Environment and Development (UNCED); further, they proposed linking DAC aid flows to limits on levels of recipient militarization. And to demonstrate its growing concern for democratization in recipient states, the Japanese government rescinded aid flows to Myanmar in 1988 and to Haiti in 1991 after military coups d'état. During the same period, they "rewarded" steps toward democracy in Nicaragua and El Salvador after years of civil conflict by approving funds for their reconstruction.

Foreign assistance was intimately related to broader aspects of U.S.-Japanese relations during the postwar period. U.S. security guarantees provided Japan with considerable leverage to pursue its economic interests, which were furthered through its aid networks, but also gave rise to bitter tensions regarding Japan's protectionist trade policies and the trade imbalance that persisted between the two states. As U.S. trade deficits continued to widen in the 1990s, these tensions increased, and the security relationship came under scrutiny. U.S. leaders encouraged Japan to support their security efforts in the name of greater "burden sharing." The Japanese government responded by providing funding, but not military personnel, to the growing number of United Nations peacekeeping efforts. The United States further urged Japan to maintain high levels of economic assistance at a time when the U.S. ODA program faced strong domestic opposition. It was widely believed that Japanese "responsiveness on foreign aid will help to deflect trade friction with Washington" (Orr, 1987: 61).

Japan's model of "guided capitalism" served as an example to NICs in an era of intensifying global economic competition. The success of Japanese leaders in engineering their own country's economic development and stimulating rapid growth among its East Asian neighbors was among the most noteworthy developments of the three decades and represented a potential model for other ODA donors. "As the political rationale for many older aid programs in the Third World collapses, Japan's more economically motivated assistance may be one of the few donor programs to grow during the 1990s" (Ensign, 1992: 4).

Sweden

As the 1990s began, Sweden's "recipient-oriented" ODA program discernibly shifted toward greater sensitivity to domestic interests. This change was due to worsening economic conditions and to the perceived failures of recipient states to implement previous aid packages effectively. As noted in Chapter 5, moderate and conservative pressure groups successfully pressed for "concerned participation" by Swedish aid officials and for greater accountability among recipients. The growing realism of Swedish ODA was reflected in the statistical linkages between its ODA flows and its bilateral trade relationships in the late 1980s. For recipients, "the hardening of terms and conditions in the aid programme of a donor who had been noted for generosity and flexibility has been received with understanding, but hardly pleasure" (Edgren, 1986: 62). Thus Sweden's foreign-aid policies, once praised for their untarnished character, became subject to "a continuous struggle to find and uphold the extremely fragile balance between continued respect for the consensus on purity of aid motives and the growing claims of national economic and commercial interests" (Jacoby, 1986: 88).

With its aid reforms largely in place by 1990, and with the easing of its economic difficulties, which extended throughout the 1980s, the Swedish government reported a 10 percent increase in ODA flows between 1991 and 1992 (OECD, 1994a). Sweden transferred $2.5 billion in real terms in the latter year, and its ODA/GNP ratio increased from .90 to 1.03 percent, placing it second only to Norway in this closely watched indicator of aid quality. Sweden transferred $1.8 billion directly to LDCs and an additional $700 million through multilateral organizations.

Swedish leaders maintained their active role within the ODA regime, participating in global negotiations over resource distribution, arms control, ecological destruction, and other emerging issues. They successfully avoided active engagement in transnational conflicts and continued to direct their energies toward the United Nations, the Conference on Security Cooperation in Europe, and other international organizations. The growing regional integration of Swedish economic activity was reflected in its proposed entry into the European Union in 1995. With the Cold War having ended, the Swedish government argued that its membership in this and other regional organizations would not violate the country's neutrality. In addition, the government announced plans to establish closer economic ties with Eastern European states, many of which received development assistance from Sweden in the early 1990s.

All of these changes suggested that Sweden's era of "splendid isolation" had come to an end. Its previous role in representing a "third way" as an alternative to superpower competition ended with the collapse of the Soviet Union in 1991. But its model of social democracy, refined by the influence of "realism" and economic reform, remained on display for developing countries. With the return to power of the Social Democrats in September 1994, some return to past practices could expected. Ingvar Carlsson, head of the Social Democratic Party, retained the post of prime minister, which he held from 1986 to 1991 before being defeated by a conservative coalition headed by Carl Bildt. The more liberal coalition was expected to limit welfare cuts and raise income taxes for many Swedes while retaining many of the pro-business reforms undertaken by the conservatives. The prospects for foreign aid were less clear beyond the ongoing consensus that future ODA commitments must be more "rational" (Swedish Government, 1994).

The United States

Despite the chronic unpopularity of its foreign-aid program, the United States regained its status in 1991 and 1992 as the largest donor of ODA, which it lost to Japan in 1989. However, its proportion of aid relative to U.S. GNP (0.20 percent) remained one of the lowest among DAC members. U.S. ODA flows in 1992 amounted to $11.7 billion, of which $7.9 billion was in the form of bilateral aid and $3.8 billion was distributed through multilateral channels (OECD, 1994a). These aid flows were among the last to be approved by Congress before a broad reassessment of USAID was undertaken by the incoming administration of President Bill Clinton.

Increasingly, the United States sought to coordinate its economic assistance program with those of other major donors in the 1990s. The United States approved aid packages to Russia, members of the Commonwealth of Independent States, and several Eastern European countries, primarily Poland and Hungary, but left it to other donors, particularly Germany, to provide most of the development assistance to this region. In addition, the United States sought contributions from many countries to implement the 1993 peace treaty between Israel and the Palestinian Liberation Organization. Aid donors attended a conference in Washington in September 1993 and committed more than $2 billion for economic development in the region. "The money is the carrot for signing the peace agreement with Israel," observed Hassan Abu Libdah (quoted in Ibrahim, 1994: A3), deputy chairman of the Palestinian Economic Council for Development and Reconstruction.[8] In October 1994, other U.S. foreign-aid "carrots" were directed toward the post-apartheid regime in South Africa and the Haitian government upon the U.S. occupation of the country (see Greenhouse, 1994: A4). Further, the passage of a peace agreement between Israel and Jordan raised the prospect of increased U.S. assistance to the Jordanian government.

The effectiveness of U.S. ODA came under intensified scrutiny during this period as critics argued that previous aid packages, which were largely driven by security concerns, had become obsolete in the post–Cold War era. Many detractors suggested that U.S. ODA be made more responsive to macroeconomic market forces and rendered more compatible with the activities of multinational corporations, trading interests, and private U.S.

investors.[9] Analyses in the early 1990s were replete with suggestions for fundamental reform of U.S. foreign assistance. Some called for the Clinton administration to "scuttle America's bilateral aid program and begin anew with a concise, clearly defined initiative to promote environmentally sound forms of economic growth" (Clad and Stone, 1993: 196).

These proposals, reminiscent of earlier calls to reconcile U.S. aid with Third World development interests, initially met with little response given the government's preoccupation with domestic economic problems. Public frustration reflected the chronic dissatisfaction with U.S. Third World foreign policy that emerged during the Vietnam War. As Schraeder (1993: 215–216) observed, "A fragmented U.S. political culture is no longer content, as it was during the 1950s and 1960s, to follow the lead of the executive branch in support of an interventionist foreign policy." Bill Clinton, who as a presidential candidate did not express a strong interest in foreign affairs, echoed this dissatisfaction with U.S. Cold War policies but failed to articulate clearly an alternative strategy. His early setbacks in Somalia, Bosnia, and Haiti were widely seen as a result of his lack of resolve. The U.S. intervention in Haiti late in 1994 was partly an attempt by Clinton to match his words with deeds. But he had yet to convince a skeptical public—and Congress—that the action was either in the U.S. national interest or that it would yield the results sought by the Clinton administration and supporters of the action within the United Nations.

For U.S. aid administrators, the central task became to convince Congress and the general public that aid flows could serve national interests that endured beyond the Cold War. In that effort, they emphasized the ongoing political and security interests served by foreign assistance and noted ominously: "While communism is shattered, its debris remains toxic. If progress is not made, reversion to totalitarianism is possible" (USAID, 1992: 21).

Among the early signs of adaptation to new global conditions, the United States under the Clinton administration acknowledged that transnational problems had emerged as the primary threats to U.S. national interests. USAID administrator J. Brian Atwood proposed to redirect the U.S. aid program in the name of "preventive diplomacy." To Atwood (quoted in Kirschten, 1993: 2370), "USAID's relevancy in the post–Cold War period will be its effectiveness in dealing with the new strategic threats to the United States." Rather than Soviet subversion, these new threats were seen as resulting from problems largely neglected during the Cold War: the rapid growth of the world's population, degradation of the global environment, political repression in many Third World countries, and the continuing obstacles to global economic growth.

The reforms proposed by Atwood were endorsed by Secretary of State Warren Christopher (1993), who reiterated the continuing need for U.S. ODA and testified before Congress that "we must now target our assistance to address today's priorities." In addition to their proposals to redirect U.S. ODA toward promoting sustainable development, Atwood and Christopher called for reducing the number of U.S. bilateral aid programs and the number of staffed overseas missions, twenty-one of which were identified for possible closure by fiscal year 1996.[10] Atwood also proposed to lower the ratio of Washington-based USAID employees to agents serving overseas and to improve the system by which USAID procures domestic goods and services, which many critics argued had been tainted by corruption. Reflecting these strategic shifts, spending categories for USAID were reorganized under such titles as "Promoting Sustainable Development," "Building Democracy," "Promoting U.S. Prosperity," and "Advancing Diplomacy." Finally, USAID proposed shifting the Economic Support Fund, which had pursued security-oriented concerns, out of the development assistance program and into a new functional category entitled "Promoting Peace." As noted in Chapter 6, the approximately $5 billion in annual ESF transfers to Egypt and Israel were primarily responsible for the statistical linkages between U.S. ODA and U.S. security interests. In addition to eliminating these linkages, however, the absence of ODA transfers to Egypt and Israel would have the additional effect of greatly reducing both the aggregate quantity of U.S. ODA and the already low qualitative measures of per capita ODA and ODA as a percentage of U.S. GNP.

These measures were collectively designed to streamline USAID and to limit its attention to international economic development, leaving other objectives of U.S. foreign policy to be pursued elsewhere. In many important respects, the proposals of agency officials suggested an alignment of U.S. priorities with those of the United Nations and the OECD.[11] Though many welcomed this reorientation, it suggested that the U.S. public and federal government would be asked to provide public funds for purposes less narrowly related to national self-interest. In an era of growing fiscal austerity and of continuing doubts about the U.S. world role, uncertainties remained about whether sufficient support could be achieved to sustain U.S. ODA at even these greatly reduced levels.

Other Stories of National Interest and Foreign Aid

By comparing the aid policies of France, Japan, Sweden, and the United States from these vantage points, I have raised many issues in hopes of provoking future cross-national analysis of this important topic. The intimate relationship between the national interests and foreign-aid programs of these countries is evident in other cases as well, and it reveals much about their general approach to world politics. Further systematic analysis may bear out these linkages and more thoroughly test the conclusions and inferences drawn in this study. Some examples may be reviewed briefly as possible avenues for future research.

Members of the Organization of Petroleum Exporting Countries ascended from aid recipients to donors with the rise of oil prices in the 1970s and established large bilateral and multilateral aid programs of their own.[12] These donors, which remained separate from the OECD and its attendant aid regime, often limited aid to Islamic countries or those that supported OPEC positions on highly charged issues such as the recognition of Israel, recognition of the Palestinian Liberation Organization, and opposition to U.S. positions in the United Nations. The OPEC countries, whose petroleum cartel fueled hopes among LDCs for their own efforts in manipulating commodity prices and supplies in other sectors, frequently "used aid as a principal instrument of their security and foreign policies" (Hunter, 1984: 7; see also Mertz and Mertz, 1983). OPEC foreign assistance, which exceeded 20 percent of global aid flows in 1980, fell dramatically throughout the ensuing decade as a result of falling oil revenues and growing internal demands for public resources. As a result, widespread expectations that OPEC would serve as a long-term source of foreign aid were not realized.

The People's Republic of China also provided economic resources to carefully selected Third World states during this period. The Chinese government often "recycled" aid it received from the Soviet Union, a practice that ended with the break between the two communist superpowers in the early 1960s. Thereafter, Chinese and Soviet officials engaged in an aid rivalry as they appealed to prospective Third World clients. Supporting revolutionary regimes involved in wars of national liberation, Chinese leaders offered foreign assistance as a means of promoting their model of communism (see Cooper, 1976; Horvath, 1976; and Bartke, 1975). In the 1980s and 1990s, the PRC accepted growing volumes of Japanese ODA even as it continued to serve as an aid donor to other developing countries. Its rapid economic growth suggested that, like Japan and South Korea before it, the PRC would soon "graduate" from the status of net ODA recipient and assume an active role in transferring development assistance abroad. China had already assumed a prominent role in the area of military transfers, exporting weaponry in record volumes in the early 1990s while expanding its own military spending by an annual average of 10 percent.

Another illustrative example is that of the United Kingdom, which, like France, utilized ODA as a functional substitute for its colonial empire. The UK annually sent more than two-thirds of its development funding to members of the Commonwealth or Sterling Area. India, once the "crown jewel" of the British Empire, annually received the largest share of Britain's development assistance. "The guiding motif has been political disengagement from the old empire, with the objective of replacing direct

British power with stable regional arrangements," observed Byrd (1991: 57; see also Morton, 1973). Reflecting their general disposition in foreign policy, British leaders favored bilateral rather than multilateral ODA channels to the Third World (Dinwiddy, 1973b). The British ODA program was the target of ongoing criticism in Margaret Thatcher's conservative parliament, especially as domestic welfare programs were being trimmed. As in the case of other donor states, observers of Britain found its aid performance in the 1980s fall in the gray area "between idealism and self-interest" (Bose and Burnell, 1991).

During this period, officials from the Federal Republic of Germany used concessional transfers to encourage self-sufficient Third World economies, targeting recipients that possessed large reserves of strategic raw materials or potential markets for West German exports (Schulz and Hansen, 1984). In addition, West Germany promoted regional stability in the Third World through selective aid allocations, a central thrust of its postwar foreign policy (Holbik and Myers, 1968; Knusel, 1968). Its general diminution of Cold War considerations in targeting ODA was shared by Canada, another U.S. ally that used its protection within NATO to pursue aid policies based largely upon social and economic considerations (Spicer, 1965). Upon its unification in 1990, the German government undertook a massive program of economic support for not only its own citizens in the former East Germany, but for those in Eastern Europe and Russia. Germany's aid commitments, the largest among DAC members for this region, contributed to the stunted growth of the German economy and, given its importance to regional stability, to strained relations within the EU.

Its controversial reputation in contemporary world politics notwithstanding, the foreign-aid regime assumed an unprecedented stature in the mid-1990s. Though its detractors pointed to donor states' pervasive manipulation of aid transfers in pursuit of selfish interests, its defenders emphasized that improvements in Third World social welfare in many areas were partly attributable to the growing concessional flows from North to South. The aid debate continued in the mid-1990s as new crises—the carnage in Rwanda, refugee boat lifts in the Caribbean, plague in India—beckoned for overseas relief. As the scope of privation and human suffering widened, and as the perils of overpopulation and environmental decay became better understood, the potential functions of economic aid multiplied as well. True to form, donor states generally responded when they had concluded that the easing of conditions abroad served their interest, however concretely or abstractly defined.

"Enlightened" National Interest and Foreign Aid

I began this book by reviewing the many ways in which the concept of national interest, a common part of the diplomatic lexicon, has been interpreted and applied by nation-states throughout history. I considered the multiple connotations of national interest in the context of the evolving relations among states, which in turn reflected shifting ties between church and state, state and society, and government and commercial concerns. A cyclical pattern was evident in which two general strains of national interest, reflecting the prevailing tenor of interstate relations of each era, were widely adopted by political leaders.

The first strain drew upon the insights of Thucydides, who observed that the decentralized political system of antiquity, unrestrained by overarching authority, was inherently prone to conflict and narrowly defined standards of national interest. His pessimistic conception, refined in modern times by Niccolo Machiavelli, Thomas Hobbes, and such leaders as Otto von Bismarck and Theodore Roosevelt, provided the basis of realism in contemporary international-relations theory. The second strain, drawing on more optimistic assumptions about human nature, endeavored to transcend the limitations of national interest and establish a basis for transnational norms and cooperation. As developed by Immanuel Kant, Woodrow Wilson, and adherents of "world-order politics" in the contemporary age, these more optimistic perspectives have framed the idealist challenge to political realism (Burton, 1972; Herz, 1951).

The practice of international relations has reflected both traditions to varying degrees in different historical periods. Prevailing notions of national interest have often influenced the worldviews of political leaders and the course of their foreign policies. When principles of collective security were prominent, such as the period following the Napoleonic wars and, however unsuccessfully, between the world wars, leaders of the most powerful states attempted to coordinate their defense policies and establish a basis for broader forms of collaboration. When transnational norms broke down, as in the late nineteenth century and again in the 1930s, leaders more aggressively pursued narrow self-interests, which precipitate systemic warfare.

In the current period, between the Cold War and the millennium, both traditions coexist uneasily, competing for the attention of world leaders. In one respect, the prevailing realism of the Cold War period has given way to a revival of universalism based on a growing sense of shared problems and solutions, the declining utility of military power, the expanding role of international organizations, and the diffusion of democratic principles as a basis of societal organization. (see Haas, 1964a, for an early elaboration). In another respect, realist expectations have been met in the resurgence of ethnic and nationalist conflict that has, in many regions, filled the vacuum left by the bipolar superpower competition. As always, the prospects of positive-sum cooperation are in many areas frustrated by the vagaries of zero-sum competition that result from economic hardship and the more general quest for finite material resources.

Though the Hobbesian struggles may draw on a more distinct legacy, the movements toward transnational cooperation and integration are by-products of modernity—advanced communication, transportation networks, and the means of global commerce. This suggests that the line between national and transnational interest has been severed to an unprecedented degree. As states have become more interdependent, transnational regimes—such as that which coordinates the flow of ODA—have arisen to advance both the interests of individual states and collective goals. Concerted efforts in controlling world population growth, stemming the AIDS epidemic, restraining weapons proliferation, conserving energy, and preserving tropical rainforests are rooted in the perceived self-interests of every participant. "We do not necessarily sacrifice realism when we analyze international relations as the products of voluntary agreements among independent actors," noted Keohane (1982: 330).

In this respect, there is a strong basis for transnational cooperation even within "the anarchical society" (Bull, 1977). Egoistic ends may often be achieved by means that benefit larger collectivities, from the community and state levels to the entire global population. This, of course, is not a novel perspective. At the time Thomas Hobbes composed his bleak *Leviathan*, the Dutch jurist Hugo Grotius examined the relations among polities and saw within their contentiousness the seeds of cooperation. Grotius foresaw states conforming to a corpus of international law, anticipating that their adherence to transnational norms of behavior would be based not upon the acceptance of universal moral codes but upon the enlarged definition of states' self-interests. This Grotian variant of the realist view, based on states' apprehension of shared problems and opportunities, may well describe the emerging framework of world politics:

> To discover that some aspects of international politics do not constitute a zero-sum game is not to sacrifice the national interest; to establish aims and devise policies that benefit other nations as well as one's own is simply to become aware of another dimension of the national interest, one that might be overlooked in an over-hasty examination of immediate advantages. That some of these unshared advantages may be eschewed is undeniable. But the state does so in the expectation that the compensating benefits of cooperation will at least as great. A policy that attempts to secure goods need not be subversive of the national interest, so long as one's own state continues to share in the goods and one's relative position is not undermined. (Clinton, 1994: 89)

The ODA regime of the post–Cold War era is located at this crossroads of national and transnational interest. More than ever, leaders of industrialized nations have explicitly acknowledged the role of economic growth—among rich and poor states alike—in enhancing their own material welfare. They have further concluded that social unrest and military conflict in LDCs undermine economic development, divert scarce resources toward unproductive uses, transform millions of able citizens into refugees, and encourage the proliferation of weapons. All of these problems perniciously affect neighboring societies and, ultimately, demand some response from abroad. Finally, the industrial nations have related the ecologically sound development of LDCs with their own long-term qualities of life. The egoistic interests of each industrialized state continue to be pursued through varying foreign policies, including those involving foreign aid, but the equation of their livelihoods with those of distant populations has become widely accepted within states both rich and poor. The aligment of the U.S. ODA program with transnational efforts to promote sustainable development offers some evidence—and grounds for optimism—that this transformation of national interest may have begun.

"A potentially powerful transformation can occur, at the point where 'my problem' and the problem of 'my adversary' are recognized by both of us as 'our problem.'" wrote North (1990: 251). These words, echoing the Grotian logic of the seventeenth century, may still seem quixotic in a world of constant tension. But in their application to the globalized threats and opportunities of the contemporary age, they may be supremely realistic.

Notes

1. In contrasting the propensity of states to participate in international organizations in the early 1970s, Ruggie (1972: 892) observed similar patterns by which the behavior of states was contingent upon their resources and systemic roles. The propensity of states to engage in transnational efforts, including economic regimes,

appears to be an issue-specific and actor-specific process. It is asymmetrical, reflecting differences in national capabilities to perform different tasks, as well as discontinuous, reflecting the differential impact of interdependence costs in different issue areas and for different states. Moreover, it appears to generate issue-specific and actor-specific collective arrangements, existing at different levels in the interstate system and compensating for different imperfections in processes and structures of the interstate system and of actors in that system.

2. The varying growth patterns represented one of many reasons for the failure of the Group of 77 and other coalitions of LDCs to engage in concerted action during the 1970s and 1980s and further the cause of Third World solidarity.

3. Among the four donors reviewed in this study, agriculture was a relatively low priority in the distribution of their ODA flows. The percentage of ODA devoted to agriculture ranged in 1985 from 9.5 percent in the case of France to 28 percent in that of Sweden; figures for the United States and Japan were 14 percent and 17.7 percent, respectively.

4. See Huntington (1968) for an early elaboration of this view.

5. The United States emerged as the "grand trafficker" of weaponry in the early 1990s as its primary competitor, the Soviet Union, disintegrated (Clairmonte,

1992: 13). Other major exporters include China, France, Germany, Great Britain, and Italy; their primary recipients are in the Middle East and South Asia.

6. Low birthrates, combined with increased African immigration into France, led to ethnic tensions and the rise of a nationalist political party determined to restrict future immigration.

7. See Howorth (1986) for a detailed analysis of the potential impact of France's domestic economic problems on its national-security policy.

8. See Marcus (1993) for the implications of these developments for ongoing U.S. assistance to Israel.

9. To some Congressional leaders, including Rep. Matthew F. McHugh (quoted in Doherty, 1992: 1354), in the post–Cold War world, "the issue is not what kind of foreign aid, but whether foreign aid." See Janssen (1991) and Stanfield (1990) for elaborations of this view.

10. These included the African countries of Burkina Faso, Botswana, Cameroon, Cape Verde, Chad, Côte d'Ivoire, Lesotho, Togo, and Zaire; the Asian states of Afghanistan, Pakistan, and Thailand; the Latin American states of Argentina, Belize, Chile, Costa Rica, and Uruguay; and the Near Eastern states of Oman and Tunisia. In addition, missions overseeing ODA to small states in the Caribbean and South Pacific were to close.

11. As Mike Crosswell, a senior policy advisor to USAID, argued in an interview, "The world is more interdependent today, and the United States is increasingly engaged in the global economy. We are interested in a global community that is open, with shared values. More than before, the United States has to count on cooperation from other countries, particularly in such areas as the environment, narcotics, and arms transfers. Cooperation is the name of the game" (USAID, 1994).

12. OPEC aid was unusual in that many of the donor states were technically LDCs themselves but were able to support overseas development with oil revenues.

Appendix 1:
Summary of
the Research Strategy

As noted in the preface, this study probes the relationship between donor interests and development-assistance flows through a combination of descriptive and statistical analysis. The former category considers the evolutionary and structural context of each state's broader foreign policies and development-aid strategies. The latter category includes both the use of descriptive statistics, which identify the aggregate volumes, direction, and qualitative dimensions of aid flows, and multivariate regression analysis, which attempts to identify the cumulative and interactive effects of possible determinants of aid allocations. It is this final research effort that will be reviewed below.

The essential structure of the McKinlay-Little foreign-policy model is adopted, particularly the utilization of multiple indicators of each potential donor interest in the ODA relationship, the repeated testing of the model over an extended period to test for temporal variation, and the use of multiple cases to demonstrate spatial variation. In an effort to construct a more parsimonious model, the range of possible interests is limited to three general categories—humanitarian, economic, and security—and the number of indicators is limited to two in each category. Larger numbers and various combinations of independent variables were previously employed in each category to test the relationship. These indicators often were highly intercorrelated and thus distorted the statistical relationships; in addition, their presence in a larger multivariate model added little to the explained variance in the dependent variable. Bivariate correlations are not included in the analysis, given that other factors are often "hidden" in bivariate coefficients and that the interactive effects of the broad range of possible influences, which are of greatest concern in this study, are not taken into account.

In the regression model the ODA commitments of each donor between 1980 and 1989, as documented and reported by the DAC, are included as dependent variables—the foreign-policy behavior we are trying to understand more fully. It is assumed that commitments, rather than actual disbursements, better reflect the behavior of donor states. Commitments of aid are considered as a more adequate expression of donor foreign-policy objectives at a given point in time. Further, the highly variable and often lengthy lag time between commitments and disbursements obscures the aid relationship. A one-year lag, most often utilized in aid research, is employed in this analysis. Such a lag represents the duration between the reported recipient characteristics and subsequent ODA commitments, which are presumably based at least in part upon those data. Though different states follow varying procedures in identifying aid recipients and making aid commitments, the one-year lag assumes that aid calculations are based upon the most recent recipient data available. It is acknowledged that officials from donor states utilize their own sources of data, which are largely unavailable to researchers; thus, data reported by international organizations such as the OECD, the World Bank, and the International Monetary Fund are utilized and cited.

The independent variables include widely adopted measures of recipient social welfare, economic development, and militarization. The data set includes these reported characteristics of ninety-four recipient states for the years 1979 through 1988. Of these recipients, forty-one are African states, twenty-one are in the Latin American region, eighteen are in the Middle East or South Asia, and fourteen are in East Asia. Developing countries with populations of less than 1 million, many of which received development assistance during the 1980s, are not included because of inadequate data. In the few cases in which data in individual categories are not provided, estimates are utilized based upon long-term averages and patterns.

For each aid recipient, the annual commitments of ODA by the four donors are included as dependent variables along with data relating to its social welfare, economic, and security characteristics. These three categories are considered as possible motivating factors underlying aid strategy; through the juxtaposition of donor ODA commitments and recipient attributes in these categories, an empirical basis for inferring the objectives of aid policy is established. First, development assistance is often rhetorically advanced as a humanitarian effort from well-endowed states to those in distress. Two widely adopted measures of humanitarian need—life expectancy and per capita income—are included in this category. More self-interested motivations for transferring development aid can be divided into two categories. Development assistance may be used to improve economic conditions within the donor as well as the recipient country. In this respect, the aggregate volume of recipient gross national product and bilateral trade between donor and recipient are considered as possible indicators of economic interest in aid relationships. Finally, calculations involving the direction and volume of development assistance may be related to donor security interests. The absolute measure of recipient military spending is utilized, along with the relative measure of recipient conscription rates.

The statistical relationships between aid flows and these recipient characteristics are presented in each of the tables. The relationships that are significant at either the .05 or the .01 level are designated as such. In-ferences are based upon consistent patterns of statistical significance; the absence of significant patterns, however, is also considered relevant in positing the relationships between donor interests and ODA commitments. Broader conclusions about the relationships accommodate other empirical patterns included in the analysis. Overall, the research strategy is designed to be readily replicated by other analysts; applications of the model to other states and other time periods are encouraged.

Appendix 2:
Primary Aid Donors to Recipient LDCs, 1988–1989

	France	Japan	Sweden	USA
Africa	Algeria Cameroon Central African Republic Chad Congo Djibouti Gabon Côte d'Ivoire Madagascar Mali Mauritania Mauritius Morocco Niger Senegal Togo Tunisia	Kenya Nigeria Rwanda Zambia Zimbabwe	Angola Mozambique	Egypt Liberia Zaire
Asia	Lebanon Syria	Bangladesh China India Indonesia Korea Laos Malaysia Nepal Pakistan Philippines Singapore Sri Lanka Turkey	Vietnam	Cyprus Israel Oman
Latin America	Colombia Mexico	Argentina Bolivia Brazil Chile Paraguay Uruguay	Nicaragua	Costa Rica Dominican Republic El Salvador Guatemala Haiti Honduras Jamaica

Source: OECD (1991b)

References

ACHESON, DEAN. (1969) *Present at the Creation*. New York: Norton.

AKIRA, KUBOTO. (1985) "Foreign Aid: Giving with One Hand?" *Japan Quarterly* 32 (April–June): 140–144.

ALDRICH, ROBERT, and JOHN CONNELL. (1989) "Francophonie: Language, Culture, or Politics?" pp. 170–193 in Robert Aldrich and John Connell, eds., *France in World Politics*. London: Routledge.

ALLISON, GRAHAM. (1971) *Essence of Decision: Explaining the Cuban Missile Crisis*. Boston: Little, Brown.

ANDERSON, STEPHEN J. (1993) "Latin America: Japan's Complementary Strategy in ODA?" pp. 275–288 in Robert M. Orr, Jr., and Bruce M. Koppel, eds., *Japanese Foreign Aid: Power and Policy in a New Era*. Boulder, CO: Westview.

ANDERSSON, CHRISTIAN. (1986) "Breaking Through: Politics and Public Opinion in the Period of Rapid Expansion," pp. 27–44 in Pierre Fruhling, ed., *Swedish Development Aid in Perspective*. Stockholm: Almquist and Wiksell.

ANDREN, NILS. (1967) *Power-Balance and Non-Alignment*. Stockholm: Almquist and Wiksell.

ARON, RAYMOND. (1966) *Peace and War: A Theory of International Relations*. Garden City, NY: Doubleday.

AUGUSTINE, SAINT. (1954 [425]). *City of God*. New York: Father of the Church, Inc.

AYRES, ROBERT L. (1983) *Banking on the Poor: The World Bank and World Poverty*. Cambridge, MA: MIT Press.

BACH, QUINTON V.S. (1987) *Soviet Economic Assistance to the Least-Developed Countries*. New York: Oxford University Press.

BAKER, ROBERT M., Jr. (1984) "Multilateral Development Banks," pp. 119–135 in John Wilhelm and Gerry Feinstein, eds., *U.S. Foreign Assistance: Investment or Folly?* New York: Praeger.

BALASSA, BELA, and MARCUS NOLAND. (1988) *Japan in the World Economy*. Washington, DC: Institute for International Economics.

BALBUS, ISAAK. (1978) "The Concept of Interest in Pluralist and Marxian Analysis," *Politics and Society* 1 (No. 2): 151–179.

BALDWIN, DAVID A. (1985) *Economic Statecraft*. Princeton, NJ: Princeton University Press.

———. (1966) *Foreign Aid and American Foreign Policy*. New York: Praeger.

BALTA, PAUL. (1986) "French Foreign Policy in North Africa," *Middle East Journal* 40 (Spring): 238–251.

BANFIELD, EDWARD. (1963) "American Foreign Aid Doctrines," pp. 10–31 in Robert A. Goldwin, ed., *Why Foreign Aid?* Chicago: Rand McNally and Co.

193

BARNET, RICHARD J. (1993) "Still Putting Arms First: The Cold War Legacy Confronting Clinton, Abroad and at Home," *Harper's* 286 (February): 59–65.
———. (1971) "The National Security Managers and the National Interest," *Politics and Society* 1 (February): 257–268.
BARTKE, WOLFGANG. (1975) *China's Economic Aid*. London: C. Hurst.
BAUER, PETER T. (1984) *Reality and Rhetoric: Studies in the Economics of Development*. Cambridge, MA: Harvard University Press.
BAUER, PETER T., and BASIL S. YAMEY (1983) "Foreign Aid: What Is at Stake?" pp. 75–115 in W. S. Thompson, ed., *The Third World: Premises of U.S. Policy*. San Francisco: Institute for Contemporary Studies.
BEARD, CHARLES A. (1934) *The Idea of National Interest: An Analytic Study of American Foreign Policy*. Chicago: Quadrangle.
BERG, ELLIOT. (1984) "The Effectiveness of Economic Assistance," pp. 187–219 in John Wilhelm and Gerry Feinstein, eds., *U.S. Foreign Assistance: Investment or Folly?* New York: Praeger.
BERLINER, JOSEPH S. (1958) *Soviet Economic Aid: The New Aid and Trade Policy in Underdeveloped Countries*. New York: Praeger.
BERTHELOT, YVES. (1973) "French Aid Performance and Development Policy," pp. 36–49 in Bruce Dinwiddy, ed., *European Development Policies: The United Kingdom, Sweden, France, EEC, and Multilateral Organizations*. New York: Praeger.
BLACHMAN, MORRIS J., WILLIAM M. LEOGRANDE, and KENNETH E. SHARPE, eds. (1987) *Confronting Revolution: Security Through Diplomacy in Central America*. New York: Pantheon.
BLACK, LLOYD D. (1968) *The Strategy of Foreign Aid*. Princeton, NJ: D. Van Nostrand, Inc.
BON, DANIEL, and KAREN MINGST. (1980) "French Intervention in Africa: Dependency or Decolonization?" *Africa Today* 27 (Spring): 5–20.
BOSE, ANURADHA, and PETER BURNELL, eds. (1991) *Britain's Overseas Aid Since 1979: Between Idealism and Self-Interest*. Manchester, UK: Manchester University Press.
BOYD, J. BARRON. (1982) "France and the Third World: The African Connection," pp. 45–65 in Phillip Taylor and Gregory A. Raymond, eds., *Third World Policies of Industrialized Nations*. Westport, CT: Greenwood Press.
BROWN, WILLIAM ADAMS, JR., and REDVERS OPIE. (1953) *American Foreign Assistance*. Washington, DC: Brookings Institution.
BRYNES, ASHER. (1966) *We Give to Conquer*. New York: W.W. Norton & Co.
BULL, HEDLEY. (1977) *The Anarchical Society*. New York: Columbia University Press.
BURTON, JOHN. (1972) *World Society*. New York: Cambridge University Press.
BYERS, R. B., and STANLEY ING. (1983) "Sharing the Burden on the Far Side of the Alliance: Japanese Security in the 1980s," *Journal of International Affairs* 37 (Summer): 163–175.
BYRD, PETER. (1991) "Foreign Policy and Overseas Aid," pp. 49–73 in Anuradha Bose and Peter Burnell, eds., *Britain's Overseas Aid Since 1979: Between Idealism and Self-Interest*. Manchester, UK: Manchester University Press.
CARDOSO, FERNANDO HENRIQUE. (1972) "Dependency and Development in Latin America," *New Left Review* 74 (July–August): 83–95.
CARLETON, DAVID, and MICHAEL STOHL. (1985) "The Foreign Policy of Human Rights: Rhetoric and Reality from Jimmy Carter to Ronald Reagan," *Human Rights Quarterly* 7 (May): 205–229.

CARR, E. H. (1939) *The Twenty Years' Crisis, 1919–1939: An Introduction to the Study of International Relations.* London: Macmillan.

CARTER, JIMMY. (1980) "U.S. Foreign Assistance," *Weekly Compilation of Presidential Documents* 16 (May 26): 941–944.

CASSEN, ROBERT, and ASSOCIATES. (1986) *Does Aid Work?* Oxford: Clarendon Press.

CASSIRER, ERNST. (1946) *The Myth of the State.* New Haven, CT: Yale University Press.

CASTLE, EUGENE W. (1955) *Billions, Blunders, and Baloney.* New York: Devin-Adair.

CERNY, PHILIP G. (1980) *The Politics of Grandeur: Ideological Aspects of de Gaulle's Foreign Policy.* Cambridge: Cambridge University Press.

CHAN, STEVE. (1992) "Humanitarianism, Mercantilism, or Comprehensive Security? Disbursement Patterns of Japanese Foreign Aid," *Asian Affairs* 19 (Spring): 3–17.

CHENERY, HOLLIS B. (1962) "Objectives and Criteria for Foreign Assistance," pp. 36–45 in Robert A. Goldwin, ed., *Why Foreign Aid?* Chicago: Rand McNally and Co.

CHILCOTE, RONALD H. (1984) *Theories of Development and Underdevelopment.* Boulder, CO: Westview.

CHILDS, MARQUIS W. (1980) *Sweden: The Middle Way on Trial.* New Haven, CT: Yale University Press.

CHRISTOPHER, WARREN. (1993) "Foreign Assistance Priorities After the Cold War," *Department of State Dispatch* 4 (May 31): 393–395.

CINGRANELLI, DAVID LOUIS. (1993) *Ethics, American Foreign Policy and the Third World.* New York: St. Martin's.

CINGRANELLI, DAVID LOUIS, and THOMAS PASQUARELLO. (1985) "Human Rights Practices and the Distribution of Foreign Aid to Latin American Countries," *American Journal of Political Science* 29 (August): 539–563.

CLAD, JAMES C., and ROGER D. STONE. (1993) "New Mission for Foreign Aid," *Foreign Affairs* 72 (Fall): 196–205.

CLAIRMONTE, FREDERICK. (1992) "The World's Top Arms Merchant," *World Press Review* (September): 13–18.

CLARK, ALAN. (1987) "Foreign Policy," pp. 107–136 in John E. Flower, ed., *France Today.* London: Methuen.

CLAUDE, INIS L., Jr. (1971) *Swords into Plowshares,* 4th ed. New York: Random House.

CLINTON, W. DAVID. (1994) *Two Faces of National Interest.* Baton Rouge, LA: Louisiana State University Press.

———. (1986) "The National Interest: Normative Foundations," *The Review of Politics* 48 (Fall): 495–519.

CONGRESSIONAL RESEARCH SERVICE. (1992) *Foreign Aid: Answers to Basic Questions.* Washington, DC: Congressional Research Service.

COOK, DONALD. (1983) *Charles De Gaulle.* New York: G. P. Putnam and Sons.

COOK, THOMAS, and MALCOLM MOOS. (1953) "The American Idea of International Interest," *American Political Science Review* 47 (March): 28–44.

COOPER, JOHN FRANKLIN. (1976) *China's Foreign Aid: An Instrument of Peking's Foreign Policy.* Lexington, MA: Lexington Books.

CRABB, CECIL V., Jr. (1986) *Policy Makers and Critics: Conflicting Theories of American Foreign Policy.* New York: Praeger.

CROPSEY, JOSEPH. (1963) "The Right of Foreign Aid," pp. 109–130 in Robert A. Goldwin, ed., *Why Foreign Aid?* Chicago: Rand McNally and Co.

DAHL, ROBERT A. (1971) *Polyarchy: Participation and Opposition.* New Haven, CT: Yale University Press.

DE GAULLE, CHARLES. (1964) *Major Addresses, Statements, and Press Conferences.* New York: French Embassy.

DEMONGEOT, PATRICK. (1984) "U.N. System Development Assistance," pp. 304–328 in John Wilhelm and Gerry Feinstein, eds., *U.S. Foreign Assistance: Investment or Folly?* New York: Praeger.

DE PORTE, ANTON W. (1984) "France's New Realism," *Foreign Affairs* 63 (Fall): 144–165.

DEUTSCH, KARL, and J. DAVID SINGER. (1964) "Multipolar Power Systems and International Stability," *World Politics* 16 (April): 390–406.

DEUTSCH, KARL W., et al. (1957) *Political Community and the North Atlantic Area.* Princeton, NJ: Princeton University Press.

DINWIDDY, BRUCE. (1973a) "The International Development Situation," pp. 7–21 in Bruce Dinwiddy, ed., *European Development Policies: The United Kingdom, Sweden, France, EEC, and Multilateral Organizations.* New York: Praeger.

———. (1973b) "United Kingdom: Performance and Policy," pp. 22–35 in Bruce Dinwiddy, ed., *European Development Policies: The United Kingdom, Sweden, France, EEC, and Multilateral Organizations.* New York: Praeger.

DOHERTY, CARROLL J. (1993) "Spending Aid Abroad," *Congressional Quarterly* (December 11): 74–84.

———. (1992) "Support for Foreign Aid Wilting Under Glare of Domestic Woes," *Congressional Quarterly* (May 16): 1351–1357.

DOHERTY, EILEEN MARIE. (1987) "Japan's Expanding Foreign Aid Program," *Asian Affairs* 14 (Fall): 129–149.

DOHLMAN, EBBA. (1989) *National Welfare and Economic Interdependence: The Case of Sweden's Foreign Trade Policy.* Oxford, UK: Clarendon Press.

DONNELLY, JACK. (1992) "Twentieth-Century Realism," pp. 85–111 in Terry Nardin and David R. Mapel, eds., *Traditions of International Ethics.* New York: Cambridge University Press.

DOYLE, MICHAEL. (1986) "Liberalism and World Politics," *American Political Science Review* 80 (December): 1151–1169.

EBERSTADT, NICHOLAS. (1988) *American Foreign Aid and American Purpose.* Washington, DC: American Enterprise Institute for Public Policy Research.

THE ECONOMIST. (1994) "Empty Promises," *The Economist* (May 7): 11.

———. (1993) "Borrowed Time," *The Economist* (May 22): 52.

EDGREN, GOSTA. (1986) "Changing Terms: Procedures and Relationships in Swedish Development Assistance," pp. 47–63 in Pierre Fruhling, ed., *Swedish Development Aid in Perspective.* Stockholm: Almquist and Wiksell.

EMMOTT, BILL. (1989) *The Sun Also Sets: The Limits to Japan's Economic Power.* New York: Times Books.

ENSIGN, MARGEE. (1992) *Doing Good or Doing Well? Japan's Foreign Aid Program.* New York: Columbia University Press.

EVANS, DOUGLAS. (1984) "New Directions Reconsidered," pp. 243–257 in John Wilhelm and Gerry Feinstein, eds., *U.S. Foreign Assistance: Investment or Folly?* New York: Praeger.

EVANS, HOWARD. (1989) "France and the Third World: Co-operation or Dependence?" pp. 126–147 in Robert Aldrich and John Connell, eds., *France in World Politics.* London: Routledge.

FALLOWS, JAMES. (1993) "Japan's Moment, and Ours," *The New York Times* (August 1): Section 4: 15.

————. (1989) *More Like Us.* Boston: Houghton Mifflin.
FARNSWORTH, LEE W. (1982) "Japan and the Third World," pp. 163–185 in Phillip Taylor and Gregory A. Raymond, eds., *Third World Policies of Industrialized Nations.* Westport, CT: Greenwood Press.
FENSKE, JOHN. (1991) "France's Uncertain Progress Toward European Union," *Current History* 90 (November): 358–362.
FERGUSON, YALE H., and RICHARD W. MANSBACH. (1988) *The Elusive Quest: Theory and International Politics.* Columbia, SC: University of South Carolina Press.
FORDE, STEVEN. (1992) "Classical Realism," pp. 62–84 in Terry Nardin and David R. Mapel, eds., *Traditions of International Ethics.* Cambridge: Cambridge University Press.
FRANK, ANDRE GUNDER. (1966) "The Development of Underdevelopment," *Monthly Review* 18 (September): 17–31.
FRANK, CHARLES R., JR., and MARY BAIRD. (1975) "Foreign Aid: Its Speckled Past and Future Prospects," *International Organization* 29 (Winter): 133–167.
FRANKEL, JOSEPH. (1970) *National Interest.* London: Macmillan.
————. (1969) "National Interest: A Vindication," *International Journal* 24 (Autumn): 717–725.
FUKUYAMA, FRANCIS. (1990) "The End of History?" *The National Interest* 16 (Summer): 3–18.
GADDIS, JOHN LEWIS. (1987) *The Long Peace: Inquiries into the History of the Cold War.* New York: Oxford University Press.
GALTUNG, JOHAN. (1991) "The New International Order and the Basic Needs Approach," pp. 287–307 in Kendall W. Stiles and Tsuneo Akaha, eds., *International Political Economy: A Reader.* New York: Harper Collins.
GELB, LESLIE H. (1992) "Not Set in Stone," *The New York Times* (November 6): Section 4: 19.
GEORGE, ALEXANDER, and ROBERT O. KEOHANE. (1980) "The Concept of National Interest: Uses and Limitations," pp. 217–237 in Alexander George, ed., *Presidential Decisionmaking and Foreign Policy.* Boulder, CO: Westview.
GILPIN, ROBERT. (1987) *The Political Economy of International Relations.* Princeton, NJ: Princeton University Press.
————. (1981) *War and Change in World Politics.* New York: Cambridge University Press.
————. (1975) *U.S. Power and the Multinational Corporation: The Political Economy of Foreign Direct Investment.* New York: Basic Books.
GIMLIN, HOYT. (1988) "Foreign Aid: A Declining Commitment," *Editorial Research Reports.* Washington, DC: Congressional Quarterly.
GOLDMAN, MARSHALL. (1967) *Soviet Foreign Aid.* New York: Praeger.
GOLDMANN, KJELL. (1986) "'Democracy is Incompatible with International Politics': Reconsideration of a Hypothesis," pp. 1–43 in Kjell Goldmann, Sten Berglund, and Gunnar Sjostedt, eds., *Democracy and Foreign Policy: The Case of Sweden.* Brookfield, VT: Gower.
GOOD, ROBERT C. (1960) "The National Interest and Political Realism: Niebuhr's 'Debate' with Morgenthau and Kennan," *Journal of Politics* 22 (November): 597–619.
GREENHOUSE, STEVEN. (1994) "U.S. Promises $1 Billion for South African Projects," *New York Times* (October 6): A4.
GROSSER, ALFRED. (1967) *French Foreign Policy Under de Gaulle.* Boston: Little, Brown.

GUESS, GEORGE M. (1987) *The Politics of United States Foreign Aid*. New York: St. Martin's.

GULUCK, EDWARD V. (1967) *Europe's Classical Balance of Power*. New York: Norton.

HAAS, ERNST. (1964) *Beyond the Nation-State: Functionalism and International Organization*. Stanford, CA: Stanford University Press.

HADLEY, ELENOR M. (1970) *Antitrust in Japan*. Princeton, NJ: Princeton University Press.

HAIG, ALEXANDER. (1981) "Secretary Haig Discusses Foreign Assistance," *Department of State Bulletin* 81 (April): 21–22.

HAITANI, KANJI. (1976) *The Japanese Economic System: An Institutional Overview*. Lexington, MA: D. C. Heath.

HALPERIN, MORTON. (1974) *Bureaucratic Politics and Foreign Policy*. Washington, DC: Brookings Institution.

HANCOCK, GRAHAM. (1989) *Lords of Poverty: The Power, Prestige, and Corruption of the International Aid Business*. New York: The Atlantic Monthly Press.

HANCOCK, M. DONALD. (1972) *The Politics of Post-Industrial Change*. London: Holt, Rinehart, and Winston.

HARRISON, MICHAEL M. (1984) "France Under the Socialists," *Current History* 83 (April): 153–156.

HASEGAWA, SUKEHIRO. (1975) *Japanese Foreign Aid: Policy and Practice*. New York: Praeger.

HAYTER, THERESA. (1971) *Aid as Imperialism*. Middlesex, England: Penguin Books.

———. (1966) *French Aid*. London: Overseas Development Institute.

HAYTER, THERESA, and CATHERINE WATSON. (1985) *Aid: Rhetoric and Reality*. London: Pluto Press.

HECLO, HUGH, and HENRIK MADSEN. (1987) *Policy and Politics in Sweden: Principled Pragmatism*. Philadelphia: Temple University Press.

HELLINGER, STEPHEN, DOUGLAS HELLINGER, and FRED M. O'REGAN. (1988) *Aid for Just Development: Report on the Future of Foreign Assistance*. Boulder, CO: Lynne Rienner.

HEPPLING, SIXTEN. (1986) "The Very First Years: Memoirs of an Insider," pp. 13–26 in Pierre Fruhling, ed., *Swedish Development Aid in Perspective*. Stockholm: Almquist and Wiksell.

HERZ, JOHN. (1951) *Political Realism and Political Idealism*. Chicago: University of Chicago Press.

HOBBES, THOMAS. (1973 [1652]) *Leviathan*. London: Dent.

HOFFMANN, STANLEY. (1984–1985) "Gaullism by Any Other Name," *Foreign Policy* 68 (Winter): 38–57.

———. (1978) *Primacy or World Order: American Foreign Policy Since the Cold War*. New York: McGraw-Hill.

———. (1974) *Decline or Renewal: French Politics Since the 1930s*. New York: Viking.

HOLBIK, KAREL, and HENRY ALLEN MYERS. (1968) *West German Foreign Aid, 1956–1966*. Boston: Boston University Press.

HOLMBERG, SUSAN L. (1989) "Welfare Abroad: Swedish Development Assistance," pp. 123–166 in Bengt Sundelius, ed., *The Committed Neutral: Sweden's Foreign Policy*. Boulder, CO: Westview.

HOLSTI, KAL J. (1988) *International Politics: A Framework for Analysis*, 5th ed. Englewood Cliffs, NJ: Prentice-Hall.

————. (1985) *The Dividing Discipline: Hegemony and Diversity in International Theory.* Boston: Unwin Hyman.

————. (1970) "National Role Conceptions in the Study of Foreign Policy," *International Studies Quarterly* 14 (September): 233–309.

HOOK, STEVEN W. (1993) "Domestic Agendas Versus Global Markets: Carter, Reagan, and U.S. Arms Sales," *Southeastern Political Review* 21 (Summer): 569–592.

HORVATH, JANOS. (1976) *Chinese Technical Transfers to the Third World.* New York: Praeger.

HOUGH, RICHARD L. (1982) *Economic Assistance and Security: Rethinking U.S. Policy.* Washington, DC: National Defense University.

HOWORTH, JOLYON. (1986) "Resources and Strategic Choices: French Defense Policy at the Crossroads," *World Today* 42 (May): 77–80.

HUDSON, MICHAEL. (1971) "The Political Economy of Foreign Aid," pp. 73–121 in Denis Goulet and Michael Hudson, eds., *The Myth of Aid: The Hidden Agenda of the Development Reports.* New York: IDOC.

HUNTER, SHIREEN. (1984) *OPEC and the Third World: The Politics of Aid.* London: Croom Helm.

HUNTINGTON, SAMUEL. (1970–1971) "Foreign Aid For What and For Whom," *Foreign Policy* 1 (Winter): 161–189.

————. (1968) *Political Order in Changing Societies.* New Haven, CT: Yale University Press.

IBRAHIM, YOUSSEF M. (1994) "PLO Pleads for Faster Disbursements of Foreign Aid Money," *The New York Times* (June 10): A3.

IKENBERRY, G. JOHN. (1988) "An Institutional Approach to American Foreign Economic Policy," pp. 219–243 in G. John Ikenberry, David A. Lake, and Michael Mastanduno, eds., *The State and American Foreign Economic Policy.* Ithaca, NY: Cornell University Press.

INSTITUTE FOR EAST-WEST SECURITY STUDIES. (1992) *Moving Beyond Assistance.* Boulder, CO: Westview.

INTERNATIONAL MONETARY FUND. (1982–1991) *Direction of Trade Statistics.* Washington, DC: International Monetary Fund.

INUKAI, ICHIRO. (1993) "Why Aid and Why Not? Japan and Sub-Saharan Africa," pp. 252–274 in Robert M. Orr, Jr., and Bruce M. Koppel, eds., *Japanese Foreign Aid: Power and Policy in a New Era.* Boulder, CO: Westview.

JACOBY, RUTH. (1986) "Idealism Versus Economics: Swedish Aid and Commercial Interests," pp. 85–100 in Pierre Fruhling, ed., *Swedish Development Aid in Perspective.* Stockholm: Almquist and Wiksell.

JANIS, IRVING. (1982) *Groupthink: Psychological Studies of Policy Decisions and Fiascoes,* 2nd ed. Boston: Houghton Mifflin.

JANSSEN, RICHARD F. (1991) "Business Role Abroad: Reagan Team Hopes to Cut Foreign-aid Burden by Encouraging Private Projects in Third World," *The Wall Street Journal* (April 14): 56.

JAPANESE GOVERNMENT. (1994) Interview with Economic Officer Kenko Sone. Japanese Embassy, Washington, DC, March 30.

————. (1993a, 1992a, 1991) *Official Development Assistance.* Tokyo: Ministry of Foreign Affairs.

————. (1993b) *Outlook of Japan's Economic Cooperation.* Tokyo: Economic Cooperation Bureau.

————. (1992b) *A Guide to Japan's Aid.* Tokyo: Association for Promotion of International Cooperation.

JERVIS, ROBERT. (1976) *Perception and Misperception in International Politics.* Princeton, NJ: Princeton University Press.

JINADU, L. ADELE. (1984) "The Political Economy of Sweden's Development Policy in Africa," *Cooperation and Conflict* 19 (No. 3): 177–196.

JOHANSEN, ROBERT C. (1980) *The National Interest and the Human Interest: An Analysis of U.S. Foreign Policy*. Princeton, NJ: Princeton University Press.

JOHNSON, CHALMERS. (1993) "The Tremor: Japan's Post–Cold War Destiny," *The New Republic* 209 (August 9): 21–27.

———. (1985) "Political Institutions and Economic Performance: The Government-Business Relationships in Japan, South Korea, and Taiwan," in Robert Scalapino, et al., eds., *Asian Economic Development: Present and Future*. Berkeley, CA: Institute for East Asian Studies.

———. (1982) *MITI and the Japanese Miracle*. Palo Alto, CA: Stanford University Press.

JOHNSON, JAMES TURNER. (1987) *The Quest for Peace: Three Moral Traditions in Western Cultural History*. Princeton, NJ: Princeton University Press.

KAPLAN, EUGENE J. (1972) *Japan: The Government-Business Relationship*. Washington, DC: U.S. Department of Commerce.

KAPLAN, JACOB J. (1967) *The Challenge of Foreign Aid: Policies, Problems, and Possibilities*. New York: Praeger.

KARRE, BO, and BENGT SVENSSON. (1989) "The Determinants of Swedish Aid Policy," pp. 231–274 in Olav Stokke, ed., *Western Middle Powers and Global Poverty*. Uppsale: Scandinavian Institute of African Studies.

KARSH, EFRAIM. (1988) *Neutrality and Small States*. London: Routledge.

KEGLEY, CHARLES W., Jr. (1987) "Decision Regimes and the Comparative Study of Foreign Policy," pp. 247–268 in Charles F. Herrmann, Charles W. Kegley, Jr., and James N. Rosenau, eds., *New Directions in the Study of Foreign Policy*. Boston: Allen and Unwin.

———. (1980) *Paradigm Lost? The Comparative Study of Foreign Policy*. Columbia, SC: Institute of International Studies.

———. (1973) *A General Empirical Typology of Foreign Policy Behavior*. Beverly Hills: Sage.

KEGLEY, CHARLES W., Jr., and STEVEN W. HOOK. (1991) "U.S. Foreign Aid and U.N. Voting: Did Reagan's Linkage Strategy Buy Deference or Defiance?" *International Studies Quarterly* 35 (September): 295–312.

KEGLEY, CHARLES W., Jr., GREGORY A. RAYMOND, ROBERT M. WOOD, and RICHARD A. SKINNER. (1975) *International Events and the Comparative Analysis of Foreign Policy*. Columbia, SC: University of South Carolina Press.

KEGLEY, CHARLES W., Jr., and EUGENE R. WITTKOPF. (1993) *World Politics: Trend and Transformation*, 4th ed. New York: St. Martin's Press.

KENNAN, GEORGE F. (1951) *American Diplomacy, 1900–1950*. Chicago: University of Chicago Press.

KEOHOANE, ROBERT O. (1984a) *After Hegemony: Cooperation and Discord in the World Political Economy*. Princeton, NJ: Princeton University Press.

———, ed. (1984b) *Neorealism and Its Critics*. New York: Columbia University Press.

———. (1982) "The Demand for International Regimes," *International Organization* 36 (Spring): 325–355.

———. (1980) "The Theory of Hegemonic Stability and Changes in International Economic Relations, 1966–1977," pp. 131–162 in Ole Holsti, Randolph Siverson, and Alexander George, eds., *Changes in the International System*. Boulder, CO: Westview.

KEOHANE, ROBERT O., and JOSEPH S. NYE, Jr. (1989) *Power and Interdependence*, 2nd ed. Glenview, IL: Scott, Foresman.

KINDLEBERGER, CHARLES P. (1987) *Marshall Plan Days*. Boston: Allen and Unwin.

———. (1973) *The World in Depression, 1929–1939*. Berkeley, CA: University of California Press.

KIRSCHTEN, DICK. (1993) "Rescuing AID," *National Journal* (October 2): 2369–2372.

KISSINGER, HENRY. (1994) *Diplomacy*. New York: Simon and Schuster.

KLARE, MICHAEL T. (1987) "The Arms Trade: Changing Patterns in the 1980s," *Third World Quarterly* 9 (October): 1257–1281.

KNORR, KLAUS. (1973) *Power and Wealth.* New York: Basic Books.

KNUSEL, JACK L. (1968) *West German Aid to Developing Nations*. New York: Praeger.

KNUTSEN, TORBJORN L. (1992) *A History of International Relations Theory*. Manchester, UK: Manchester University Press.

KOLKO, GABRIEL, and JOYCE KOLKO. (1972) *The Limits of Power: The World and United States Foreign Policy, 1945–1954*. New York: Harper and Row.

KOLODZIEJ, EDWARD A. (1974) *French Foreign Policy Under De Gaulle and Pompidou: The Politics of Grandeur*. Ithaca, NY: Cornell University Press.

KOTANI, TORU. (1985) "Africa and Japan: Rising Sun Over Africa?" *Africa Report* 30 (November–December): 68–71.

KRASNER STEPHEN D., ed. (1983) *International Regimes*. Ithaca, NY: Cornell University Press.

———. (1982) "Structural Causes and Regime Consequences: Regimes as Intervening Variables," *International Organization* 36 (Spring): 185–206.

———. (1978) *Defending the National Interest: Raw Materials Investment and U.S. Foreign Policy*. Princeton, NJ: Princeton University Press.

KRATOCHWIL, FRIEDRICH. (1982) "On the Notion of 'Interest' in International Relations," *International Organization* 36 (Winter): 1–30.

KRAUTHAMMER, CHARLES. (1991) "The Unipolar Moment," *Foreign Affairs* 70 (Fall): 23–33.

KRONHOLZ, JUNE. (1981) "France's Role in Africa: The Colonial Master Who Didn't Go Home," *The Wall Street Journal* (July 22): 1, 26.

KRUZEL, JOSEPH. (1989) "Sweden's Security Dilemma: Balancing Domestic Realities with the Obligations of Neutrality," pp. 67–93 in Bengt Sundelius, ed., *The Committed Neutral: Sweden's Foreign Policy*. Boulder, CO: Westview.

LAIRD, ROBBIN F. (1984) "The French Strategic Dilemma," *Orbis* 28 (Summer): 307–328.

LAIRSON, THOMAS D., and DAVID SKIDMORE. (1993) *International Political Economy: The Struggle for Wealth and Power*. Fort Worth, TX: Harcourt Brace Jovanovich.

LAKE, DAVID A. (1988) *Power, Protection, and Free Trade: International Sources of U.S. Commercial Strategy, 1887–1939*. Ithaca, NY: Cornell University Press.

———. (1983) "International Economic Structures and American Foreign Economic Policy, 1887–1934," *World Politics* 36 (Summer): 517–543.

LAL, DEEPAK. (1985) "The Misconceptions of Development Economics," *Finance and Development* 22 (June): 10–14.

LAPPÉ, FRANCES MOORE, RACHEL SCHURMAN, and KEVIN DANAHER. (1987) *Betraying the National Interest*. New York: Grove Press.

LAPPÉ, FRANCES MOORE, JOSEPH COLLINS, and DAVID KINLEY. (1981) *Aid as Obstacle: Twenty Questions About our Foreign Aid and the Hungry*. San Francisco: Institute for Food Policy.

LEBOVIC, JAMES H. (1988) "National Interests and U.S. Foreign Aid: The Carter and Reagan Years," *Journal of Peace Research* 25 (June): 115–135.

LELE, UMA, and IJAZ NABI, eds. (1991) *Transitions in Development: The Role of Aid and Commercial Flows.* San Francisco: ICS Press.

LENIN, VLADIMIR I. (1939) *Imperialism, the Highest Stage of Capitalism.* New York: International Publishers.

LEWIS, JEAN C. (1984) "A Historical Look at Objectives of Foreign Aid, Congressional Action, and Legislative Changes, 1961–1982," pp. 24–28 in John Wilhelm and Gerry Feinstein, eds., *U.S. Foreign Assistance: Investment or Folly?* New York: Praeger.

LINEAR, MARCUS. (1985) *Zapping the Third World: The Disaster of Development Aid.* London: Pluto Press.

LISKA, GEORGE. (1960) *The New Statecraft: Foreign Aid in American Foreign Policy.* Chicago: University of Chicago Press.

LJUNGGREN, BORJE. (1986) "Swedish Goals and Priorities," pp. 65–83 in Pierre Fruhling, ed., *Swedish Development Aid in Perspective.* Stockholm: Almquist and Wiksell.

LOUTFI, MARTHA. (1973) *The Net Cost of Japanese Foreign Aid.* New York: Praeger.

LOW, O. A. (1980) "Francophone Africa and France: A Special Case of North-South Relations," *Barclay's Review:* 85–88.

LUCAS, ROBERT E. (1988) "On the Mechanics of Economic Development," *Journal of Monetary Economics* 22 (July): 2–42.

LUMSDAINE, DAVID H. (1993) *Moral Vision in International Politics: The Foreign Aid Regime, 1949–1989.* Princeton, NJ: Princeton University Press.

LUTTWAK, EDWARD. (1990) "From Geopolitics to Geoeconomics," *The National Interest* 20 (Summer): 17–23.

MACHIAVELLI, NICCOLO. (1985 [1532]) *The Prince.* Translated by Harvey C. Mansfield, Jr. Chicago: University of Chicago Press.

MACRIDIS, ROY. (1992) "French Foreign Policy: The Quest for Rank," pp. 32–67 in Roy Macridis, ed., *Foreign Policy in World Politics.* Englewood Cliffs, NJ: Prentice-Hall.

MADISON, JAMES. (1938 [1787]) "Federalist 10," pp. 53–62 in *The Federalist Papers,* edited by Edward Mead Earle. New York: The Modern Library.

MANNING, PATRICK. (1988) *Francophone Sub-Saharan Africa, 1880–1985.* New York: Cambridge University Press.

MARCUS, AMY DOCKSER. (1993) "Israel Takes Steps Toward Closer Ties with EC, Partly Due to U.S.'s Uncertain Mood on Aid," *The Wall Street Journal* (August 24): A6.

MARTIN, GUY. (1985) "The Historical, Economic, and Political Bases of France's African Policy," *Journal of Modern African Studies* 23 (June): 189–208.

MARX, KARL. (1989) *Basic Writings on Politics and Philosophy.* Edited by Lewis S. Feuer. New York: Anchor Books.

McCORD, WILLIAM. (1991) *The Dawn of the Pacific Century: Implications for Three Worlds of Development.* New Brunswick, NJ: Transaction Publishers.

McCORMICK, JAMES M., and NEIL J. MITCHELL. (1989) "Human Rights and Foreign Assistance: An Update," *Social Science Quarterly* 70 (December): 969–979.

McGUIRE, MARK F., and VERNON W. RUTTAN. (1990) "Lost Directions: U.S. Foreign Assistance Policy Since New Directions," *Journal of Developing Areas* 24 (January): 127–179.

McKINLAY, ROBERT D. (1979) "The Aid Relationship: A Foreign Policy Model and Interpretation of the Distribution of Official Bilateral Economic Aid of the United States, the United Kingdom, France, and Germany, 1960–1970," *Comparative Political Studies* 1 (January): 411–463.

McKINLAY, ROBERT D., and RICHARD LITTLE. (1979) "The U.S. Aid Relationship: A Test of the Recipient Need and the Donor Interest Models," *Political Studies* 27 (June): 236–250.

———. (1978) "A Foreign Policy Model of the Distribution of British Bilateral Aid, 1960–1970," *British Journal of Political Science* 8 (July): 313–331.

———. (1977) "A Foreign Policy Model of U.S. Bilateral Aid Allocation," *World Politics* 30 (October): 58–86.

McKINLAY, ROBERT D., and ANTHONY MUGHAN. (1984) *Aid and Arms to the Third World: An Analysis of the Distribution of U.S. Official Transfers.* London: Francis Pinter.

McNEIL, D. (1981) *The Contradictions of Foreign Aid.* London: Croom Helm.

MEIER, GERALD M. (1984) *Emerging from Poverty: The Economics that Really Matters.* New York: Oxford University Press.

MEINECKE, FRIEDRICH. (1957) *Machiavellianism: The Doctrine of Raison D'état and Its Place in Modern History.* London: Routledge and Kegan Paul.

MENDE, TIBOR. (1973) *From Aid to Re-Colonization: Lessons of a Failure.* London: Harrap.

MERTZ, ROBERT ANTON, and PAMELA MACDONALD MERTZ. (1983) *Arab Aid to Sub-Saharan Africa.* Boulder, CO: Westview.

MICKELWAIT, DONALD R., CHARLES F. SWEET, and ELLIOT R. MORSS. (1979) *New Directions in Development: A Study of U.S. Aid.* Boulder, CO: Westview.

MIKESELL, RAYMOND F. (1983) *The Economics of Foreign Aid and Self-Sustaining Development.* Boulder, CO: Westview.

MILLIKAN, MAX F. (1963) "The Political Case for Economic Development Aid," pp. 90–108 in Robert H. Goldwin, ed., *Why Foreign Aid?* Chicago: Rand McNally and Co.

MILNER, HENRY. (1989) *Sweden: Social Democracy in Practice.* New York: Oxford University Press.

MITRANY, DAVID. (1946) *A Working Peace System: An Argument for the Functional Development of International Organization*, 4th ed. London: National Peace Council.

MOISI, DOMINIQUE. (1981–1982) "Mitterrand's Foreign Policy: The Limits of Continuity," *Foreign Affairs* 60 (Winter): 347–357.

MONTGOMERY, JOHN D. (1962) *The Politics of Foreign Aid.* New York: Praeger.

MOON, BRUCE E. (1991) *The Political Economy of Basic Human Needs.* Ithaca, NY: Cornell University Press.

MOORE, MICK, and MARK ROBINSON. (1994) "Can Foreign Aid be Used to Promote Good Government in Developing Countries?" *Ethics and International Affairs* 8: 141–158.

MORGENTHAU, HANS J. (1963) "Preface to a Political Theory of Foreign Aid," pp. 70–89 in Robert H. Goldwin, ed., *Why Foreign Aid?* Chicago: Rand McNally and Co.

———. (1951) *In Defense of the National Interest.* New York: Knopf.

MORGENTHAU, HANS J., and KENNETH W. THOMPSON. (1985) *Politics Among Nations: The Struggle for Power and Peace*, 6th ed. New York: Knopf.

MORLEY, LORNA, and FELIX MORLEY. (1961) *The Patchwork History of Foreign Aid*. Washington, DC: American Enterprise Institute.

MORSE, EDWARD L. (1973) *Foreign Policy and Interdependence in Gaullist France*. Princeton, NJ: Princeton University Press.

MORSE, ROBERT. (1987) "Japan's Drive to Pre-eminence," *Foreign Policy* 69 (Winter): 3–21.

MORTON, KATHRYN. (1973) "Britain's One Per Cent," pp. 74–89 in Bruce Dinwiddy, ed., *European Development Policies: The United Kingdom, Sweden, France, EEC, and Multilateral Organizations*. New York: Praeger.

MOSLEY, PAUL. (1987) *Foreign Aid: Its Defense and Reform*. Lexington, KY: University of Kentucky Press.

MOST, BENJAMIN, and HARVEY STARR. (1989) *Inquiry, Logic, and International Politics*. Columbia, SC: University of South Carolina Press.

MUELLER, JOHN. (1989) *Retreat from Doomsday: The Obsolescence of Major War*. New York: Basic Books.

MULLER, KURT. (1967) *The Foreign Aid Programs of the Soviet Bloc and Communist China*. New York: Walker and Co.

MYRDAL, GUNNAR. (1971) *Economic Theory and Underdeveloped Regions*. New York: Harper and Row.

————. (1960) *Beyond the Welfare State*. New Haven, CT: Yale University Press.

NORTH, ROBERT C. (1990) *War, Peace, Survival*. Boulder, CO: Westview.

NUVEEN, JOHN. (1962) "Social and Political Aid," pp. 46–69 in Robert H. Goldwin, ed., *Why Foreign Aid?* Chicago: Rand McNally and Co.

NYE, JOSEPH S., Jr. (1990) *Bound to Lead: The Changing Nature of American Power*. New York: Basic Books.

OBEY, DAVID R., and CAROL LANCASTER. (1988) "Funding Foreign Aid," *Foreign Policy* 71 (Summer): 141–155.

OHLIN, GORAN. (1973) "Swedish Aid Performance and Development Policy," pp. 50–62 in Bruce Dinwiddy, ed., *European Development Policies: The United Kingdom, Sweden, France, EEC, and Multilateral Organizations*. New York: Praeger.

————. (1966) *Foreign Aid Policies Reconsidered*. Paris: OECD.

O'LEARY, MICHAEL KENT. (1967) *The Politics of American Foreign Aid*. New York: Atherton Press.

OLSEN, GREGG M. (1992) *The Struggle for Economic Democracy in Sweden*. Aldershot, UK: Avebury.

OLSON, MANCUR. (1971) "Increasing the Incentives for International Cooperation," *International Organization* 25 (Fall): 866–874.

ORGANIZATION FOR ECONOMIC COOPERATION AND DEVELOPMENT (1981a–1994a, 1979, 1974). *Development Co-operation: Efforts and Policies of the Members of the Development Assistance Committee*. Paris: OECD.

————. (1981b–1994b). *Geographic Distribution of Financial Flows to Developing Countries*. Paris: OECD.

————. (1983). *World Economic Interdependence and the Evolving North-South Relationship*. Paris: OECD.

ORR, ROBERT M., Jr. (1993) "Japanese Foreign Aid: Over a Barrel in the Middle East," pp. 289–304 in Robert M. Orr, Jr., and Bruce M. Koppel, eds., *Japanese Foreign Aid: Power and Policy in a New Era*. Boulder, CO: Westview.

————. (1990) *The Emergence of Japan's Foreign Aid Power*. New York: Columbia University Press.

————. (1987) "The Rising Sun: Japan's Foreign Assistance to ASEAN, the Pacific Basin, and the Republic of Korea," *Journal of International Affairs* 41 (Summer–Fall): 39–62.

ORR, ROBERT M., JR., and BRUCE M. KOPPEL. (1993) "A Donor of Consequence: Japan as a Foreign Aid Power," pp. 1–18 in Robert M. Orr, Jr., and Bruce M. Koppel, eds., *Japanese Foreign Aid: Power and Policy in a New Era.* Boulder, CO: Westview.

OSGOOD, ROBERT E. (1953) *Ideals and Self-Interest in America's Foreign Relations.* Chicago: University of Chicago Press.

PACKENHAM, ROBERT. (1973) *Liberal America and the Third World: Political Development Ideas in Foreign Aid and Social Science.* Princeton, NJ: Princeton University Press.

PADDOCK, WILLIAM, and ELIZABETH PADDOCK. (1973) *We Don't Know How: An Independent Audit of What They Call Success in Foreign Assistance.* Ames: Iowa State University Press.

PALME, OLAF. (1982) "Sweden's Role in the World," pp. 234–253 in Bengt Ryden and Villy Bergstrom, eds., *Sweden: Choices for Economic and Social Policy in the 1980s.* London: George Allen and Unwin.

PALMLUND, THORD. (1986) "Altruism and Other Motives: Swedish Development Aid and Foreign Policy," pp. 109–125 in Pierre Fruhling, ed., *Swedish Development Aid in Perspective.* Stockholm: Almquist and Wiksell.

PARKINSON, JOHN R. (1983) "A Window on the World," pp. 1–11 in John R. Parkinson, ed., *Poverty and Aid.* New York: St. Martin's.

PASTOR, ROBERT A. (1980) *Congress and the Politics of U.S. Foreign Economic Policy, 1929–1976.* Berkeley, CA: University of California Press.

PATERSON, THOMAS G. (1974) "Foreign Aid as a Diplomatic Weapon," pp. 69–81 in Thomas G. Paterson, ed., *The Origins of the Cold War.* Lexington, MA: D. C. Heath.

PIERRE, ANDREW J. (1982) *The Global Politics of Arms Sales.* Princeton, NJ: Princeton University Press.

POGGI, GIANFRANCO. (1978) *The Development of the Modern State.* Stanford, CA: Stanford University Press.

PREBISCH, RAÚL. (1959) "The Role of Commercial Policy in Underdeveloped Countries," *American Economic Review* 49 (May): 251–273.

PRICE, HARRY BAYARD. (1955) *The Marshall Plan and Its Meaning.* Ithaca, NY: Cornell University Press.

PRLJA, ALEKSANDER. (1982) "France Between East and West," *Review of International Affairs* 33 (April): 18–21.

QUANSHENG, ZHAO. (1993) "Japan's Aid Diplomacy with China," pp. 163–187 in Robert M. Orr, Jr., and Bruce M. Koppel, eds., *Japanese Foreign Aid: Power and Policy in a New Era.* Boulder, CO: Westview.

RAPPAPORT, ARMIN. (1966) *Sources in American Diplomacy.* New York: Macmillan.

REAGAN, RONALD. (1981) "Statement at the First Plenary Session of the International Meeting on Cooperation and Development," *Weekly Compilation of Presidential Documents* 17 (Nov. 2): 1185–1188.

REILLY, JOHN E. (1988) "America's State of Mind: Trends in Public Attitudes Toward Foreign Policy," pp. 45–56 in Charles W. Kegley, Jr., and Eugene R. Wittkopf, eds., *The Domestic Sources of American Foreign Policy.* New York: St. Martin's.

RICHARDS, ANNE. (1992) "The Developing Countries and the World Trading System," *The OECD Observer* 177 (August/September): 23–25.

RICHARDSON, NEIL R. (1978) *Foreign Policy and Economic Dependence.* Austin: University of Texas Press.

RIDING, ALAN. (1994) "French Socialist Leader Faces Unrest in Party," *The New York Times* (June 16): A4.

RIX, ALAN. (1989–1990) "Japan's Foreign Aid: A Capacity for Leadership?" *Pacific Affairs* 62 (Winter): 463–464.

———. (1980) *Japan's Economic Aid: Policy-Making and Politics*. New York: St. Martin's.

ROBINSON, LINDA. (1991) *Intervention or Neglect: The United States and Central America Beyond the 1980s*. New York: Council on Foreign Relations.

ROCHESTER, J. MARTIN. (1978) "The 'National Interest' and Contemporary World Politics," *Review of Politics* 40 (January): 77–96.

ROEDER, PHILIP G. (1985) "The Ties that Bind: Aid, Trade, and Political Compliance in Soviet Third World Relations," *International Studies Quarterly* 29 (June): 191–216.

ROPER, BURNS W. (1979) "The Limits of Public Support," *Annals of the Academy of Political and Social Science* 442 (March): 40–45.

ROSATI, JEREL. (1987) *The Carter Administration's Quest for Global Community*. Columbia, SC: University of South Carolina Press.

ROSECRANCE, RICHARD. (1986) *The Rise of the Trading State: Commerce and Conquest in the Modern World*. New York: Basic Books.

ROSECRANCE, RICHARD, and JENNIFER TAW. (1990) "Japan and the Theory of International Leadership," *World Politics* 62 (January): 184–209.

ROSENAU, JAMES N. (1990) *Turbulence in World Politics*. Princeton, NJ: Princeton University Press.

———. (1987) "Roles and Role Scenarios in Foreign Policy," pp. 44–65 in Stephen G. Walker, ed., *Role Theory and Foreign Policy Analysis*. Durham, NC: Duke University Press.

———. (1980) *The Study of Political Adaptation*. New York: Nichols.

———. (1968) "National Interest," *International Encyclopedia of the Social Sciences*. New York: Free Press.

———. (1966) "Pre-Theories and Theories of Foreign Policy," pp. 27–92 in R. Barry Farrell, ed., *Approaches to Comparative and International Politics*. Evanston, IL: Northwestern University Press.

ROSENSTEIN-RODAN, PAUL N. (1943) "Problems of Industrialization in Eastern and South-Eastern Europe," *Economic Journal* 53 (June): 202–211.

ROSTOW, W. W. (1985) *Eisenhower, Kennedy, and Foreign Aid*. Austin: University of Texas Press.

———. (1971) *Politics and the Stages of Growth*. New York: Cambridge University Press.

———. (1960) *The United States in the World Arena*. New York: Clarion.

RUBIN, SEYMOUR J. (1966) *The Conscience of the Rich Nations: The Development Assistance Committee and the Common Aid Effort*. New York: Council on Foreign Relations.

RUDEBECK, LARS. (1984) "Swedish Development Aid in Times of Economic Realities," *Scandinavian Review* 72 (Winter): 49–55.

———. (1982) "Nordic Policies Toward the Third World," pp. 143–176 in Bengt Sundelius, ed., *Foreign Policies of Northern Europe*. Boulder, CO: Westview.

RUGGIE, JOHN G. (1972) "Collective Goods and Future International Collaboration," *American Political Science Review* 66 (September): 874–893.

RUSSETT, BRUCE M. (1990) *Controlling the Sword: The Democratic Governance of National Security*. Cambridge, MA: Harvard University Press.

RUSSETT, BRUCE M., and JOHN S. SULLIVAN. (1971) "Collective Goods and International Organization," *International Organization* 25: 845–865.

SAMUELSON, KURT. (1975) "The Philosophy of Swedish Welfare Polities," pp. 335–353 in Steven Koblik, ed., *Sweden's Development from Poverty to Affluence, 1750–1970*. Minneapolis: University of Minnesota Press.

SCALAPINO, ROBERT A. (1992) "The Foreign Policy of Modern Japan," pp. 186–221 in Roy A. Macridis, ed., *Foreign Policy in World Politics*, 8th ed. Englewood Cliffs, NJ: Prentice-Hall.

SCHLESINGER, ARTHUR M., Jr. (1989) *The Imperial Presidency*, 2nd ed. Boston: Houghton Mifflin.

SCHMOOKLER, ANDREW B. (1984) *Parable of the Tribes*. Berkeley, CA: University of California Press.

———. (1983) "An Overview of Japan's Economic Success: Its Sources and Implications for the United States," *Journal of East Asian Affairs* 3 (Fall–Winter): 356–377.

SCHRAEDER, PETER J. (1993) "'It's the Third World Stupid!' Why the Third World Should be the Priority of the Clinton Administration," *Third World Quarterly* 14 (No. 2): 215–237.

———, ed. (1992) *Intervention into the 1990s: U.S. Foreign Policy in the Third World*, 2nd ed. Boulder, CO: Lynne Rienner.

SCHULTZ, GEORGE. (1984) "Foreign Aid and U.S. Policy Objectives," *Department of State Bulletin* 84 (May): 17–22.

SCHULZ, BRIGITTE, and WILLIAM HANSEN. (1984) "Aid or Imperialism? West Germany in Sub-Saharan Africa," *Journal of Modern African Studies* 22 (No. 2): 287–313.

SEITZ, J. L. (1980) "The Failure of U.S. Technical Assistance in Public Administration: The Iranian Case," *Public Administration Review* 40 (No. 5): 407–413.

SEIZABURO, SATO. (1977) "The Foundations of Modern Japanese Foreign Policy," pp. 367–389 in Robert A. Scalapino, ed., *The Foreign Policy of Modern Japan*. Berkeley, CA: University of California Press.

SEWELL, JOHN, and CHRISTINE CONTEE. (1985) "U.S. Foreign Aid in the 1980s: Reordering Priorities," pp. 95–118 in John Sewell, Richard Feinberg, and Valeriana Kallab, eds., *U.S. Foreign Policy and the Third World: Agenda 1985–86*. New Brunswick, NJ: Transaction Publishers.

SHANNON, THOMAS RICHARD. (1989) *An Introduction to the World-System Perspective*. Boulder, CO: Westview.

SHINSUKE, SAMEJIMA. (1982) "Can Japan Steer its Foreign Aid Policy Clear of Militarism?" *Japan Quarterly* 29 (January–March): 30–38.

SINGER, MARSHALL. (1972) *Weak States in a World of Powers*. New York: Free Press.

SMOUTS, MARIE-CLAUDE. (1983) "The External Policy of François Mitterrand," *International Affairs* 59 (Spring): 155–167.

SNYDER, RICHARD C., H. W. BRUCK, and BURTON SAPIN. (1962) "Decision-Making as an Approach to the Study of International Politics," pp. 14–185 in Richard C. Snyder, H. W. Bruck, and Burton Sapin, eds., *Foreign Policy Decision-Making*. Glencoe, IL: Free Press.

SOROOS, MARVIN S. (1988) "Global Interdependence and the Responsibilities of States: Learning from the Japanese Experience," *Journal of Peace Research* 25 (March): 17–29.

SPANIER, JOHN, and STEVEN W. HOOK. (1995) *American Foreign Policy Since World War II*, 13th ed. Washington, DC: CQ Press.

SPICER, KEITH. (1965) *A Samaritan State? External Aid in Canada's Foreign Policy*. Toronto: University of Toronto Press.

SPROUT, HAROLD, and MARGARET SPROUT. (1969) "Environmental Factors in the Study of International Politics," pp. 41–56 in James N. Rosenau, ed., *International Politics and Foreign Policy*. New York: The Free Press.

STANFIELD, ROCHELLE L. (1990) "Fixing Foreign Aid," *National Journal* 22 (May 19): 1223–1226.

STANILAND, MARTIN. (1987) "Francophone Africa: The Enduring French Connection," *Annals of the American Academy of Political and Social Science* 489 (January): 51–62.

STEENE, MICHAEL S. (1989) "Role Model or Power Pawn? The Changing Image of Swedish Foreign Policy, 1929–1987," pp. 167–194 in Bengt Sundelius, ed., *The Committed Neutral: Sweden's Foreign Policy*. Boulder, CO: Westview.

STEVEN, ROB. (1990) *Japan's New Imperialism*. New York: M. E. Sharpe.

STIRLING, JOHN. (1981) "Japan and Asia: A 'Business Foreign Policy,'" *Asian Affairs* 8 (July–August): 353–363.

STOHL, MICHAEL, and HARRY R. TARG. (1982) "United States and the Third World: The Struggle to Make Others Adapt," pp. 115–141 in Phillip Taylor and Gregory A. Raymond, eds., *Third World Policies of Industrialized Nations*. Westport, CT: Greenwood Press.

SUNDELIUS, BENGT. (1990) "Sweden: Secure Neutrality," *Annals of the Academy of Political and Social Science* 512 (November): 116–125.

———. (1989) *The Committed Neutral: Sweden's Foreign Policy*. Boulder, CO: Westview.

SUNDELIUS, BENGT, and DON ODOM. (1992) "Scandinavia Security, Prosperity, and Solidarity Amidst Change," pp. 303–329 in Roy Macridis, ed., *Foreign Policy in World Politics*. Englewood Cliffs, NJ: Prentice-Hall.

SWEDISH GOVERNMENT. (1994) *Is Swedish Aid Rational? A Critical Study of Swedish Aid Policy in the Period 1968–1993*. Stockholm: Secretariat for Analyses of Swedish Development Assistance.

———. (1993) *Sweden's Development Assistance, 1992/93*. Stockholm: Ministry of Foreign Affairs.

———. (1992) *Swedish Development Co-Operation*. Stockholm: The Swedish Institute.

———. (1962) Government Bill 100. Stockholm: Public Documents of Swedish National Government.

TENDLER, JUDITH. (1975) *Inside Foreign Aid*. Baltimore: Johns Hopkins University Press.

TERRILL, TOM E. (1973) *The Tariff, Politics, and American Foreign Policy, 1874–1901*. Westport, CT: Greenwood Press.

THOMPSON, WILLIAM, ed. (1983) *Contending Approaches to World-System Analysis*. Beverly Hills, CA: Sage.

THUCYDIDES. (1951 [ca. 402 B.C.]) *The Complete Writings of Thucydides*. New York: Penguin.

TINT, HERBERT. (1972) *French Foreign Policy Since the Second World War*. London: Weidenfeld.

TODARO, MICHAEL P. (1977) *Economic Development in the Third World*. New York: Longman.

TONELSON, ALAN. (1985–1986) "The Real National Interest," *Foreign Policy* 61 (Winter): 49–72.

TREVERTON, GREGORY F. (1987) *The Limits of Intervention in the Postwar World*. New York: Basic Books.

TRUMAN, DAVID. (1951) *The Governmental Process*. New York: Knopf.

U.S. AGENCY FOR INTERNATIONAL DEVELOPMENT. (1994) Interview with Mike Crosswell. U.S. State Department, Washington, DC, March 30.

———. (1993a, 1991, 1990) *U.S. Overseas Loans and Grants, and Assistance from International Organizations*. Washington, DC: U.S. Government Printing Office.

————. (1993b) "Preventive Diplomacy: Revitalizing A.I.D. and Foreign Assistance for the Post-Cold War Era." Washington, DC: U.S. Government Printing Office.

————. (1992) *Why Foreign Aid?* Washington, DC: U.S. Government Printing Office.

————. (1989) *Development and the National Interest: U.S. Development Assistance into the 21st Century.* Washington, DC: U.S. Government Printing Office.

U.S. ARMS CONTROL AND DISARMAMENT AGENCY. (1990–1992) *World Military Expenditures and Arms Transfers.* Washington, DC: U.S. Government Printing Office.

U.S. GENERAL ACCOUNTING OFFICE. (1983) *Donor Approaches to Development Assistance: Implications for the United States.* Washington, DC: U.S. Government Printing Office.

U.S. HOUSE OF REPRESENTATIVES. (1989) *Report of the Task Force on Foreign Assistance.* 101st Congress, 1st Session. Washington, DC: U.S. Government Printing Office.

————. (1948) *Public Law 793: The Foreign Assistance Act of 1948.* 80th Congress, 2nd Session. Washington, DC: U.S. Government Printing Office.

U.S. NATIONAL SECURITY AGENCY. (1993 [1950]) "United States Objectives and Programs for National Security (NSA 68)," reprinted in Ernest R. May, ed., *American Cold War Strategy.* Boston: Bedford Books of St. Martin's.

VANCE, CYRUS. (1979) "Foreign Assistance and U.S. Policy," *Department of State Bulletin* 79 (March): 34–38.

VAN WOLFEREN, KAREL. (1989) *The Enigma of Japanese Power.* New York: Knopf.

————. (1986–1987) "The Japan Problem," *Foreign Affairs* 65 (Winter): 288–303.

VIOTTI, PAUL, and MARK KAUPPI. (1987) *International Relations: Realism, Pluralism, Globalism.* London: Macmillan.

VITORIA, FRANCISCO de. (1934 [1532]) *The Spanish Origin of International Law.* Oxford: Clarendon Press.

VOGEL, EZRA. (1986) "Pax Nipponica?" *Foreign Affairs* 64 (Spring): 752–767.

WAITES, NEVILLE. (1982) "France Under Mitterrand: External Relations," *World Today* 38 (June): 224–231.

WALKER, STEPHEN G. (1987) "Role Theory and the International System: A Postscript to Waltz's Theory of International Politics?" pp. 66–79 in Stephen G. Walker, ed., *Role Theory and Foreign Policy Analysis.* Durham, NC: Duke University Press.

WALLERSTEIN, IMMANUEL. (1979) *The Capitalist World-Economy.* Cambridge: Cambridge University Press.

WALTZ, KENNETH. (1979) *Theory of World Politics.* Reading, MA: Addison-Wesley.

————. (1964) "The Stability of a Bipolar World," *Deadelus* 93 (Summer): 881–909.

WATKINS, FREDERICK M. (1934) *The State as a Concept of Political Science.* New York: Harper and Brothers.

WEISKEL, TIMOTHY. (1988) "Mission Civilisatrice," *Wilson Quarterly* 3 (Fall): 97–113.

WEISSMAN, STEVE. (1975) *The Trojan Horse: A Radical Look At Foreign Aid.* Palo Alto, CA: Ramparts Press.

WEST, FRANCIS J., Jr. (1984) "The Security Setting," pp. 29–41 in John Wilhelm and Gerry Feinstein, eds., *U.S. Foreign Assistance: Investment or Folly?* New York: Praeger.

WESTWOOD, ANDREW F. (1966) *Foreign Aid in a Foreign Policy Framework.* Washington, DC: Brookings Institution.

WHARTON, CLIFTON. (1993) "USAID and Foreign Aid Reform," *U.S. Department of State Dispatch* 4 (July 26): 526–531.

WHITE, DOROTHY SHIPLEY. (1979) *Black Africa and De Gaulle.* University Park, PA: Pennsylvania State University Press.

WHITE, JOHN. (1974) *The Politics of Aid.* New York: St. Martin's.

WILHELM, JOHN, and GERRY FEINSTEIN, eds. (1984) *U.S. Foreign Assistance: Investment or Folly?* New York: Praeger.

WILLIS, F. ROY. (1982) *The French Paradox.* Stanford, CA: Hoover Institution Press.

WISH, NAOMI BAILIN. (1987) "National Attributes as Sources of National Role Conceptions: A Capability-Motivation Model," pp. 94–103 in Stephen G. Walker, ed., *Role Theory and Foreign Policy Analysis.* Durham, NC: Duke University Press.

WITTKOPF, EUGENE R. (1975) "Containment Versus Underdevelopment in the Distribution of United States Foreign Aid: An Introduction to the Use of Cross-national Aggregate Data Analysis in the Study of Foreign Policy," pp. 80–95 in William D. Coplin and Charles W. Kegley, Jr., eds., *Analyzing International Relations.* New York: Praeger.

———. (1973) "Foreign Aid and United Nations Votes," *American Political Science Review* 67 (September): 868–888.

WOLFSON, D. J. (1979) *Public Finance and Development Strategy.* Baltimore: Johns Hopkins University Press.

WOOD, ROBERT E. (1986) *From Marshall Plan to Debt Crisis: Foreign Aid and Development Choices in the World Economy.* Berkeley, CA: University of California Press.

———. (1980) "Foreign Aid and the Capitalist State in Underdeveloped Countries," *Politics and Society* 10 (No. 1): 1–34.

THE WORLD BANK. (1993) *The East Asian Economic Miracle.* New York: The World Bank.

———. (1980–1994) *World Development Report.* New York: Oxford.

YANAGIHARA, TORU, and ANNE EMIG. (1991) "An Overview of Japan's Foreign Aid," pp. 37–69 in Shafiqul Islam, ed., *Yen for Development.* New York: Council on Foreign Relations Press.

YASUTOMO, DENNIS T. (1993) "Japan and the Asian Development Bank: Multilateral Aid Policy in Transition," pp. 305–340 in Robert M. Orr, Jr., and Bruce M. Koppel, eds., *Japanese Foreign Aid: Power and Policy in a New Era.* Boulder, CO: Westview.

———. (1986) *The Manner of Giving: Strategic Aid and Japanese Foreign Policy.* Lexington, MA: Lexington Books.

ZAHARIADIS, MIKOLAOS, RICK TRAVIS, and PAUL F. DIEHL. (1990) "Military Substitution Effects from Foreign Economic Aid: Buying Guns or Butter?" *Social Science Quarterly* 71 (December): 774–785.

ZIMMERMAN, ROBERT F. (1993) *Dollars, Diplomacy, and Dependency: Dilemmas of U.S. Economic Aid.* Boulder, CO: Lynne Rienner.

Index

211

About the Book and the Author

Foreign assistance has taken on a central role as an instrument of foreign policy for rich and poor states alike. The topic remains, however, an enigmatic and controversial one.

Seeking to advance the understanding of aid as a foreign-policy tool, *National Interest and Foreign Aid* provides a comparative, data-based evaluation of the varying roles served by the development assistance programs of four major donors: France, Japan, Sweden, and the United States. Although the focus of the book is on the 1980s, Hook also contrasts the ongoing evolution of the four aid programs and assesses their adaptation to world politics beyond the Cold War. His analysis contributes to an enhanced appreciation not only of foreign aid, but of comparative foreign policy in the contemporary international system.

Steven W. Hook is visiting assistant professor of political science at the University of Missouri.